Pandora's Hunnert Januarys

Watching 20th Century Women

Fly Out of the Box

a novel by
Val Dumond

First edition
Published by
    Muddy Puddle Press
    P O Box 97124
    Lakewood WA 98497

ISBN: 0988750651
ISBN 9780988750654

Printed in the United States of America

Contents

Dedication

To the women who know
that freedom has always been their right:

Mary Belle and Nelle Marie
Mary Dawn
Lisbeth
Eleanor
Girl Scouts
(Sally, Ginny, Pat, and Wanda)
The Mala Siete
(Donna, Bug, Char, Cookie, Marge, Margie)
Electa, Jo, and Claudia
Dorothy
The B.I.R.
(Ann, Vera, Jackie, Sally, Terry, Judy)
Janelle
Kathy
Suezy
BMae
Maha
...and all the women I have
met and worked with... ever!

Introduction

The hullabaloo over the impending fearsome arrival of the 21st century is building as I write this. How I have lived this long is a mystery to me. Whether it's good genes or stubbornness, or a combination of both with a big pile of luck tossed in, the fact remains: I am about to turn 100 years old.

You may be interested in what prompted me to write this book in the first place. I was listening to someone on television talking about "thinking outside the box" when it hit me: *Why stay inside the box to think? Why not escape — get the heck out of there?*

When I was born, women still hid inside their boxes (some still do), fearing to move out and live full lives, fearing to break some of society's codes (mostly imposed by men), and fearing to trust themselves and their gifts. Thank god (male or female) that I chose to nudge open the lid so other women could peek out at the world and decide whether or not to join the fun.

Pandora isn't my real name; it's every woman's name. The woman in my story was born at the turn of the 20th century and is about to celebrate her 100th birthday at the turn of the 21st century. In some ways, she is a combination of the Storyteller and my mother; Mother lived the first seventy years of the 1900s, and Storyteller lived the last seventy years.

I admit, sometimes I feel as if I've lived two lives — one as a very lucky girl and woman whose life turns in and out without too much drama, and another life as the magical Pandora who could wave her hands and make things happen. (Our dream lives often exceed our comfort zones, which keeps dreams inside our heads.)

Along the journey through the historic century, my awe increased as I watched women climb out of their boxes, first poking out their heads in quiet curiosity and then blatantly throwing open the lid and joining in the joy of life — reaching for the stars, realizing their dreams, and enjoying every minute of fulfilling their own expectations.

The Greek goddess Pandora was right: Curiosity is a gift to be cherished. As the song says, "once you've seen Kansas City, your life will never be the same again."

—Pandora Whaley
December 1999

1900-1909

*Hello. My name is... I don't have one since I haven't been borned yet
and I don't know if I'm a girl or a boy, so you mayn't have heard about
me. All I know is that I'm tired of this dark cramped place and looking
for a way out. Around me, I sense whispering, rhythmic sounds, strange
smells, colorful lights, tastes of sweet fluids, and a very soft feeling on
my skin — something I will learn to call l-o-v-e. Maybe if I stretch and
kick some more, I can attract attention. I like attention — and I'm only
nine months in the making. Look out, World. Here I come!*

The entire world celebrated the arrival of both the 20th century and a baby girl
on that snowy early Tuesday morning, January 1, 1900. Of course the world
hadn't heard of the baby girl yet, but then they hadn't heard of the impending
marvels, innovations, pain, crises, and magic of the new century either.

Nine months after Spring, new life always increases. Nine months
earlier, Mary Belle Taylor and Fayette Whaley had celebrated the coming of
spring with a bottle of new wine and a night of love that whirled dust into
spirit and spirit into the body of a new baby soul. In the dark early morning
hours of New Years Day 1900, they saw the face of that miracle for the first
time.

There had been arguments about whether the new century actually
began with the first day of 1900 or the first day of 1901. "Technically, the
new century begins in 1901," was Fayette's contention.

"Not so," claimed Mary Belle. "The numbers change from 18-something
to 19-something. That's the end of the old century and the beginning of a

new one. Now think of the end of this new century," she added, "when all of the numbers will change from 19-something to 20-something."

"I won't be here," Fayette grumped.

"Maybe our children will be."

The hullabaloo over the new century was barely underway when the infant girl announced her arrival. Labor began on a very cold New Years Eve, and by the time Baby New Year was just two hours old, Mary Belle had pushed a nine-pound baby of her own through a very tiny cervix.

The new mother soon lay half-asleep, holding a gurgling infant near her breast, her small body listless from its work, now contracting gently to pull itself back together. "You're barely a baby yourself," her mother whispered, half to herself but loud enough for her son-in-law to hear.

"She's strong, Rosella," Fayette countered.

"Strong, yes… but so young. Only sixteen."

"How old were ye when Mary Belle was born?"

"Eighteen. There's a big difference."

"Well, she'll be eighteen afore long and then she can have another, okay Ma?" The new father, his long reddish mustache drooping from his cheeks, lifted his face and laughed that hearty Irish laugh that had attracted his wife and, yes, if truth be told, her mother. Fayette was closer to Rosella's age and already had fathered five children when he met Mary Belle. His first wife had been laid to rest less than a year earlier, leaving him alone with five grieving children.

Grace, his eldest, came into the room and motioned the others to leave. "Let her sleep, Papa," she whispered. "I'll put the babe in the cradle."

Grace lifted the small bundle and gently placed it into the oak cradle her father had put together before she herself was born 15 years earlier. "Come, Mrs. Taylor, Pa, let the girl sleep." The *girl*, now a mother, stirred beneath the comforter as Grace lowered the oil lamp and shooed the reluctant grandmother and proud father out of the room.

Mary Belle watched them leave through half-open eyes, looked at her baby in its cradle, then gave way to her exhausted body and dropped into a deep sleep. Baby Girl was left to dream her first worldly dreams. She moved her lips in and out and let her fingers curl and uncurl, occasionally flexing a leg to feel her new freedom. Reds and greens and blues wove themselves into wisps of memory to form the beginning of a lifelong collection of dreams.

In the early morning darkness, Mary woke to hear her husband rummaging about the bedroom. "Morning," she whispered.

Fayette stopped looking for his suspenders and walked over to the bed. "Top o' the marnin' to ye," he told her, using his best Irish brogue remembered from his youth in the Old Sod. "That'll be a fine-lookin' wee 'un ye gave me, Mrs. Whaley," he winked at her. "Sorry she weren't a man-child, but maybe the next one. Isn't she pretty? She's altogether the fittin' image of her pretty mother. Maybe she'll learn to milk cows too."

"Away with yer blarney, Mr. Whaley," Mary came back at him. "I'm too tired."

"I heard ye up twice in the night. Is she sucklin' all right?"

"A very hungry babe, that one. I'm so sore." She cradled her breasts, which were once again full and seeping milk. "It's time again. I hear her wiggling about. Would you bring her to me?"

"C'mon, woman, that ain't no job fer a man." The tall man, dressed only in long underwear and a wool flannel shirt, leaned over the cradle and reluctantly pulled up the bundle. He caressed the baby as he leaned over and kissed his wife on the lips with a passion that told her how happy he was. "Here's yer new daughter, our firstborn," he said, his voice soft through his mustache. "I never quite get over the miracle of this new livin' thing, a flamin' miracle, 'tis." He ceremoniously handed over the bundle as Mary pulled down her nightshirt and lifted out the overflowing breast. The baby quickly seized it and began to work her mouth.

Mary looked up into the face of her husband, his eyes fixed on the two of them. "Isn't she beautiful?" she asked again.

"Fer a gal, I guess so. But the next one…"

"Oh Fay, let's get this one grown before thinking of…"

"My boys are growed and they'll be leavin' soon; I have to think of the farm."

"She needs a name, Fay."

"That she does. How about Mary Ann? Always liked that name."

"Too much like mine. We'd never know who you was callin'. How about Rose... Rosie... like my mamá?"

"Then how'd her and baby Rose know who I'm callin'?"

"Your mother's name then. Wasn't it Nancy or Nellie or something like that?"

"Nell. It was Nell, N-E-L-L, and how she hated bein' called Nellie."

"Nell it is, for her middle name. And for the first name something... like..."

"Ye ain't thinking of namin' her like yer cats... in Greek, are ye?"

"I always liked the name Pandora. What do you think? Pandora Nell... Whaley!" The baby pulled back her head releasing the breast, as if she recognized her name. Mary wiped her daughter's mouth with her gown and looked back at her husband.

Fayette gave up. "Has a nice sound, darlin'. Yeah, a real nice sound. But add an 'e' to Nell and make it more French. B'gorra, we got a dotter named Pandora Nelle Whaley."

Pandora Nelle Whaley took one last tug of milk and dozed off to sleep.

By the time the sun was up, Mary had pulled herself out of bed and wrapped a warm bathrobe about her body. She moved one foot in front of the other, holding onto chairs, doorways, and determination, until she reached the kitchen table. There she eased herself into a chair. Grace already had fed Fayette and the boys who helped with the morning milking. Since her mother died, Grace had taken over the household chores, rising before the men, stoking the kitchen stove, making the coffee and frying the griddle cakes, eggs, and sausages. Now she was combing the girls' hair and sending her younger siblings off to school. Billie, not yet four years old, was putting on a warm coat to follow her father back to the barn.

"Morning, Mary," Grace greeted her step-mother. "Have some nice eggs?" she teased, knowing that Mary had been deathly upset when cooking eggs during her pregnancy. Mary shook her head, smiling and moaning at the same time.

"Oatmeal then, how about oatmeal?"

"That sounds better. Yes, that sounds very good. Suddenly I have an appetite. I think I could eat a horse."

Fayette, pulling on his boots at the door, turned and shouted, "Don't ye dare. We'll need 'em come spring."

"If it ever comes," shouted Billie. "Come on, Papa, let's go. I gotta see if Artemis had her kittens."

Billie was supposed to be another boy to help Fayette with the farm. So was Pandora, for that matter. But the jolly Irishman swallowed his disappointment and half-heartedly welcomed the little girls into the family. "Guess I'll have to teach the girls how to hitch up horses," he joked. And that was what he was doing — teaching Billie how to farm.

Mary softly rubbed her tummy as she and Grace sipped coffee. "Did Mama stay very late last night?"

"No, she left right after you fell asleep. Helped me clean up, then went home." The younger girl, nearly the age of her step-mother, clasped her fingers together nervously before asking, "Did it hurt much?"

"Sorta, but I don't remember. I still feel sore, but it's a good kind, you know?"

"I couldn't do it, have a baby… I'd be too scared… I mean… remembering how it was with Mama when Billie was born."

"I'm sorry. How awful it must be for you to have to go through that again."

"I wasn't scared with you… like I was with Mama… before. I knew something was wrong with her, even before it was time for the birthing. I think Mama was tired of having babies, tired of the farm, tired of just about everything."

"I'm so sorry, Grace. She was very young."

"Oh, don't mind me. Just mind that wee one that's sleeping in there." Grace walked to the large kitchen range for the coffeepot and refilled their cups. "By the way, what are you and Papa going to name this new one?"

"We already did. Pandora Nelle. Like it?"

"Nell… oh, like Grandma Whaley. She'd have liked that." Grace replaced the coffeepot on the warming side of the stove. "But Pandora? Where'd you get that?"

"Pandora was my choice. I heard tell about a famous dancer that my sister Edith saw when she was in Chicago. The name just stuck in my head." Mary Belle paused for a sip of warm coffee. "I've always loved the story of the Greek goddess who lifted the lid of that magical box and let loose the spirits into the world. I learned to read from Mama's book of Greek mythology." Mary Belle took another sip of coffee. "Your pa added an 'e' to make *Nelle* look French. Do you like it?"

"Yes, I'm glad. He did the same with my name. My middle name is S-u-z-a-n-n-e, the French version of my mother's name, Susan. I wonder why that old Irishman keeps falling in love with French women."

"I hope I'm the last one he falls for." Mary rose slowly and walked over to the rocking chair that her husband had made especially for his new wife to nurse their first child. She settled back and began to rock, humming a little French tune. After a moment, she told Grace, "I'm going to call her Pandora."

Grace lifted the lid from the back of the iron stove and stirred the coals with a long-handled poker. "These coals are about right for my bread," she spoke half to herself. She lifted the towel from the bread pans and stuck her finger into the yeasty tops before brushing them with butter and placing them in the oven. "There! They ought to be done in time for lunch." Grace turned and watched Mary sip her coffee as she rocked.

Mary returned her gaze. "I never did think I could have a baby; I thought I was too young. Do you believe me, Grace? I didn't know where babies came from. I just knew I loved your father and he loved me."

"When your mother has five children, like mine, you get to know where babies come from real fast."

"I knew how cows and pigs and cats got babies, but I never thought people were like that. I shouldn't be talking to you like this. You aren't even married."

Mary fingered her cup nervously. She had never talked to anyone about sex before she talked to her mother that night last spring. It was after the school graduation picnic when the two of them sat on the bank of the river, watching the sun drop below the horizon, leaving its golden shadow on the water.

Mary closed her eyes as she remembered.

"Mamá, something is happening to me that I don't understand."

"Oh?" the older woman replies. "Just what might that be?"

"My periods have stopped. You told me I'd have them the rest of my life. But they've stopped."

Rosella Taylor's whole body shudders; her eyes search her daughter's face. The innocence blinks back at her. "Do you feel queasy sometimes?" she asks.

"Yes. Sometimes, when I wake up."

"*Ma foi!*" the mother cries out. Then more calmly, "Have you and Mr. Whaley... I mean, have you... do you... have you been... intimate?"

"Of course we're intimate. We love each other."

"But he's so much older than you. I thought you were just good friends."

A silence from her daughter causes Rosella to ask, "Do you know what it means to be... intimate?"

"Umm, I'm not sure. We kiss and hug and..."

"Has he... oh good gracious, why am I asking all these questions. It's obvious he has."

"You mean like that warm night last spring under the blanket in the hayloft?"

Rosella gulps. "I guess I do."

"But it was just that once. We were foaling the mare and the air smelled like spring."

"That's all it takes." Rosella grasps her daughter's hands. "Mary Belle Taylor, you're going to have a baby. We're going to get you married... right away."

Mary brought her eyes back to Grace. "I didn't know where babies came from. Here you are, not much younger than me, and you help deliver them..."

"Did you hear that?" Grace interrupted.

Mary stopped rocking and lifted herself slowly. "Time for another breakfast for little Pandora Nelle." Grace helped her step-mother walk back to the bedroom.

Little Pandora was still in diapers when her baby brother Jason Matthew was born the next year. By the following summer, Mary Belle was expecting again. Her only discomfort during her pregnancies seemed to be her aversion to eggs and the queasiness that disappeared in the third month. This time Mary developed a short temper. She'd fly off the handle without warning, shouting at Fayette, scolding the children, fussing over which cats were allowed in the house and which weren't. There were always cats around the Whaley place, but some belonged in the barn and only a select few were allowed to enter the house.

"Darned cats," Mary wailed and nudged two tabbies with her foot. "*Allez! Allez!* Get out of my house."

"Me take them out, Ma," Pandora offered. "I take kitties out for you."

The toddler scooped up the two cats in her arms and carried them dangling out the door. "Bad kitties," she scolded. "You made Ma mad."

Pandora dropped the cats just outside and wandered over to the woodpile. The cats followed, rubbing against her unsteady legs and nearly tripping her. She climbed up the stacked wood that towered twice as high as her small self, picking her way along the edge, making use of steps she had fashioned by using the woodpile often as her thinking place.

"Come on, Persephone," she called to the gray kitten that scratched at the log behind her. "You're big enough; jump up here with me." The kitten sprang from one log to another, scrambling awkwardly with all four legs over the big logs until it reached the child. Pandora cradled the furry ball in her arms and bent over it. "What a good kitty," she purred, stroking its head.

The morning sun felt warm on her back. Soon she removed her sweater and tossed it to the ground. The kitten had fallen asleep in her lap and Pandora amused herself with games she dreamed up. With Billie and the older children in school and her little brother still a baby, Pandora often was overlooked in the crowd.

"Pa lets me help him in the barn," she told the sleeping kitten. "But Mamá's so busy with her chores she doesn't see me. And lately she's cranky. I think it's me. I heard Grace and Pa talking the other day and she says Mamá is afraid she'll die when the new baby is born. I don't know if Ma is afraid or if Grace is afraid for her. Grace works down at Hartung's store, and Pa said she don't know what Ma thinks anymore. Oh, Persi, they had a terrible fight. Grace's mother died borning Billie. She said so."

The child closed her eyes. "But I know that my Mamá isn't going to die. She's going to live forever and ever. Pastor Nichols said so in church last Sunday. 'Life everlasting,' he said, as long as you're good. And we know Ma is good. So she'll live everlasting."

The small girl on the woodpile gazed upward at the sky. "Do you hear that, God? My mamá is going to live everlasting. And so am I. Pa said so. He said I could live through the whole new century and not rest in peace until the next century… if I want to. And I do.

"You'll see, Persi, I'm going to live a hunnert years — that's what a century is — a hunnert years. I have to live that long 'cause there's lots I want to do. Maybe I can even be king some day. And when I'm king, I'll change the world." The child closed her eyes for a moment to let the dream sink in.

"Mamá says I was born on the cuss of the new decade and she says I have a whole new clean century to live in. Pa says, 'Don't count yer chickens afore they hatch,' but I don't know what that means. Because our chickens are out pecking in the yard, where I can count them.

When you're born in the middle of two families of children, you often feel ignored. Pandora was such a child, although she didn't seem to mind. She had her kittens to care for, her chores in the house, and her chores in the barn — she tended the cow named Miss Moo. In time she had school to keep her occupied.

Even before she started school, she was learning to read. She sat quietly and watched the homework sessions around the big kitchen table. Her half-brother, Andrew, seven years older, taught her the A-B-Cs. Then he dug around and found some easy books and listened while Pandora read, hesitating over the big words and sounding out the rest.

School for the lonely child gave Pandora a place to shine. She had been enrolled in the nearby one-room Arkansaw school soon after Christmas and her sixth birthday.

When the snow was deep, she got to ride one of the horses to school; as spring melted the snow, she took to walking the muddy rutted path into town. In school, she became fascinated with the lessons of all the older kids. She'd pretend to be engrossed in her *McGuffey Reader* while she listened to stories about Magellan and Marco Polo and Alexander the Great and Julius Caesar. Teacher would never have caught onto his wandering pupil if Pandora hadn't blurted out one day, "Where are the girls?"

"What do you mean, Pandora?" Teacher asked, overlooking the interruption by the first grader in the midst of the fifth grade history lesson.

"I hear you talking about all the men who explored and ruled and fought battles, but I never hear you talk about the girls. Where are they?"

"Um, well, history is made by men… I guess," Teacher had mumbled. Then, "You're supposed to be parsing sentences for tomorrow's lesson, Pandora. I suggest you place your attention in front of you."

The question remained in Pandora's mind and she thought she'd ask her mother, but never got around to it.

By the time Pandora was ready to leave third grade, she had read more books than any of her brothers. Most farm families did not own many books. They had their Bible, of course, and perhaps a book about treating ailments, animal and human. In spite of the difficulty in finding books in rural areas, Mary Belle and her sisters had taught each other to read by borrowing books from Madame Pouquette, who brought her father's library with her when she moved from Canada to the village of Arkansaw, Wisconsin.

One of the books Pandora loved was her mother's copy of *Greek Mythology*, where she found stories of gods and goddesses that did exciting things. One of her favorites was the story of Pandora. Intrigued by the story of the release of "evils" into the world, she asked her mother one day, "What are *evils*?"

"Something bad. All the bad things."

"Am I bad?"

"Of course not." Mary watched her child's face. "Why do you ask?"

"When I told Teacher I read the story of Pandora, he said she filled the world with evils. And he called me a Pandora because I was always asking questions. 'Curious killed the cat,' he said, and told me I had too much curious. Am I filled with evils?"

Mary Belle took a deep breath. "Of course not, my dear one. I read that book too, you know. I thought Pandora was very brave for releasing such long-lost secrets. And…"

"But they were *evils*! You said they were bad."

"Well… that isn't exactly the way I saw it. Did you ever wonder how those *things* got locked away in a box?"

"Uh, no. I thought that was just the way it was."

"And that is what intrigued me. It took awhile, but I figured out that those evils were stuffed away because they bothered people — therefore, they must have been truths. Truth bothers lots of folks, some more'n the evils do."

Pandora closed her eyes for a moment, then opened them, squinting at her mother. "That must mean that what she did was good. Hmmm. I like that better. My Pandora released the Truths in the world." She stood up and skipped to the door. "I like that. Thanks, Mamá."

Little Pandora pondered the question of evils often, especially after the day Andrew, her half-brother, called her that name. It wasn't so much the word, but the way he spit it out at her.

"You're a *tomboy*."

"No I'm not."

"Yes you are. Everybody says so. Tomboy! Tomboy!"

"You're… nuts!" Pandora screamed wildly. She didn't know what a *tomboy* was, but she knew it sounded bad.

Andrew at fourteen had let his little sisters play baseball with him, his brothers, and friends. It was a new game they learned from Teacher, and they were getting good at it. But it took a bunch of kids to play. Since there weren't enough boys to make two full teams of five, they allowed two of the girls to play — Pandora was eight and Billie was eleven. The girls were the best hitters and the boys knew it, each wanting at least one of them on their team at choose-up time. After a new family with four young boys came to town, Andrew engineered a baseball players' revision, making up and enforcing the new rule that girls can't play.

"After all, we only let you play because we didn't have anybody else," Andrew explained to the girls. "Now we've got enough boys, we don't need you."

"Yes you do," Pandora squealed. "You need us to hit 'cause we're better."

"Nah, we just told you that so you'd play."

"We are too!" Billie stomped her foot. "We're better'n anybody."

"Sorry, girls, go on home, tomboys, your mama's calling."

Tears streaming down her face, Pandora stuck out her tongue at her brother and yelled, "You'll be sorry!"

"Ooh, I'm scared. Now go home, cry baby."

"I'm not a cry baby."

"Are too. A tomboy and a cry baby!"

Pandora cried her way home as Billie morosely kicked up sand along the road. Billy had been called *tomboy* before. After all, she carried a boy's name, did a boy's chores, and wore her brother's knickerbockers. She couldn't remember wearing a dress except at Easter time, and then she felt silly.

Billie and Pandora both knew their Pa wanted boy children. Billie was the baby who resulted in her mother's death. Her place as youngest in the family was replaced by Pandora Nelle and Mary Belle's other kids. Life wasn't fair and Billie accepted it that way — a lot for a little girl nearing those dangerous teen-age years.

Pandora couldn't accept the epithet as easily. She was a girl and didn't want to be called *tomboy*, not by her brother or anyone else. Her mother met her at the door and cradled her sobbing head as she finally blurted out, "What's a tomboy, Mamá?"

"Is that what you're crying about? I thought you'd been hurt."

"Am I one?"

"No, you're my big girl."

"But what *is* a tomboy, Ma?"

"I guess it's a girl who plays like a boy. I'm not sure if that's as bad as you make it sound; I rather envy you. I never could…"

"But Andrew called me one, and he said it like he hated me for it."

"Andrew is becoming a man and his… er… he has other problems that interfere with his good judgment right now. You'll have to be patient with him."

"What problems?"

"Maybe we'll talk about this later. Right now, you need to wash your face and comb your hair and come help me with dinner."

The subject was forgotten by everyone except Pandora. Billie let it pass; Mary Belle had dinner to prepare; Andrew never gave it another thought. Only young Pandora went to sleep that night wondering why she felt squishy inside when she was called *tomboy* by her big brother.

Pandora loved school, but she always looked forward to spending more time with her mother during the summer. The two sat in the shade of the front porch culling strawberries one such warm day in June. The little girl and her mother had spent the early morning over in the strawberry patch picking the berries they would preserve later that day.

"Why can't I cut my hair, Mamá? It gets in my eyes and tangles in trees when I run through the woods and climb trees with Billie."

"Proper little girls don't cut their hair, sweetheart," Mary Belle answered. "If you'd like, I'll braid it for you. Your pa likes his girls with long hair; it says you're a lady."

"But it's hot and sweaty. And I don't want to be a *lady*." She sneered at the word.

"Hush, dear. 'Sweaty' isn't a proper word. Pa doesn't like…"

"It's how I feel."

"One more thing, *ma fille chère*. You must stop dressing up in Andrew's knickerbockers. They're boys' pants. What will folks think if you look like a boy?"

"Folks don't think about Billie as a boy."

"Perhaps, but… Pandora! Watch what you're doing. You just put leaves in the strawberry bowl and tossed out the berry."

"Sorry." The two concentrated on their berries for a moment.

"I know it's difficult being a girl," Mary Belle began, "but your pa thinks…"

"Why is it always what Pa thinks? I don't give a tinker's damn what Pa thinks!"

"Pandora Nelle Whaley!" Her mother's head shot back, her eyes stretched wide. "Pan-dor-ah! Watch your language. Wherever did you hear that word?"

"Andy says it, and so do his friends."

"Proper young ladies do not use cuss words, and you are not to use them, ever. As for what your pa thinks, he's… your father."

"I don't care. He's wrong. It isn't fair for him to tell me how to wear my hair. It's my hair."

"And he's your father. He keeps you safe and provides for you. He's the head of this house and he tells us whatever he wants to."

"But it isn't fair," Pandora continued to whine.

"Fair or not, *that's the way it is*." Mary Belle accented her words by standing up and carrying her bowl of strawberries into the kitchen. Pandora began to rock in her chair, letting the stirred-up breeze dry her teary eyes. Her girlish rage had found a voice. And it shouted, "I hate *the way it is*; I hate it!"

The Whaley family gathered on Saturday nights after the week's work was done and before Sunday soul time began. Fayette pulled out his banjo and Mary Belle sat down at her beloved piano — the one loaned to her by her sister.

Sister Edith had run away to marry a traveling man, Mr. Anderson, a life that little Pandora considered glamorous. Ede agreed to loan Mary Belle the treasure she had bought for herself from earnings she saved from her job at the Arkansaw Feed Store.

Billie had devised a kind of drum set from a collection of pans and barrels, and played percussion in the family band. When Grace was home, she added her fiddle. And Pandora sang. She had a lilting sweet voice for "Amazing Grace", but her voice could be strong and vibrant when they swung into "Onward Christian Soldiers".

Pandora took a natural shine to Aunt Ede's piano and soon was playing as well as her mother.

During one such music session just before Christmas and Pandora's tenth birthday, Mary Belle asked her family to learn a new song that Ede had told her about, called "Good Morning To You". The family listened to her sing, and soon were accompanying her young voice. When they finished, she suggested they change the words a bit.

"How come, Ma?" Billie asked. "What words?"

"Let's sing, 'Happy birthday to you; happy birthday to you...'" Mary Belle said, smiling a mysterious grin.

It took only a few moments for Fayette to get the message. "Are you...? Are we...?"

"Yes. I'm going to have another baby."

A previous pregnancy had aborted in 1905 in the midst of her fourth month, and Mary Belle had been afraid to begin another life since. Baby Iris Rosella was born on a very hot and humid morning the following July.

By autumn Pandora was way ahead of the other fifth grader. The new teacher, a German woman who had brought many books with her, encouraged her students to read all of them. Pandora had read Rudyard Kipling's *Pourquoi* and *Jungle Book*, and the *Wonderful Wizard of Oz*. "All stories about boys," she wailed to Teacher as she searched for a new book to read. "Aren't there any books about girls?"

Teacher looked up from her desk, put down her red marking pencil, and sighed. "Oh Pandora. Of course there are stories about girls. There is Sacajawea, and Queen Victoria, and… and…" she tried to think of another. "You know, you may be right. There aren't many stories about girls. Perhaps you ought to write one. Yes, that's your next assignment. Write a story about a girl or a woman you know. Tell me all about her." Teacher sat back with an eerie smile on her face.

Pandora responded by turning in a four-page story a week later, written in very careful script, all about her extraordinary mother who was smart and pretty and could play the piano and make wonderful blueberry pancakes and sew dresses for her daughter and knit sweaters for her children and tell intriguing bedtime stories and who knew the real story about Pandora and the escaping Truths. Teacher sat back after reading it, astounded. She had no other choice. She placed a bright A+ at the top of the page, adding "well written", and returned the story to the anxious child.

Teacher soon had her writing essays about science and history and geography. By the end of fifth grade, Pandora knew all forty-five, no forty-six states (Oklahoma had just been added) and their capital cities, all the capitals of the world, and she knew about astronomy.

"Pandora, you're doing so well, I'm thinking of moving you ahead one grade," Teacher said as she made out report cards.

"Oh no," the child objected. "No! I like school and want to stay here forever and learn everything there is to learn."

"Everything? To do that you must go to college and study long hours. Even then you may not learn everything."

"I saw a book at Madame Pouquette's that said it contained everything, all the knowledge of the world. She called it a cyclo… cycle…"

"Encyclopedia?"

"Yes, that's it. She said if I read that book cover to cover, then I'd know…"

"Oh my dear child. You will have facts, some facts. But you won't have information, and you won't know where to find all the things you don't know. To do that, you must develop your curiosity."

"Curiosity?"

"Curiosity also opens doors. It opens worlds to you. Develop your curiosity. Ask questions… about everything you want to know. Keep looking for new ways to learn. You may never learn it all, but at least you'll know how."

"I will, I will," Pandora shouted. "I'll go to college and I'll open doors… with cur-ee-os-ity."

"That's very ambitious," Teacher said. "You have a marvelous curiosity, and that's a very good thing."

"Except for the other Pandora," the child added.

"What do you mean?"

"Old Teacher said that Pandora had too much curiosity and turned evils loose in the world."

"Oh he did, did he? Not everyone agrees what came out of that box was evil."

"Mamá said that the box was filled with truths. She said that the goddess Pandora did good."

"I've always loved the stories of the Greek gods and goddesses messing around… it was kinda fun," Teacher said. "I especially loved the story of the Greek goddess who lifted the lid of the magical box and let loose the spirits into the world. I enjoyed the idea of a woman freeing her spirit like Pandora did… the other Pandora. I never pictured the spirits as evil, like some stories tell, only as spirits that threatened the imagination."

"Oh yes." No one had spoken like that to Pandora before. She took a chance and added, "Sometimes I feel as if I'd like to open such a box. And then I'd know everything in the world."

"You indeed have the curiosity to do just that, Pandora, if you choose to."

"Yes, oh yes, I choose to."

Teacher gasped, thought a moment, then carefully wrote on Pandora's report card: "Excellent student. Promoted to 6th grade."

On starlit nights Pandora Nelle liked to lie atop the woodpile and trace the constellations with her outstretched hands. "There's Orion, the Bears, and the Big Dipper," she relayed to her new kitten. "See, Ophelia? The stars stay up there in order — the same every night. And Teacher says that explorers find their way by reading them. And Teacher says they haven't changed in eons — that's lots and lots of years, centuries — and they won't change ever… ever… everlasting, like Grace's mom and my mamá." She paused to contemplate *eons* and *everlasting*. "Even Grandma's friend, that cranky old Mrs. Martin who just died, is using the stars to guide her. Everybody does, Ophelia. Teacher says so." Awed silence enveloped the young mind blanketed that fall evening with the wonders of the universe.

In just ten short years, Pandora had learned much about the boundaries placed on women. Young ones had to keep their hair long and be quiet when company came to call. Little girls were not to use rude language, and they weren't supposed to climb trees or run in the fields. She had learned in Sunday School that all the evils of the world were let loose by a woman with a different name — Eve. *Did the goddess Pandora use a nickname?*

Pandora also learned that men were gods and The God was male, and that women were punished, nay doomed, to bear the pain of childbirth because of that evil Eve. The child's conclusion: a woman was responsible for the problems of the world. A new question arose: Which one? Pandora or Eve?

All by herself, she had concluded that women were merely house servants, placed on earth to please men and to bear children who would become farm laborers. She knew that women arose early and worked late to prepare food, wash and iron clothes, clean the house, care for sick children (and husbands), educate those children, wait on those men, and keep their families on the straight and narrow. Women were the ones who paid attention to Pastor Nichol's sermons and translated them to their families over Sunday dinner.

Oh yes, and Pandora knew that when everyone else was taking a rest on that seventh day (like it said in the Bible), it was the women who still prepared meals, dressed the family for church, saw that they stayed awake during sermons, and cleaned up the house at the end of the day of "rest".

Pandora's Notes of the 19-aughts

Women had not sat around idly before 1900, but the new century certainly stoked more activity. Women were sticking their toes into medicine, education, politics, government, journalism, literature, and art. Social feminism was on its way.

[For more about "What Women Were Doing Before 1900", see Chapter: "Pandora's Hundredth January".]

None of this touched Pandora. Her home had no way to hear news of the world except what arrived in stories from travelers whose horse or carriage gave out, or who stopped for a meal and respite from journeying. Only rarely did a newspaper from the city find its way to the Arkansaw Creek farming community. When it did arrive, the newspaper generally was a few weeks old. None of the towns around Arkansaw were big enough for daily papers.

Therefore, she didn't know an electric washing machine had come into being, or that **FANNY FARMER**, who published her first cookbook with standardized cooking measurements in 1896, had opened a "School of Cookery" in Boston MA (1902).

Nor did she know that a physicist named **MARIE CURIE** in France had discovered radium (1903), the same year the **U.S. WOMEN'S TRADE UNION LEAGUE** was established.

ZELIA NUTTALL, a Mexican-American anthropologist and archaeologist, uncovered ancient art that explored religious rites and the military action of early Mexicans (1902).

Inventor **HERTHA MARKS AYRTON**, a mathematician, began her career with a study of electric arcs that led to her book, *The Electric Arc* (1902) and continued through her development in 1915 of the anti-poison-gas fan that saved thousands of lives in The Great War. Yet, she was denied admission to the scientific establishment that showered her work with honors.

Inventor **MARY ANDERSON** received a patent for a car window cleaning device (1903), later called the *windshield wiper*.

And since Pandora had no idea that dark-skinned people existed, she couldn't know how **MARY MCLEOD BETHUNE** had opened the first school for dark-skinned students in Daytona Beach, FL (1904).

ELLA E. RYAN, a black woman, became publisher, owner, and manager of *The Forum*, a high quality weekly newspaper in Tacoma WA, writing forceful editorials attacking discrimination against blacks in the nation (1903).

ANNA JEANES established the Negro Rural School Fund, aimed at improving education for blacks in the South (1907).

NANNIE HELEN BURROUGHS founded the Women's Convention of the National Baptist Convention and convinced the NBC to establish the National Training School for Women and Girls (1909).

MAGGIE LENA WALKER founded the *St. Luke Herald* in Richmond VA (1902), and was the first woman to open a bank in America — St. Luke Penny Savings Bank (1903); she later opened the St. Luke Emporium (1905), offering black women opportunities for work and providing the black community access to affordable goods.

HARRIET MARSHALL founded the Washington (DC) Conservatory, admitting African American students (1903).

HARRIOT STANTON BLATCH founded the Equality League of Self-Supporting Women to aid women in the trade unions and the women's suffrage movement (1907).

SARAH WALKER (MADAM C.J.), entrepreneur, philanthropist, and America's first woman self-made millionaire, invented a line of hair care products for blacks, and established Madame C.J. Walker Laboratories (1905).

MAUD POWELL, internationally recognized as America's greatest violinist, was chosen to be the first solo instrumentalist to record for the Victor Company (1904). At a time when musicians were mostly male, she soloed with the New York Philharmonic Orchestra and later formed her own string quartet, bringing music to audiences who had never heard classical music.

META VAUX WARRICK FULLER received the first federal art commission awarded to an African American woman — for figurines of African Americans to be used at the Jamestown Tercentenniel Exposition (1907).

HELEN KELLER, both deaf and blind, graduated cum laude from Radcliffe College (1904).

African American crusading journalist **MARY WHITE OVINGTON,** social reformer **FLORENCE KELLEY**, both white women, and anti-lynching crusader **IDA B. WELLS-BARNETT,** an African American, were among the ten or so founders of the National Association for Coloured [sic] People (NAACP) in 1909. Other women included **JANE ADDAMS, ANNA GARLIN SPENCER,** and **HARRIOT STANTON BLATCH** (daughter of **ELIZABETH CADY STANTON**).

FANNY GARRISON VILLARD was a wealthy active supporter of women's rights, who joined the American Woman Suffrage Association (1906).

MARGARET SLOCUM SAGE inherited a sizeable fortune upon the death of her husband and became the nation's largest individual taxpayer (1907), thirteen years before women had a right to vote. Her Russell Sage Foundation generously gave away millions of dollars in support of women's education, among them founding the Teachers College for Syracuse University, and helping to overcome poverty of women and children.

EMMA SMITH DEVOE helped achieve voting rights for women in Washington State, conducting the Great Women's Campaign (1905). The first woman to serve on the State Republican Committee, she became known as the "Mother of Women's Suffrage".

After Congress passed the Pure Food Act in 1906, the **WOMEN'S CHRISTIAN TEMPERANCE UNION** (WCTU) began a campaign against the use of alcohol in medicine.

ESTHER ALLSTRUM, outspoken suffragist, was running a printing business when she launched into educating lackadaisical grocers about successful food sanitation programs, enforcing license requirements, even setting fire to decaying food and destroying tainted food displays (1908).

ANNIE EDSON TAYLOR, a schoolteacher from Michigan, became the first person to go over Niagara Falls in a barrel (1901).

LUCIA AMES MEAD co-founded the American School Peace League (1908) after supporting the international court proposed at the Hague Conference in 1899.

THE INTERNATIONAL LADIES' GARMENT WORKERS UNION (ILGWU), founded at the turn of the century, called a general strike in 1909, "The Uprising of 20,000", precipitated by a bold speech made by a young Russian Jewish woman named **CLARA LEMLICH.**

Women were not allowed to smoke in public in the U.S., according to a law passed in 1908.

1910-1919

Hello. My name is Pandora. I go to school; I am in the sixth grade, but I'd rather be outside ice skating. Santa brought me new white figure skates for Christmas. (Shhh! Don't tell; I know it was Mama.) I'm going to get another brother or sister. I told Mama I'm not going to get married and have children. They would keep me from having a career, which Aunt Ede says I can have. Not sure what a career is, but I'm going to find out.

After her tenth birthday, Pandora asked her schoolmates to call her *Dora*. She made other choices, opting to choose what clothes she'd wear and how she wanted to live her life. The former came after reading a *Harper's Bazaar* magazine at Madame Pouquette's library that showed women in tight corsets and hobble skirts; who could possibly run and play in such garb?

The latter was decided after a talk with her mother one afternoon following a day when Mary had ironed a pile of clothes, prepared three meals, canned eighteen jars of applesauce, and helped her children with their homework. When Mary Belle closed her eyes for a moment, Pandora asked, "Mamá, are you tired?"

"No, *ma chere*… well actually yes, I'm plumb worn out. It's been a long day."

After a moment, Mary Belle put her arms around her daughter and spoke quietly, "Pandora Nelle, don't marry too soon. I think you might like a career some day."

"What's a *career*, Mamá?"

"Well, it's work… but the kind that may take you away from the duties of keeping a house. Men seem to enjoy careers."

"Oh Ma, I'd like a career. Is that like Miss Gloria's Beauty Shop?"

"Not that kind of career; it's too risky. But I hear some girls work in offices and stores and get salaries, like Grace does."

"Teacher said she'd like an office job. What's that?"

"Well, sort of like the bank… like the one in Durand where Pa goes to vote. He said he once saw a woman behind the counter there."

"Teacher said some girls are typewriters. And they get paid money for it. Is that a career?"

"Hmm. I'm not sure either. But you're too young to be thinking about such things yet."

Pandora put her mother's weary comments in her memory collection and knew she'd give the career topic more consideration later.

School was uppermost in Dora's life, even though she became bored without enough challenges. She missed the times she and Pa hung around the barn or tromped through the fields. She hated being indoors and she hated having to wear skirts. Winters were the worst. She was happiest from spring to fall, when warm breezes beckoned her to roam the woods and hike along the creek.

For her eleventh birthday, Dora received a box of watercolors, brushes, and thick drawing paper. Teacher had told Mary Belle that she thought Pandora needed "an artistic pursuit". Teacher thought Pandora was playing with the boys too much. "She tears the school yard around like one of the lads, her skirts flyin' in the breeze. 'At's not a proper activity for a proper young lady," said Teacher.

Teacher was herself a very proper young woman. Lillian Horne came from a German family and still spoke English with a slight accent and occasionally reversed her sentences. Her family had come to America straight from Germany in the 1890s, homesteading on farmland near the Whaleys. At fourteen, Lillian went to work as a housekeeper for a family who took the time to teach her proper English in exchange for her teaching them German. She learned so well that when she was eighteen, she taught neighborhood immigrant children, until enough gathered to form a school of sorts. She had to convince the town council that she could teach as well as the men who, until that time, had done most of the teaching.

By 1911, Teacher had reached the grand old age of twenty-four and realized, as did her pupils, that she probably would never marry. She enjoyed teaching and loved the children. What more could she ask? (*A husband to love me*, she frequently told herself. But that was not to be.)

Dora had taken to tutoring her brothers, who were eager for her help. Andrew at seventeen was still struggling with numbers and spending most of his time at farm work. Jason, only a third grader and big for his age, hated to read.

"How do you squelch a tornado?" Mary Belle asked Teacher.

"Pandora Nelle has many talents," Teacher responded. "She observes; she always knows what's going on around her. And curious! I never saw such a girl with so much curious in her. Send her into the world to learn."

Mary Belle spoke to Dora of Teacher's comments about "artistic pursuits" only once, and was greeted with a sneer from her daughter. "I can't just sit and sew like some of those girls," she whined.

No matter, Mary Belle had much too much work to worry about Pandora. "She'll find her way," she assured her husband. "Teacher says she's curious."

"Hrumph!" was Fayette's response.

The watercolors didn't remain in their container for long. They seemed to be just what Dora needed to express some of the new feelings she was discovering inside herself. She spent hours with the tiny brushes, fashioning pictures of bouquets of flowers, detailed insects, and horses — galloping, rearing, whinnying horses.

"They don't look like our Ned and Moll," Fayette told his daughter.

"That's 'cuz they're not Ned and Moll," Dora explained proudly. "They're racing steeds with swift legs and strong lungs. They gallop at full speed over the plains looking for Indians to take care of them."

"That's a pretty picture," cooed her mother. "You fixin' to let some Injuns haul you off to their teepees to raise you?"

"Ma," Dora shot back. "You don't understand."

Dora had taken an interest in her dad's horses, the ones that pulled the family wagon to town for groceries, tugged harrows across spring fields, and harvesters and hay wagons through the same fields at the end of summer. She had tried to ride them once or twice, but either they threw her off their backs or they plodded too slowly down the narrow dirt roads. Her dreams turned to dashing steeds whinnying and leaping, raising up on hind legs to paw the air with authority.

It wouldn't be long before her fascination with speed would be transferred to a new fangled invention — a horseless carriage called an *automobile*. Aunt Ede, just back from a trip to her husband's home office in New York, had brought tales of the belching machines that "were causing a ruckus in city streets as they sputtered and roared, frightening horses, women, and children."

Edith always brought spectacular gifts along with her stories to her nieces and nephews when she returned from a trip. Those were special times when all the family gathered to hear her tales and to open her gifts.

For Pandora's twelfth birthday, Aunt Ede's gift struck up another fire in her niece. "It's a camera, a Kodak," Dora announced proudly as she showed it around the family. "See how this part pulls out? You aim the shutter at what you want a picture of and then you take a deep breath and click this gadget here."

"Whew! I didn't realize you knew that much about cameras, Dora," her mother said. "Now say *thank you*."

But Dora was still too breathless to speak. She had heard about cameras, even had her picture taken when she graduated from Sunday School's Summer Class last year. But she never dreamed of having her own, her very own camera. She wouldn't let go of it long enough to let even her mother handle it.

"No need for thanks, Dora," Aunt Ede whispered. "Here, take our pictures. It's all loaded with film." The family dutifully followed Dora onto the porch where a wan winter sun offered its frosty light.

"Stand still, everyone," Dora commanded. "Mother, hold little Iris Rosella. I wish Grace were here to be in the picture. Everybody stand real still now. No fussing, Iris. Jason, look at the camera! Take a deep breath everyone and hold it while you count to ten slowly. Hold it... and... eight, nine, (click) there! You can breathe again."

Once back indoors, Aunt Ede, reaching around her niece to show her how to wind to the next film stop, could feel the young girl's heart pounding.

"You really like this camera, don't you."

"Yes, oh yes, oh yes. Thank you, Aunt Ede. Thank you, thank you, thank..."

"Whoa, that's enough. Take some good pictures and I'll try to find you an album to put them in. I'm told the Five-and-Dime over at Durand has some. It's difficult to find places that carry film. So here," she handed Dora a small sack. "I brought you four rolls of film to start."

Dora carried the camera wherever she went. After school, she and her friends went out to the woods and cavorted in the snow, aping at the camera. Some of the girls wanted their pictures taken hanging from trees. Dora's favorite pose was when one of her friends put on boys' clothing, tucked her long hair under a cap, and posed holding a cigar. Dora snapped pictures at school and church pageants, at holiday parades, picnics, Sunday School parties, and around the farm. The only hitch was that she had to take pictures outdoors on clear days or they didn't *turn out*. She tried an indoor shot once in a room at church with all the lights on, but it didn't work. Neither did the shots she took outside on cloudy days.

Those lights at church? Yes, Arkansaw had acquired access to electrical wires. REA was a household word (in some households). It meant Rural Electrification Association and fed electricity to those rural areas that could pay for it. The Whaleys wouldn't take advantage of it until after the Great War.

Dora's camera helped her capture the likenesses of family members who were beginning to disappear. Her half-sisters, Grace and Lynna, had married Durand men and moved away with their new husbands. Andrew joined the army in 1914 when Europe was rumbling with the early throes of what would turn into a world-wide war. Adam, Fayette's oldest son, married and moved onto his own farm. He and his wife Laura invited Billie to live with them as a housekeeper, following a family dispute about Billie's newly found freedom after she graduated from eighth grade.

Dora took to wearing her brothers' clothes more and more often. Jason's knickerbockers offered her the freedom and individuality she sought. "If I'm going to be called a tomboy, I might as well dress like one," she told her mother. Mary Belle started to lift her voice, but restrained herself.

Dora learned more about women's roles in the family when two more babies joined the Whaley brood. Selene Nicolette was born in 1912, and Apollo Ralph followed early in 1914. Both times, Dora helped her mother through the birthings; each time she swore never to have children of her own.

She'll become a real woman soon, Mary Belle told herself. *Then she'll understand.*

And that's exactly what happened. Dora's sexuality clearly came into bloom — one day as she was wearing her brother's trousers. She was frightened at first by the menstrual blood. She ran to her mother, who showed her how to tear up an old sheet and roll up the pieces to form pads. Dora carefully lined her underwear with the "pads" and hobbled off to her room.

Mary Belle followed and sat down on her daughter's bed. "You can expect this every month now; this is what makes it possible for women to have babies," she began. "You'll experience 'the curse' until you're an old woman."

"But animals don't bleed. Moll just gets big and round and then lies down until the new foal is born."

"Well, we humans are animals, but we're a bit different, in several ways."

"Do old women bleed? Did Grandma Rose?"

"Menstruate," her mother corrected. "Not past a certain age. No need when the childbearing is over. But no, Mother Rosella was not that old when she died."

"I remember. That was a long time ago; I was just seven years old. Do you?"

"Do I what?"

"You know, menstate?"

"Of course. Women men-stru-ate…" she pronounced it carefully again "…until they are too old to bear children."

"Are you expecting more babies?"

"No. Your pa says that five's enough. Ten, counting his first family." Mary paused, then added, "I had two miscarriages before little Iris was born."

"I didn't know that," Dora whispered. "Are you okay now?"

"Yes, it's not an illness you know… menstruation. It's part of life — like having children. But I'm small and that makes it hard to bear them. You know, Pandora, that you're able to have children now — you've begun your years as a woman. And you're a good size."

The very idea of childbirth panicked the young girl after witnessing the births of her younger sister and brother. "I guess I'd like to have a baby — someday, but not five. Maybe two, a boy and a girl."

"Good luck, ma fille." Mary Belle patted her daughter's head as she walked past her out of the room. "Good luck."

Schooling ended for Pandora after the eight years considered enough for girls. Still, Teacher had encouraged her to consider going away to business school where she could learn skills as a secretary. Because that meant leaving her family and moving alone to the big city, Dora could see no possibility when the idea first came up. Dora helped out Teacher at the school the following year, but she knew there were more important things she wanted to do.

"Papá, did you go away to school?" she asked Fayette one morning as they sat hunched over milking pails.

"Naw. Didn't yer mother ever tell ye? I finished third grade, but I know how to read real good. My mum made sure I larned."

"What do you want me to be when I grow up?" she asked.

"Well now, let's see. Ye can be the mum of some very pretty grandchildren for me..."

"Oh Pa!"

"...or ye could be a princess and marry the new king of England..."

"Or I could go to business school," Dora finished quickly so she wouldn't lose her nerve. She held her breath.

"Or ye could go to... well now, is that what ye want to do? Ain't niver had a bizness girl in the family."

"Oh Pa, could I? I'd really like to go to business school, even if it means I have to leave you and Ma... I wouldn't like that much."

"Come on now, little Pandora. Ye and me had too many good times together to talk like that. Ye can leave here and go anywhere in this gosh-darned whole wide world..."

"Papa, don't swear."

"Ye know what I mean. Ye can go anywhere and ye won't be out of our hearts." The old man sat back on his milking stool, patted the fat cow belly near his face, then leaned his head against the cow's warm soft hide. "Aw, what's the use! Of course I'll miss ye, my lovely Pandora. I'm nigh onto 60 years soon and there ain't much more for me. But ye... there's more to life than just milking cows and cooking supper. Ask yer ma!"

"Ooh, thank you, thank you," Pandora cried as she rushed to hug her father, nearly upsetting the pail of warm milk in front of him.

That fall, 1915, Pandora packed the new dresses that her mother had made from the flowered cloth that once formed the large sacks of flour they used for baking bread. Since her daughter had entered Arkansaw's school, Mary Belle had carefully saved flour sacks, washing and folding the cloth and stashing it into a drawer near her treadle sewing machine. All her daughters wore new dresses on the first day of every school year.

Now she had a daughter going away to business school. She had already packed three sets of brand new undergarments, cotton stockings, a new hair brush and several sets of combs. Dora would have to wind up her hair in a bun or braid it loosely on top of her head from now on. Only little girls let their hair fly in the wind. And only strumpets cut their hair short.

Pandora Nelle, a confident young woman, perched a new hat on top of her new rolled-up hairdo, fitted her small hands into the new gloves, slung her camera by its strap over her shoulder, and set off for the Menomonie Business School. She quickly learned the meaning of "office" and "typewriter", words not generally spoken on farms.

Dora's easy smile and tendency to giggle at the wrong time earned her new friends quickly. Her camera helped too; she could always find something funny to photograph, and she didn't hesitate to share the fun. She took pictures of her new friends, some with pencils behind their ears and some glowering at the intrusive camera. One girl wore a man's hat balanced on her head and horn-rimmed glasses perched atop her nose. If anyone stood lifeless in front of her lens, Dora simply waited until something made them laugh or they made a face at the camera before she clicked the shutter.

"Have you heard about the new instructor?" her friend Ginger asked one afternoon as the two of them carried their books to the ice cream shop.

"No, but I heard he has something to do with telephones."

"You're right. We're going to learn how to use the telephone... and..."

"That sounds exciting."

"... and learn how to be telephone... operators." She spoke slowly so the weight of her words would sink in.

Dora listened, waiting for more, then asked, "What do telephone operators do?"

"Don't you have telephones in that backwater town you're from?" Ginger teased.

"Of course we do... I think. Yes, I know we do. Hartung's Mercantile has one. I heard it ring... once...." Dora recalled how excited she became when the strange sound interrupted, ringing throughout the store. Grace explained how the town's general store had installed the gadget only the week before and this was the second time it had rung. Needless to say, the customers were impressed.

"Do you want to be a telephone operator?" Dora asked her friend. "It must be terribly complicated."

"Don't you? Heck, Dora, let's sign up and find out."

"Watch your language, Missy," Dora imitated their instructor. "What a way for a typewriter to talk."

"Heck!" Ginger repeated defiantly. "I don't want to be just a typewriter. I want to work in a bank and operate a calculator, or work in a store and run a cash drawer. I like machines, but not just typewriting machines." Ginger and Dora had reached the shop and ordered their daily sarsaparilla with ice from the electric ice machine. Life in the city was very different from Arkansaw.

The telephone instructor offered not only a fascinating new career opportunity, but he was good looking too. Dora and Ginger weren't the only two who suddenly switched career goals to join the Bell Telephone Company. Within a week, several model telephone boards had been moved into the classrooms, and students began to learn about the equipment.

"Each set of cords represents one call," the instructor explained carefully. "One cord responds to the blinking light — that's an incoming call." He plugged the tip into the flashing receptor. "And the other cord connects with the proper number inside the office — or home." The young man pulled the matching cord and plugged it into another slot. He blushed constantly as he attempted to show these adoring young women the intricacies of the telephone system. Dora felt sorry for him.

Somehow they learned how to operate the boards. Dora and Ginger and their friends also learned there were good wages connected with their new technological profession. Bell Telephone would assign them six- or eight-hour shifts and pay them by the hour — more than they would ever receive as typewriters or cashiers. Dora began to dream of administering the telephone board back home — if Arkansaw ever got one.

In the wide world beyond Arkansaw and the college town of Menomonie, the second decade of the 20th century was to witness a great war — "the war to end all wars". Many changes in a roiling world led up to the conflagration.

Inventions in the ways people moved about the globe — automobiles and aeroplanes — brought people of the world closer together. And the worlds clashed.

Horseless carriages turned cities into noisy places to live. "They won't last long, just a passing fad," exclaimed the naysayers about the "autos". Still, European immigrants escaping the turmoil of their own countries, sought out America's manufacturing cities.

The "passing fad" label was soon shifted to the flying machines beginning to appear overhead, spotted by observant children in various corners of the country. "There's a… a… thing in the sky making a buzzing noise," was the usual warning of approaching aircraft. And everyone turned out if one came close to the ground or landed. People claimed the airplane was the cause for the Great War; "If it weren't for flying machines, the war wouldn't have spread," they said. And yet, when America entered the battle with its fleet of aircraft, they shot the German fleet out of the air.

During their first year at Menomonie, Ginger had dragged Dora to a suffragists' meeting on one of those very cold clear spring nights. About two dozen women huddled in the drafty hall behind the town's only theater and waited nearly an hour before the guest speaker arrived. A group of women entered the hall grandly, kicking their long black skirts high as they walked to the stage. Behind them, several young women carried placards on sticks that read: *Votes For Women* and *Give Women The Vote*. The audience stood up and clapped their hands — vigorously to keep warm — until one of the women on stage motioned for them to stop.

When the room was silent, she began. "Ladies. Thank you for coming out tonight to hear one of the nation's most famous women speak on the subject of rights for women. I'll let her tell you what is happening across our country. Please greet Mrs. Sarah Burnham Leighton, president of the state's Women's Right To Vote movement."

Dora applauded before, during, and after the speech as she recognized the truths spoken by this overpowering woman. Women indeed were as good as men. Women had the right to cast their ballots in elections. Women didn't have to spend their lives tied to their kitchens. Women had the right to pursue their own lives and careers. And who gave men their power over women anyway? Yea! Yea!

Afterwards, Dora and Ginger walked home in the brisk starlit night, ignoring the cold as they talked excitedly about what they were going to do with their new-found freedom. After all, they had rights!

The following morning, as the young women waited for their breakfast in the large dining room of the boarding house, chatter turned to suffragists. Dora had wakened to visions of last night's meeting and was eager to learn more about what suffragists do. *Look at me,* she thought, *a 15-year-old farm girl having breakfast with city girls who are arguing who will wear the six banners left behind by last night's speaker.*

"They're asking us to walk with them in a show of strength," said the girl at the head of the table. "We have only six banners. How'll we decide who'll wear them?"

"I'm the tallest. They can read the words better on someone who stands tall," called out another.

"I'm older," shouted the 20-year-old at the end of the table. "I've been here the longest."

"The school's newest student, wanted to join the fray. Her heart beat a rhythm inside her as the argument continued amid discord, the girls shouting over each other, trying to be heard. Only the entry of the girl pouring fresh cups of coffee quelled their voices, but only for a moment. Once she left, the chatter continued. Voices reached a breathless high pitch, or they wouldn't have heard her.

Quietly, from Dora's corner of the table came her small voice. "I can jump high."

The room froze, forks in mid-air, as all eyes turned toward the newcomer. The girls hadn't heard much from her in the weeks since she joined them. Her voice startled them.

Dora stood up, waving her arms as she jumped — toes tucked under her, about two feet off the ground, shouting, "Give women the vote!"

When she sat down again, the other girls looked at each other, then as one, they applauded, calling out, "She speaks!" The little girl has a voice." "Whadayaknow?" and "Jeez! That girl can jump!"

When they ran out of phrases, a surprised Ginger asked, "Jump high, huh? What good will *that* do?"

"They'll notice me… er, my banner. I can shout the words too." Her courage reached a pitch that raised her blood and her voice. "Just standing still with a banner won't get attention."

Ginger turned to the others and nodded, adding, "You know, Dora has a good idea. Can anyone else jump?" Blank faces stared back. "Well good then, Dora gets a banner and a chance to… jump."

Amid applause, Dora smiled at her friends and said, "I would be honored to wear the banner and jump for the cause."

When they left for class, Ginger placed a friendly arm around her friend's shoulders. "You're quite a gal, Dora. Where'd you get the nerve?"

"I had to say something. After last night's meeting, the cause is all I could think about. I hardly slept."

"Me too, but today is now. C'mon, Dora, we don't want to be late for class."

The parade that marched boldly down Main Street the following Saturday featured almost thirty young women dressed in long white dresses, their hair primly pinned on top of their heads. The six in front wore banners proudly across their chests declaring, "Give Women the Vote!" But one of the marchers garnered the most applause from an awed crowd.

"That one!" they shouted. "Watch her. Gee, can she jump!"

"I'd vote for her!"

During her second year at Menomonie, Pandora Nelle officially became a telephone operator, accredited by the Bell Telephone Company. Leo Carlson, the self-conscious instructor, finally worked up enough nerve to invite her to see a Mary Pickford film. And love came to Pandora for the first time.

Her letters home contained bland accounts of her classes, without a single mention of the suffragist meetings she attended regularly. Nor did they mention the telephone class instructor. It wasn't until she was ready to move back to Arkansaw at graduation that she summoned up the courage to write about Leo.

Her mother's admonitions arrived by return mail. "You're too young to get serious about anyone. Are you planning to stay there and work? Hartung's is looking for a new clerk. Or maybe you could work as a typewriter and nurse for the new doctor."

Dora wrote back, "I'm eighteen now, an accomplished telephone operator and I'll probably operate the new Arkansaw telephone office. People back home are about to get their own telephones."

"Pshaw!" responded her mother when she read the letter.

Durand already had a telephone exchange and Arkansaw would have its own by summer; Leo would see to that. The young salesmen who were caught up in selling this new convenience spread the word about telephones. "In a very few years, everyone will have a telephone in their house," they promised. "Everyone!"

"Impossible," said the detractors. "This fad will pass and folks will go back to visiting one another and writing letters."

"What would happen if we could only talk to people's ears and never see their faces?"

Still, seven new telephones were installed in Arkansaw by spring 1918, and ten more were scheduled by the time the Arkansaw Telephone Office opened. Most of the new customers were the French Canadians, Dora noted. "Somehow they always seemed way ahead of the Irish and the Germans."

At the end of the school year, right after Dora's graduation, Leo decided to move from instructing to selling telephones, even if it demanded he learn to be aggressive in dealing with customers. The Bell company, always eager to move enterprising young men into the field, complied, giving Leo the territory that included Arkansaw, where he trained new hires in "the art of sales", with the power to hire and fire.

Dora and Ginger were hired as Operators that summer — Dora because she knew everyone in town, and Ginger because Leo figured they were good friends who belonged together. Besides, he was eager to make Dora happy.

The young women moved some of their belongings into the upstairs rooms of the new *office*. Ma Bell had secured a house in which to set up business. Ginger was to live there, and Dora would have a sleepover room if she was too tired to go home. While Fayette was delighted to have his daughter back under his roof, he couldn't help but wonder if she'd ever find a husband and have her own home.

The telephone office had been fashioned from the house that belonged to the Methodist Church as a manse for the pastor. When Pastor Nichols' family agreed to pay for half of a newly built manse, the church offered the old house to the telephone company. Bell was a good renter and paid top dollar. Equipment occupied the first floor, and the upstairs rooms were outfitted for the operators.

A small wood cooking range warmed the kitchen in the back of the house and a small wood-burning Franklin stove heated the office in front. Leftover heat rose upstairs to warm the bedrooms, which were drafty and cold in winter and stuffy and hot in summer. But the rooms belonged to the operators, to furnish and decorate as they pleased.

Pandora found the telephone switchboard a magical box made for her. She felt satisfaction in connecting people with only a pair of cords. And she knew she could connect people to any place in the world — as far away as Chicago and even Cleveland and maybe even New York. She could also connect people with the inside of another's heart. Hers was indeed a precious treasure box of magic.

Sleeping over at the telephone office provided Dora privacy she didn't have at home. Her father had taken to talk constantly about his friends' daughters who were getting married and having children. For a time, even her mother joined the chorus.

Dora was happier than she had ever been. She saw Leo more than she had at school, and realized he had taken a special liking for her. Quite often he invited her to spend her free time driving around the countryside with him as he made sales calls to prospective clients.

By fall, second and third operators were hired part-time for emergencies — should Dora or Ginger become ill or when they wanted to get away for a few hours. It would be nearly another year before the town had enough telephones to warrant twenty-four-hour service. As it was, Dora was awakened only three times to answer a night-time call (Ginger slept too soundly to respond).

In mid-October, Bell offered Leo a job as installer of telephones, at a slight raise in pay. He took it, even if it kept him tightly tied to a schedule.

Dora spent most of her time at the telephone office, returning to the family farm for an occasional visit. She had been trying for months to convince her father the family needed a telephone of their own.

"You can contact me whenever you want — at five-cents a call, of course," she suggested. "You can talk for three minutes, and you can say a lot in three minutes. And what about emergencies?"

"Who would I call, dotter?" her pa countered. "Nobody I know got a telly-phone."

"What if you needed a doctor in Durand in a hurry?"

"Yer ma takes good care of me."

"And what if Ma or the children need care?"

That did it — Fayette gave in and ordered the phone. Leo made the installation himself, giving Dora's mother time to question him about how it worked.

"See this handle here? You lift it off the hook and place it next to your left ear. You take that crank on the right and turn it… away from you. Here try it!"

Mary Belle approached the box on the wall. "Go on," Leo urged. "Give it a try."

"Oh dear. Well, all right." She reached for the receiver, lifted it cautiously and placed it near her ear. She gave the handle a twist and jumped back as she heard the sound. "It's buzzing," she called out. Then her eyes opened wide and her jaw dropped as she heard her daughter's voice ask, "Is that you Mamá?"

Leo pointed toward the mouthpiece and Mary Belle yelled into it, "Pandora?"

"You don't have to holler, Ma, I can hear you just fine. I guess Leo has installed your telephone."

In a quieter voice, her mother tried to sound as if she had always used a telephone and they chatted for a few minutes. Leo pointed to the clock on the wall and showed his new customer how to disconnect the call.

"Mercy me," Mary Belle sighed. "Will wonders never cease?"

She insisted that Leo stay for a cup of coffee, giving her the opportunity to question him about his work and what he perceived as his "destiny".

"I'm making the best money possible right now," Leo responded. "And don't worry about Pandora. She's my girl and I want to see she has a good life."

Mary Belle poured another cup of coffee and sat back, smiling.

Arkansaw had met its own destiny. The first words proclaiming the end of the Great War came through the telephone office and convinced the town that telephones might be more useful than originally thought. Pandora wasn't on duty, but she was close enough to her family's new phone to hear the message relayed within minutes. Ginger had sounded the coded ring — three-short — to the Whaley house. Upon hearing the wild sounding rings, Dora called out, "Sounds like the town is on fire" as she lifted the receiver.

"The war has ended. It's over!" Ginger shouted into the phone.

"Are you sure? Oh, that's great. Wait, I'll tell Pa; he's out in the barn."

"Can't wait. Must call the rest of the town."

"Of course. Need help?"

"Naw, I've got this. Good news is fun to spread. Does this mean Andy will be coming home soon?"

"I guess. He's stationed down south, someplace in Georgia. When he came back from France, they sent him to a hospital there. He should be home soon."

"Gotta go, Dora. I'm ringing all the phones on the exchange."

"Call back if you need help."

"I've got things under control. One ring on the party line and I get the message to a lot of people. Thanks anyway."

Dora called out to her family and told them the good news. "Just in time too," she told her mother. "Leo and his crew were about to be sent to Europe to install telephone communication for troops."

"Ye mean they're takin' this fad to Europe?" her father chided as he removed his boots at the door.

"You mean you two were about to get married?" Mary Belle asked.

"Ma! Don't be gross. I'm a career woman now. And he's very busy with his job. Although he says he's about to be made regional manager of the Bell system."

"A big move up, eh?" suggested Fayette. "Means more money. Now he can afford a wife. Nice going, Dora."

"Pa!" Dora wailed. "Don't you start too."

The Great War ended on a cold November day in 1918. News spread rapidly through the new telephones, across ticker tapes to newsrooms, and then to newsboys on the streets crying, "Extra! Extra! Read all about it! The war is over!" The Durand newspaper hired three newsboys to carry the special edition to the townspeople.

Pandora greeted the good news with her own mark of independence. With the war ended, hope rose for a world working together, a nation of peaceful progress, and for her, a future full of choices.

Leo continued installing telephones, but the area had expanded and required more of his attention. Now that Dora was back working in Arkansaw, Leo found his new Ford Model-T automobile useful. Several of the telephone people had them, painted a special dark green to match the Ma Bell logo that was painted on the door.

The only problem was that when Leo drove to Arkansaw to visit *his girl*, everyone knew it. He'd pick up Pandora when her shift ended, and they'd drive over to Durand for a soda. Whenever the "telephone man" came to town, people wondered whether someone was getting a new telephone or if Dora was being courted.

On one trip into the country with Dora, Leo pulled over to the side of the dirt road and got out of the vehicle. "Come on, get behind the wheel. You should know how to drive this thing," he encouraged.

"Aw no, I couldn't," she began. "Really? You'd let me drive your tin lizzie? You gotta tell me how."

Leo showed her how to engage the spark on the steering wheel, then move the gearshift on the floor, then press on the accelerator ever-so...

"Slow, Dora! Just a little at a time. That's a gasoline engine under there and it needs just a little... whoa... all right now, just a bit more... don't let 'er die... more gas, Dora... more..." But the engine died anyway.

Leo grabbed the crank from under the seat and climbed out. He gave the crank a twist, and the engine coughed. "Once more..." he muttered to himself and turned the crank again. This time the engine coughed twice. "And one more time..." he gave the crank a hefty turn-and-a-half and the engine sputtered to life. "Give it a little gas, Dora, the choke!" he called as he hopped back into the car.

"What's a choke?" Dora yelled over the sputtering engine.

"That thing there." Leo pointed behind the steering wheel.

"Like this?"

"Good. Now, do everything you did before, but this time feel the accelerator. Feel the gas that's feeding the engine."

Dora started up again, moving very slowly, but more smoothly. "Beginner's luck," she called as the car took to the narrow rutty road and chugged happily on its way. "Steering a car is easier than steering horses, except I have to keep my eyes on the road. A horse knows where to go, even if the driver isn't watching."

After the first driving lesson, she couldn't wait to try it again. Within a few trips, she was driving the Model-T almost as well as Leo did. In time, and by necessity, she learned to patch tires, re-fill the gas tank, replace spark plugs, and pull the car out of a mud puddle. Her challenging side roads often were muddy traps for automobiles, and just when she thought she had found a shortcut road, she'd find her rear wheels sunk deep in a mud hole.

One of these days, she'd have her own car and drive back and forth wherever and whenever she wanted.

Although Dora worked all the telephone shifts, she preferred the mornings. She loved to walk to the telephone office with the rising sun as the early rays warmed up the town. In summer, the streets of sand retained heat from the previous day. In winter, she carefully picked her way in the dark along the tracks in the snow laid by sleighs and teams of horses the night before. When she worked the six a.m. to two p.m. shift, she had hours free to paint or sew, to play around with her growing nieces and nephews, or go driving with Leo.

That winter following the end of the war, Mary Belle's eyes were giving her more trouble, and she depended more and more on Pandora to do the weekend baking. "Cataracts," said the doctor. "Your eyes will only get worse. But with care you could still see, maybe for years." Dora tried to give her mother the care she needed, carefully bathing her eyes with a special mixture, keeping lights low, and monitoring her mother's movements in the sun.

Andrew finally came home from war, with a slight limp and minus a few fingers on his left hand, the toll taken by an exploding mine in France. "It's a small matter when you realize how many minds were lost from the poison gas and how many bodies were lost," he told the family. "Some of my buddies lost legs and arms. I'm the lucky one. Besides, Dora's the piano player, not me," he joked. Still, Andy had to learn new ways to do the simple things, especially milking cows.

Leo and Dora became regular fixtures at the Sunday after-church dinner table. At Christmas in 1918, Leo proposed, placing a small diamond ring on Dora's finger. "I love you, Dora," he said quietly.

She didn't need time to think before responding, "I love you too."

Dora felt her years as she approached her nineteenth birthday. She had seen Mary Belle grow old with her five-plus children, all born before she was 30. Dora remembered last summer, when everyone helped with the haying, how she had seen the fatigue in the lines on her mother's face as she worked to feed the haying crew, lines that a woman that young shouldn't have.

"Can we wait until next summer to get married?" Dora asked.

"Sure, if that's what you want," Leo replied. "Is June summer?"

Dora laughed. Sharing life with this man would be fun. Perhaps housework wouldn't be so bad now that electricity was being installed around town. Imagine, electric stoves instead of having to chop wood all the time. And electric refrigerators to replace the ice boxes and chilled pantries. How bad could it be with such fine appliances? Besides, Leo wouldn't expect her to give up her job... would he?

Grace had come home for a weekend in February with three little daughters tugging at her skirts. She agreed to be Pandora's matron of honor. Ginger, Billie, and Iris would be bridesmaids. Dora's youngest sister, Selene, nearly seven, was designated the flower girl and baby Apollo, at four, the ring bearer.

With Mary Belle's eyes bothering her more, the girls decided to sew their own dresses — their mother had taught them well. They made a trip to Durand and bought out the store's supply of dress patterns and several yards of pale blue silk. Dora chose to make her own wedding dress, with her mother helping on good days.

Dora had never been happier as the wedding plans progressed. Until the day in May she responded to the long-distance blinking light.

"Arkansaw Telephone Office. Number please."

"Dora? That you? Call Durand and have them send over an ambulance. There's been an accident," a voice shouted. Dora recognized Leo's co-worker. The two were out at the Schneider place on the Durand road, wiring the house for a new phone.

"What's wrong? What should I tell the hospital?" She already knew the answer.

"Sorry, Dora. It's Leo. We were... looking for a place... electric shock... he's not breathing..."

Dora's numb body did what she had been taught to do in emergencies. She called the hospital and asked for an ambulance. Then she called upstairs to Ginger and asked her to finish the shift. She waited, hands frozen on cords and switches until Ginger raced down the stairs.

"I'm so sorry, Dor! I'm so sorry." The two young women cried, hugging each other and rocking back and forth.

Late spring of 1919 witnessed a funeral instead of a wedding at the Whaley house. Dora felt a piece of herself fall away, lost in the flurry of amenities. The Whaleys entertained Leo's parents for two days after the funeral, the first time the Carlsons had met Pandora. It was a sad summer of might-haves for the young woman: she might have had a partner for life, someone funny and smart and serious and wild and adventurous and well-behaved. She might have had a gentleman to accompany her to church picnics and family get-togethers, a gentle man to hold her close and take away her fears, a loving soul to wrap her in comfort and familiarity… all gone. She'd never hear his cheery voice call her name as he drove up to the telephone office at the end of her shift. Never again.

When the Carlsons went home, they left Leo's automobile with Pandora.

Men returning home after winning a major war sat back and looked at the world around them. Men were educated; men wrote books; men formed history; men led businesses, ran the government, painted the pictures, protected their country, healed its citizens, and for leisure activities developed ways to keep the women out.

During the year 1919, Congress-*men* may have thought: *This is 1919! Women have been hollering for the vote for a hundred years — why not toss them a crumb? Besides, they seem satisfied to have their men home again, taking charge of things; the women will be content to stay home and raise children; they probably won't vote anyway.*

Pandora's Notes of the 19-teens

The decade that would turn into a cauldron of political movement began in March 1911 with a tragic fire that killed scores of women who worked for the TRIANGLE SHIRTWAIST COMPANY in New York. Only a year after a strike failed to improve dangerous working conditions and low wages, fire trapped workers on upper floors. Because it was Saturday, payday, the exits had been locked to keep the women working until the shift was over.

An all-male jury failed to indict the company's management, suggesting the women *were not as intelligent as other workers and may have contributed to their own deaths because of panic.* A total of 146 women with an average age of 19 were killed in that fire, either through suffocation, flames, or by jumping out of windows. Four years later, following numerous investigations, new laws were written to govern safety standards for states throughout the U.S.

EMILY GREENE BALCH served as secretary-treasurer of the Women's International League for Peace and Freedom (WILPF) (1915), first established as the Women's Peace Party. She received the Nobel Peace Prize for her work in 1946.

CRYSTAL EASTMAN, an organizer of the Woman's Peace Party (1915) and leader of the American Union Against Militarism, authored model legislation, which led to co-founding the National Civil Liberties Bureau (later to become the ACLU) to fight government suppression of dissenters during World War I (1917).

JOVITA IDAR, Texas journalist, wrote articles criticizing Hispanic-Anglo relations. Her efforts led to the First Mexican Congress to discuss educational, social, labor, and economic matters. One outcome was the formation of the League of Mexican Women (1911).

FANNIE ANDREWS co-founded the American School Peace League (1908) and developed a peace curriculum (1913) used until 1950.

The year Pandora turned ten, **CAMP FIRE GIRLS** was founded by **CHARLOTTE VETTER GUILICK** as the first interracial, non-sectarian American organization for girls (1910).

ALICE STEBBINS WELLS, a formal social worker became the nation's first female police officer with arrest powers (Los Angeles, 1910).

BLANCHE STUART SCOTT became the first American woman pilot to solo in an aeroplane. She wore classy bloomers created by a Fifth Avenue (NYC) tailor (1910).

JULIETTE GORDON LOW founded the Girl Scouts of America (1912).

HENRIETTA SZOLD founded Hadassah, the largest Jewish organization in U.S. history, focusing on education and health care in Israel and the U.S. (1912).

The second Sunday of May was designated by presidential proclamation as **MOTHER'S DAY** (1914).

VIRGINIA ESTELLE RANDOLPH, an innovative teacher and daughter of former slaves, became the first Jeanes Supervisor Industrial Teacher in Virginia (1908) and was honored when the first vocational training school for African Americans was named after her (1915).

JENNIE MARIE HOWE, a New York journalist, formed The Heterodoxy Club, which provided women with a forum to discuss issues without the worry of derision and scorn from the public (1912).

LAURA BELLE DOWNEY BARTLETT, mining engineer and president of the Oregon State Mining Association, wrote songs and books in the Chinook Indian language (1916).

BEULAH LOUISE HENRY, a housewife and inventor known as "Lady Edison", registered 49 patents and is credited with more than twice that number of inventions. Her first was the vacuum ice cream freezer (1912), followed by changeable umbrella covers to coordinate with clothing (1924), soap-filled sponges for children (1929), a "protograph" (typewriter accessory that could make four copies of a document) (1932), a bobbin-less sewing machine (1940), and linked envelopes to simplify mass mailings (1952).

IMOGEN CUNNINGHAM, photographer specializing in portraits, held her first one-person exhibition at the Brooklyn Institute of Arts and Sciences (1914).

GEORGIA O'KEEFE'S paintings were exhibited at the famous gallery of Alfred Stieglitz in New York (1916).

FRANCES ELLIOTT DAVIS was the first African American nurse to enroll with the American Red Cross (1918).

LENA MADESON PHILLIPS promoted opportunities for women in professional and white collar work by founding the **NATIONAL FEDERATION OF BUSINESS AND PROFESSIONAL WOMEN'S CLUBS (BPWC)** (1919).

BRENDA VINEYARD RUNYON founded the First Woman's Bank in Clarksville TN — the first bank run entirely by women (1919).

NELLIE CENTENNIAL CORNISH founded the Cornish School of Music and Art in Seattle WA (1914).

MARGARET H'DOUBLER, dance educator, founded the American University's first dance class (1917).

MARY DAVENPORT ENGBERG took up her baton for the Bellingham (WA) Symphony to become the first female symphony conductor in the U.S. (1914). She moved on to the Seattle Symphony (1921).

MARGARET SANGER and her sister **ETHEL SANGER BYRNE** (known as the Birth Control Sisters) opened the first U.S. birth control clinic in Brooklyn NY and were arrested a few days later in violation of The Comstock Law of 1873, that outlawed the sale or distribution of materials that could be used for contraception or abortion (1916).

ALICE BALL, black pharmaceutical chemist in Hawaii, formulated the "Ball Method" treatment after studying the effect of chaulmooga oil on Hansen disease (leprosy) (1915). Her findings relieved symptoms of the disease and are still used in some areas. Professor Ball, the first African American to graduate and the first woman to receive a Master of Science degree from the University of Hawaii, died at age 26 "from unknown causes".

A new garment for women was re-designed by **MARY PHELPS JACOB**, a New York socialite, who patented her "backless brassiere", an invention she came up with at the age of 19, to replace steel corsets (1914).

Dancer **ISADORA DUNCAN** rose to fame by appearing at the Metropolitan Opera House in New York (1917).

FEMALE PHYSICIANS were called into service during the Great War, as were WOMEN AVIATORS (1918).

The WOMEN'S LAND ARMY was formed to train women to plow fields, drive tractors, plant and harvest crops, to replace male farmers going to war. From 1917-1919, the WLA put about 20,000 women to work on farms in 25 states.

ILLINOIS WOMEN celebrated the passage of a state women's suffrage bill allowing women to vote in presidential elections (1913).

EDNA BUCKMAN KEARNS, an ardent suffragist, drove a horse-drawn suffrage campaign wagon, the "Spirit of 1776", for the first time in a suffrage movement parade in New York (1912).

Much political maneuvering preceded the passage of the 19th Amendment to the Constitution, including a protest led by ALICE PAUL before the 1912 election of Woodrow Wilson; the following year she founded the NATIONAL WOMAN'S PARTY (the forerunner of NOW) and marched on the Capitol the day before Wilson's inauguration. On Bastille Day 1917, women picketed the White House to demand voting rights for women. Sixteen were arrested for obstructing traffic.

The first female member elected to the House of Representatives in Congress was JEANNETTE RANKIN (R-MT), who was seated in March 1917. There were no women in the Senate. Montana was one of four (of 48) states or territories with voting rights for women before 1919.

THE LEAGUE OF WOMEN VOTERS was founded in 1919. About one-third of eligible women, or about 20 million, exercised their voting right in 1920. Twenty-one states gained voting rights for women following passage of the 19th Amendment to the Constitution.

A footnote to the women's vote was a *New York Times* article that quoted the observation of **Mrs. Nettie Shuler**, of the National American Woman Suffrage Association: "No groups of women I know of refrained from voting. The only groups which seemed uninterested were the women who belong to the bridge-playing classes — the parasitic women who do nothing except amuse themselves…."

Pandora, in deep mourning for her lost love, barely noticed the passing of The 19th Amendment to the Constitution by Congress on June 4, 1919, guaranteeing all American women the right to vote. Ratified in August 1920, it allowed little time for women to register and vote in the fall presidential election. Besides, Dora was not yet of voting age.

1920-1929

Hello. My name is Pandora. I'm in love... again! And I'm going to bob my hair. Pa says if I do he'll disown me, but Ginger and my school friends say it's the new fashion. I'm back in Arkansaw and busy at the telephone office. I don't want to get married right away, maybe never, although Ginger says that's a mistake. She's always telling me, "Grab him before some floozy gets her hooks into him." I tell her I'm going to have a career, and not just answering telephones. When I lost Leo, I felt as if I would never love again, but then along came Barry. He may help me get out of this one-horse town.

Pandora threw herself into her work to occupy that long bleak winter after Leo died. It was the first time in her life she had nothing to look forward to. She still lifted her head and listened when she heard a rare automobile chugging up the street.

As a telephone operator, Dora felt important. Her job was the center of the community. She knew everyone's phone line, who was on it, when they were home, when somebody needed help, when somebody wanted to be left alone. Arkansaw didn't have a newspaper; they didn't need one; it had the telephone office.

Folks called the Operator to report a straying cow. Dora knew just whose it was and how to contact them. Some called to ask the time, or even the date. Or to seek help for an emergency when somebody fell on a farm or was gored by a bull or stepped on the tine of a pitchfork. They'd call the

Operator, who immediately contacted the doctor. Sometimes she'd have to urge a party-liner to hang up so she could put through the call.

Party lines held up to six or eight customers, which often required the Operator to mediate whose call was more important. "I need to call the hardware for a new hammer so we can fix the fence." "I'm out of sugar and I have to bake muffins for the church supper." "I'm having folks over for lunch today and my electric refrigerator just quit." "I'm in the middle of laundry and there's a leak in the plumbing." Ah, those wonderful appliances and the luxury of electricity!

She told herself she was glad to be living at home again, her family moving around her, constantly watching her fight the loneliness. They barely reacted when, in her depression, she cut off her hair, opting for one of the new bobs with marcelled waves.

One morning in October, after she had worked the late shift, Dora slept in — until almost eight o'clock. When she managed to haul herself out of bed, she found Mary Belle reading a newspaper, the *Arkansaw Journal*, at the large oval kitchen table, squinting at the print and using a small magnifying glass when she needed it. Dora shuffled in, rubbing the sleep from her eyes.

"What's that?" she inquired, reaching across her mother for a freshly picked apple.

"Newspaper! What's it look like?"

"Something new?"

"Seems so. It supposed to come weekly from Durand. Got it in the mail yesterday. Get yourself some oatmeal — saved some for you on the back of the stove." Mary Belle pushed herself up and walked over to the ironing board next to the wood stove. She spread out a hand towel and reached for the iron warming on the back of the stove. "Go ahead, read it — catch up on what's happening in the world."

Dora mixed some sugar with her oatmeal and picked up the newspaper. After a few moments, she looked up. "Ma, did you know that women can vote? Says so right here in the *Journal*. There's to be an election this fall and you can vote. I can't — I'm not 21 yet.

"Vote? Vote for what?"

"You know, Ma, take part in electing the men who govern us."

"Humph! Why'd I want to do that? I'm a woman. Seems it should be their business, not us women."

"Ma! This is 1920. Women are doing all kinds of things. Since the war, lots of women have been going into business. We demonstrated to get the vote for years, and we finally got it. We actually got Congress to let women vote — and now it's up to us to do it." Pandora was reciting parts of lectures she heard when she was away at business school.

"Doesn't seem right."

"You didn't know it, but I demonstrated. Wore a banner and marched in a suffragists parade, in Menomonie."

"Naw! My daughter marching in public? Shame, shame!"

"It must have helped women get the vote." She pointed to the newspaper headlines.

"Who takes care of their children while they're out gallivanting around?"

"Who?"

"Those women going into business. Just doesn't seem right." Mary Belle set the iron down heavily on the stove for emphasis, then finished folding a towel before she picked up another. "You thinking of installing telephones now? Or opening your own telephone office? And what does your... what's his name?... Barney... think?"

"Barry, Ma. It's Barry. And he says that women belong in the kitchen with the children, but I think I'm changing his mind. You don't understand. Women are as capable as men. We know how to do things — like telephone installing. I think I know as much about telephones as any of the men who install them now."

"Humph!" Mary Belle pushed the iron back and forth furiously.

Dora could see she wasn't changing her mother's mind, but she pressed on. "Can't you see how men keep women locked up at home, bearing babies, one after another? Can't you see how they do that so they can stay free to run everything? Men need to run things." She was getting wound up as she echoed the words of the suffragist Sarah Burnham Leighton.

Mary Belle sprinkled more water on a pillowcase and reached again for the iron, almost burning herself as she fumed, "Careful your pa don't hear you."

"Look what happens when men are threatened; they start a war! Wasn't so long ago they were fighting another war, in Cuba or Spain or someplace. Men get bored or angry and they start a war! What's happened to your thinking, Ma?"

"Where do you get these ideas?"

"It's the truth! When I was in Menomonie, I heard some suffragists speak. They're the women who go around the country telling other women how men are keeping them from taking their rightful places in society. They said that…"

"Never heard tell of such hogwash."

"But, Ma, it's true. The women of the world are rising up, they're…"

"Hush, Pandora Nelle. That's enough. I don't want to hear that kind of talk in this house again. It's bad enough when you cut your hair so you look like… like a… a… jezebel, but now this!"

"Ma!"

"Enough, I said. Enough."

"Are you angry? At me? Or at the men?"

"I'm angry that you would say such things about your pa. He has never once lifted a hand against any woman or any of you children. And he doesn't leave us alone while he goes off gallivanting. He's…"

"No, not Papá. But men in general. They're the ones who…"

"No! I don't live with 'men in general', I live with your pa and he's…"

"I'm what?" Fayette had walked into the kitchen. "I'm hell to live with? I'm…"

"Fayette! Your language!" Mary Belle dropped the iron back onto the stove and reached out to hug her husband. "I was just saying that you are a good husband and father and that you don't deserve to be lumped with all the men that Pandora's yowling about."

"Dora? Ye yowlin' agin?"

"Come on, Pa. I was just telling Mamá some of what I heard in Menomonie from the suffragists."

"What in tarnation are suff-ra-gists?" Fayette dipped into the water pail for a drink. He held the dipper in front of his face while he asked the question, then placed the dipper between his mustached lips and drank.

"Suffragists are people, mostly women, who believe women should vote. And they won. Women can vote now, except you have to be twenty-one."

"Well I'll be… never woulda thought… Mary Belle? Ye going to run down and vote now?" he teased.

"'Course not. Stop your joshin', get your water, and get back out to the barn. You get that wheel back on the wagon yet?"

"You just tend to yer ironing, Mrs. Whaley. I'll take care of the farmin' business… *and* the votin' in this family." He winked at his wife, hugged his daughter, and opened the screen door. "Yup, ye just keep at yer wimmin's work." He emphasized *wimmin*, threw back his head and laughed to the sky. "Votin'. What'll they think up next?"

"Pa, you're…" but Pandora had run out of her audience.

Mary Belle spread out a pillowcase and picked up the iron; Fayette headed toward the barn, and Dora sat quietly wondering how she was going to convince anyone she was smart and in control of her life. *I'm beginning to think Barry doesn't get it either.*

Dora was nearly late getting to the telephone office for her afternoon shift. She stopped at the library — a special room at Madame Pouquette's home library — to pick up a copy of a Mark Twain book.

On the walk back up the hill to the office, Dora pondered the talk with her mother and the reaction of her father. She cradled *A Connecticut Yankee in King Arthur's Court* in her arms and wondered why she couldn't find a book at Madame P's that was written by a woman, or even about a woman. *We must be invisible, like the suffragists said. Well, we aren't going to stay invisible if I have anything to say about it.*

The afternoon shift was the busiest. She didn't have time to read until nearly suppertime, when the phones stopped ringing as women peeled potatoes and put them on the stove to cook, as men finished up the last of their day's work, as the old folks dozed in their chairs, as children… well, they weren't allowed to use the telephones anyway, except in emergencies.

She had read only a few pages of her Twain book when the idea struck her. Quiet time... people at home... what a good time to remind the women...

Dora carefully started at the left side of the board and worked her way across to the right, ringing each party line with the ring that would have every woman picking up. Men never bothered with the telephones unless they needed to call a vet or the tractor store.

Ring-ring, two-short for gabby Mrs. Olsen. She knew everyone on the Olsen party line would be listening. "Hello, Mrs. Olsen, I'm calling from the telephone office to remind you to vote in the upcoming election. Women can vote now. Be sure you vote."

The responses came in groups from the party line customers. "Huh?" "What'd she say?" "Vote? for what?" "Pandora? That you? What are you calling for?" "What's this about voting?"

"Mrs. Olsen, yes, it's me, Pandora. I'm reminding you that women can vote. Did you see the newspaper this morning? It's your duty to vote now. I hope you do. It's important that we women take part in our government. Agreed, ladies?"

In response to their questions, she attempted to convince the women of the importance of elections by reciting what she had read that morning. "You can help elect the next President," she said. "You know that President Roosevelt just died, and running in his place is James Cox, the governor of Ohio, with Roosevelt's cousin, Franklin Roosevelt, as his Vice President. The Republican candidates are Warren Harding and a guy named Calvin Coolidge. Let's show men that we women are good voters...." She could hear the clicks as the women returned to peeling potatoes.

Arkansaw women had to travel to the First National Bank in Durand to cast their votes, enduring the cigar smoke and taunts of men. But first they had to get there; most of their fathers, husbands, and brothers said they were too busy to take them. Still, about seventeen women managed to meet the challenge that year, thanks to Pandora. She offered her car to transport women voters, making the trip four times through a cold snow flurry with only thin blankets to warm the women and their chattering teeth. Mary Belle stayed home.

Pandora had to wait to cast her first vote until the election of 1922 when she helped elect Horace Wright as mayor of Durand. He had campaigned with the motto, "Vote For the Wright Man."

In the 1924 election for President of the United States, she read all she could about the candidates and, again, rang up all her women customers to remind them to be sure to vote.

She cast her precious vote for Calvin Coolidge, mostly because she felt sorry for him. She knew her father would vote for Robert LaFollette, a Wisconsin politician who ran in the Progressive Party, and she hoped to convince her mother to vote along with her for "Silent Cal".

"Who're you going to vote for?" she asked Mary Belle every morning during the week before the election.

The answer was always the same. "None of your beeswax. It's a secret ballot, remember? I'm going to vote. Isn't that enough to make you happy?"

"Ma! You have to vote for Coolidge. You read what the *Journal* said about him. He's done a good job since President Harding died. And now, with his son dying, he needs our support."

"Never you mind," Mary Belle told her daughter. "I'll vote for the best man."

"Man, yes. Why don't women run for office now that we can vote? Florence Harding could probably do as good a job as her husband did."

"Pandora! Where do you get ideas like that? Women in politics? Ugh! Smoky cigar-smelling places."

"How do you know?" Dora asked.

Was Mary Belle blushing as she confessed? "I went to a caucus once. Your father was going and I insisted he take me along. Ugh! Never again. No thank you. I'll let the men handle the politics."

The look Dora saw on her mother's face exposed a combination of guilt and bravery. "I never knew that. You mean you actually were interested in the election process?"

"Had to know what this voting thing was about, didn't I?"

"Really?"

"Not really, Dora. I was just tired of staying home all the time while Fayette roamed the countryside."

After the flurry of the election died down and the Christmas holidays were still weeks away, Arkansaw discovered another new fad — a new-fangled contraption that Fayette called the *rah-dee-oh*. Adam brought one to the family one day, calling it a *wireless*. He explained how it worked: "by snatching sounds from the air and pushing them through the speaker." He showed Dora how to work the dial and managed to bring in music from a station in Minneapolis.

"What'll they think of next?" Mary Belle exclaimed.

"Just think, Ma, maybe one day we may be able to *watch* the music being played on this box... one day," Dora responded.

"Not likely," said Adam. He knew how the radio worked.

"Don't bring that thing, that rah-dee-oh around here," Fayette warned. "It'd scare the cows."

Came spring, Dora often took her free sunny afternoons as an opportunity to jump into Leo's car and wander about the hills. Because most roads were still mostly dirt, she kept to the sunny days so she wouldn't get trapped in a muddy rut. The most traveled roads soon became reliable mud-packed routes, but only state-maintained roads were paved with gravel or tar. The country lanes were another matter.

Barry's objection to her driving by herself was the final straw that sent him scurrying out of her life. "No wife of mine is going to be roaming those lonely roads by herself. No wife of mine..."

"I feel sorry for whoever that is. Maybe 'no wife' is what you deserve," Dora replied. "I'll drive where I want, when I want, and how I want. Thank you very much." And Barry was sent packing.

Dora preferred the back roads, the winding ones that wove their way up and down hills and through lush forests and farmland — as long as they remained dry. Most people didn't own cars, and she enjoyed the solitude.

A few weeks before Easter, Dora was speeding along paved roads, merrily singing about *Lucille* in her merry Oldsmobile — *Down the road of life we'll fly, automobubbling, you and I... You can go as far as you like with me in my merry Oldsmobile.*

This was one of those days when the snow had nearly melted away, except on the north side of the barn. Dora swerved off the paved county road to explore a country lane. It took only a half-mile before mud left behind from a spring shower became so thick the car faltered, then died — the nose pointing down into a deep mud puddle.

The singing stopped. "Drat and darn!" Dora howled. She sat for a moment before she hitched up her skirts and jumped out, her feet sinking deep into the mud. Hands on hips, she looked around for a building, another car, a person — anyone, anything. She was alone.

Well, the sun is going down and I won't be stuck out here. How can I do this? The back wheels hadn't yet met the mud. Only the front wheels were bogged down. *Dry stuff under the front wheels. That's what I need.*

First she removed her soaked shoes and stockings. *No one around to care*, she thought, *and ooh, the mud feels so squooshy warm between my toes.* Then she folded her skirt around her waist and used a piece of rope from the car box to hold it. She scoured the woods for sticks and leaves, anything that would be dry and small enough to catch the wheels. She found a small flat board and used that to hold down the thatch. Standing back to admire her work, she nearly fell into the puddle herself.

"Now, you flibbertigibbet! You will follow my directions and haul yourself backward out of this mudhole." She fairly shrieked her directions, then thinking again, she repeated her orders in a very calm soothing voice, addressing "my dear sweet darling little flibbertigibbet".

She cranked the car, climbed back in, and paused before repeating the order aloud, "You *will* haul us out of this mudhole!" She set the gears in Reverse and pulled gently on the throttle, feeling the wheels searching for traction. Then, with a violent jerking motion, the car backed up a full six yards before Dora could let up on the gas. She found a grassy plot where she turned around and headed for home.

"Glad there's nobody out here to see me," she said to the steering wheel. "I'm a mess."

The words had barely left her mouth when her head turned in surprise, hearing another motor as she maneuvered the narrow road alongside the river. She turned and checked behind her, but saw nothing. She looked around for a side road, but there were none. Then she looked up — and pressed on the brake at the same time. There right over her head was a small two-winged aeroplane, passing so close she could see the aviator waving at her. She climbed out and waved back as the aeroplane made a wide circle and returned, dipping its wings.

"I've heard of aeroplanes, but never thought I'd see one myself," she said aloud. "And right here in Plum County." She watched the fragile airship skim off above the trees until it disappeared behind the hill and the buzz of the engine faded out of earshot. She got back into the car and turned homeward.

"I saw it, I saw it! Did it come here?" she called out as she ran breathlessly toward the house.

"Saw what?" asked Fayette. He put down the newspaper and sat rocking on the porch. Two of Andrew's youngsters came racing through the screen door shouting at Aunt Pandora.

"The aeroplane," shouted Pandora, dropping onto the porch steps.

"My gawd, ya look awful. Ya been playing in the mud?" her father said.

"Had a bit of trouble with a mudhole."

"I saw it! See? I told you I saw it," yelled Marcus. "I told you I saw an aeroplane. It was way over beyond the Red Barn silo, but I knew it was an aeroplane. Wasn't it, Aunt Dora?"

"Yup! That's what I saw. Only it flew right over my head."

"Gee whiz. I'd sure like to see that," Marcus returned.

"Yeah, me too," added little Troy. "Can I go too, Marcus?"

"Where are you going?" Dora asked.

"How 'bout Sunday?" Fayette smiled at his grandsons, then at his daughter. "I just read there's a barnstormer flyin' in here and taking folks fer rides. Says so right here in the *Journal*. See? Sunday, June 5, 1921, behind the old Cheese Factory up near Durand, two to four p.m."

"Can we go, Grandpa?" the boys shouted together.

"Don't see why not. That is, if 'n yer folks say it's all right and if Dora... er... Aunt Dora... will clean herself up and give us a ride in her automobile." He looked at his daughter.

Just then Mary Belle pushed open the screen door and asked, "What's all the yowlin' out here?" After a double-take, she asked, "Pandora Nelle, how'd you get so dirty? Are you all right?"

"Just a tussle with a mudhole, Mamá, not to worry."

"We're going to see an aeroplane, Grandma, and Aunt Dora is going to drive us, aren't you... Aunty Dora... dear," the boys wheedled.

"I'd say we could all go. Ma? You coming too? To see the aeroplane?"

"Mercy. Don't know as I'd miss that."

On Sunday, Mary Belle, Dora and Andrew's wife Laura packed a picnic hamper with sandwiches, potato salad, and a jar of canned peaches. They filled the water jug and tucked the bundles neatly into the auto box. Andrew and Laura slid into the front seat next to Dora; the boys sat on their grandparents' laps in the rumble seat. And off they drove to Durand.

To hear them tell it years later, no two could agree which was more fun, seeing the aeroplane doing loop-the-loops over the cornfields, riding in the automobile all the way to Durand, or stuffing themselves with the picnic and finding room for strawberry ice cream sundaes afterward. Pandora had no trouble choosing the outstanding, most memorable event of the day.

As the family piled back into the auto for the return trip, a strange young man dressed in leggings and white shirt walked over to the car. "You, you're the driver I spotted out on River Road the other day," he said to Pandora as she bent over to crank up the car.

She looked at him closely. "Oh, the aeroplane. You're the aviator?"

"Yes, I guess I am. And you're the barefoot girl with the muddy clothes."

"Could you see that clearly?"

"I could see clearly enough to know you are a beauty… under the mud. And I saw the markings on your car. I figured you worked for the Telephone Company. And here you are in the same car."

"Yes," she responded. "Here I am."

He cleared his throat and looked at the astonished family. "I'm sorry. My name is Dan Chesterfield. I'm a pilot… er… aviator. I fly the plane." He waited for a reaction. "I mean… I just, you know… flew…"

Pandora finally spoke. "I know. We recognized you from the posters and your white scarf. We saw you fly… the *plane*." The family waited to be introduced.

Marcus jumped out of the car and stuck out his hand, saying, "I'm Marcus. This is my brother Troy. That's my dad and mom and my grandparents."

Embarrassed at the omission, Marcus added, "and that's Aunt Dora; it's her car."

Dan Chesterfield bowed again and took Dora's hand. "So very *very* nice to make your acquaintance, Aunt Dora."

"Pandora, if you please," she corrected. "Pandora Whaley."

"And where does Pandora Whaley live? Here in…" he looked around and spied the banner over the Milton Hardware Store, "er… Milton?"

Everyone laughed. "That's the Milton Hardware Store… in Durand," Dora corrected him.

"Sorry. I never know where I am — they don't paint town names on rooftops yet. Do you live in… Durand?"

"No, we have a farm over in Arkansaw." She stood, smiling at the aviator as Marcus took the crank, turned it, and hopped back in the car. Dora blinked away her stare and climbed in behind the wheel. With a wave at the aviator, she drove off.

The Tuesday before the Fourth of July, Pandora worked the afternoon shift with Ginger. The town's phone service had enlarged enough to require two boards, which were both busy as townspeople made plans for the holiday. Seemed like everyone was calling everyone else to see who would make which potato salad (German, French, or American) and who would bring the lemonade.

"Operator. Arkansaw Exchange. Number, please?" Pandora responded to a light from an incoming line.

"Yes, if you please, Operator. Can you connect me with Miss Pandora Whalen?"

"I believe you mean Pandora Whaley."

Ginger finished her call at the second board and pushed her headset behind her ear to listen.

"Yes, oh yes, that's right. Do you know her? Can you give me her number?"

"One moment puleez," Dora cooed in her best Oper-a-tor voice. She closed the receiver and tried to place the voice. Her years at the switchboard had given her an ear for voices. Where had she heard that one before?

"Who is that?" Ginger asked.

Pandora shrugged and re-opened the key. Using her best "operator" voice, she said, "I'm sorry, that line is busy. May I take a message and tell her who called?"

"Sure, sure. I guess. Tell her that Dan Chesterfield called… the aviator… the one she met in Durand a few weeks ago… Dan…"

"Oh, one moment. That line is free now." She closed the key again. "Ginger, can you take my board? I want to take this call."

"Sure, but who the heck is it?"

"Tell you later, Gingersnap." Dora re-opened the line and turned her back to her friend, whose board immediately lit up with three new calls.

"Hello, this is Pandora." She tried to lower and relax her "operator" voice, hoping he wouldn't notice.

"Pandora?" Dan shouted. "Pandora, is that you? I can barely hear you."

Great, the lines are crackling. "Yes, this is Pandora," she shouted back. "Who is this?"

"Dan… Dan Chesterfield… the aviator. We met in Durand at the airfield."

"Dan? Oh yes." She noticed her hands had become sweaty and she was sure her cheeks had turned red. She hoped Ginger would stay busy.

"I'm glad to reach you. I just found out I'm coming back that way for the Fourth of July — to your Durand. I was wondering if you could meet me after the show. Maybe we could take a walk or see a film or something. That is… if you're… if you're… you aren't, are you?"

"Aren't what?" Dora felt like teasing.

"You know… busy… or taken… or spoken for."

"Well…" she couldn't resist teasing him some more. "I was planning an exciting afternoon with the family and then a band concert… perhaps in Durand… and then the fireworks out on River Road."

"Oh." Dan's voice dropped.

"But then, if you would go with me, that might be fun," she grinned into the mouthpiece. She could hear him let out a sigh and smile too. Actually, it was more of a "Whoopee!"

"Our barnstorming show is over about four. We could get a bite to eat and listen to the band concert. I'd really like to see the fireworks too."

"I look forward to it. I'll meet you there… at four."

"Twenty-three-skidoo! I'll see you."

"What?" Dora wasn't sure what she had heard.

"I'll see you on Friday. Bye for now, Miss Pandora."

"Goodbye, Dan." She sat smiling into space for just a moment, her hands covering her warm cheeks, before she heard Ginger call for help. Both boards were lit up like a Fourth of July sparkler.

The holiday fireworks appeared as bright lights in the sky overhead for everyone else in Durand. But for Pandora and her new beau, they were showers of stars surrounding them, reflecting the stars in their eyes.

"Okay, Dora. Tell all," Ginger demanded when Pandora reported for work the next day.

"Tell you what?" Pandora asked innocently.

"Come on. Tell me. What's he like? Where'd you go? What did you do?"

"Oh that," she teased. She broke down and recounted the entire day, ending with, "He's so wonderful, Gingersnap. I think I'm in love."

The two women kept their heads together all through the afternoon shift. By ten o'clock, Ginger knew as much about Dan as Pandora did. He flew his airplane on weekends and off days from his regular job as a high school science teacher over in River Falls. He wanted to make a career out of flying, but needed the teaching job to buy parts and fuel.

Dan had taken Dora up in his plane to watch the fireworks from the sky, and as much as Dora talked about it, she didn't feel that Ginger fully understood just how magnificent it was.

"Showers and showers of colored bursts of light below us, in front of us, off on the horizon. I could see all the way to Pepin and their fireworks. And black sky like velvet all around, the most beautiful sight I shall ever see. It was like opening the doors to heaven."

"You really got it bad. Did you see a film? Or what afterwards?"

"Not even a Barrymore film could top that display. We landed the plane; he walked me to the car, and then we sat and talked and talked." Dora silently stared across the switchboard. Ginger had to nudge her when two lights appeared simultaneously. "Number please," she responded automatically from outer space.

The Dan and Dora romance bloomed over the next few months. They spent Christmas with his family in River Falls and her birthday (New Years Day) with her family in Arkansaw. A year later, in spring, he announced he was being considered for a job as assistant principal. The only hitch was that the school was two counties away from Arkansaw.

"Why don't you two get married and move to his new job?" Ginger urged. "Haven't you had enough of this career thing yet?"

"Maybe. Dan says he wants to be a full principal before he considers settling down. And I'm not too sure I'm ready to marry yet either."

"Dora, you're nearly twenty-three years old. You were ready to marry Leo."

"That was different. Or maybe it isn't. Maybe I'm just scared."

"Scared? Of what?"

"Not sure. Seems I feel like there's something else I have to do before I settle down." She drifted into thought for a few moments. "Settle down. *Settle down.* Isn't that a strange phrase? It sounds almost like settling for something less than you want. It sounds…"

"…like getting stuck somewhere. Is that what you're afraid of?"

"Maybe. *Settle down* sounds so… final."

Another summer and winter passed. Dan took the new job and flew to see Pandora as often as he could get away. During the next two summers, he barnstormed all over the state, and by the following summer he had added a second plane and a partner. He even considered starting a flying club and training others to fly.

Pandora dated a couple of young men she met at church parties, but kept her holidays open when Dan could get away. Between working at the school and flying his aircraft, that didn't happen often.

The next Fourth of July found Dan returning to Durand for a command performance. Dora joined him again, and he took her for a joy ride when business slowed at lunchtime. Dan taxied the plane to the edge of the runway, then motioned to Dora to take hold of the stick. He revved up the engine and released the brake. With his hand on hers, he showed her how to gently pull back, lifting the plane off the ground.

"I'm flying," she squealed over the noise of the motor. "I'm flying."

In the sky over the rolling hills, she took the controls again as Dan showed her how to bank and turn and steer the plane, keeping an eye on the altitude and keeping the wings level.

When she turned up for work the next day, she jabbered on and on about how she had flown a plane. "I'll never forget how that felt, Gingersnap. It was so… so…" but a buzzing switchboard cut short her description. She couldn't have found the words anyway.

A strange Indian Summer had prolonged the autumn outdoors that year. Pandora spent warm weekends driving friends through the hills to see the glorious red and yellow foliage. Picnics under the trees in late September added special emphasis to the beauty of the countryside.

At the same time, the warm weekends gave Dan and his new barnstorming company added hours of work. "We took forty-two people up this afternoon for rides, and gave flying lessons to three people this morning," he told Dora during a late evening telephone call. "How about I fly down next Saturday and take you for a ride?"

"Swell. You can use Dad's grazing pasture for a landing strip again. I'll meet you there with the car. At noon?"

"I'll be there."

Noon on Saturday came and went and Dan's plane didn't appear. Dora waited. After a couple hours, she waited longer and began to worry. Then she returned to the house and worried some more. *Was she going to lose the love of her life again?*

By suppertime, she had lost her appetite and sat near the telephone waiting for it to ring. Once the neighbor's phone rang… two shorts and a long… and she reached for it, but didn't pick it up.

What if he's lost interest in me? What if I've put him off too long? What if he's hurt? What if his plane crashed and he's lying hurt somewhere… or… dead? Oh no! I can't go through that again… please, God, not again.

Twice she started to call Dan's parents, but decided not to worry them. She felt so alone.

"Come eat something," Mary Belle prompted. "You have to keep up your strength. Your young man will show up. Perhaps the first thing in the morning."

"But why hasn't he called? Why hasn't he let me know he's all right?"

"Perhaps he can't. Perhaps he's not near a telephone. Why don't you lie down and try to sleep? You'll hear the telephone if it rings. With the all-night service now, he can get through anytime."

"I know, Ma. Thanks. I'll lie down here on the daybed. You go to bed. Pa's waiting. I'll be all right."

The next morning, Pandora followed her family to church service to do some heavy praying. Just as Pastor Nichols was winding up his sermon, the familiar drone of an airplane sent her rushing out the door. Until that moment, she hadn't been sure how much she loved this man and how much she needed to know he was all right.

As he crawled out of the plane, he called to her, "Sorry about yesterday. Had trouble getting this old machine to go. And I wanted to call, but…"

"I love you, Dan Chesterfield," she moaned and fell into his arms. Cows lowed in harmony as they watched the two young people hold each other and whisper their fears.

That summer of 1927 sent Charles Lindbergh and the airplane business into the headlines. His spectacular flight to Europe opened up the doors for aviation's future. People talked about sending mail to out-of-the-way places with airplanes, using planes to reach distant places quickly, and eventually providing a plane for every family. Airplanes would replace the automobile and trains to become the next way to move people and goods around the country.

Women got into the act too — finding airplanes fun and as easy to operate as automobiles. Many participated in cross-country races and competed for all kinds of flight records. In 1929, a group of women pilots established The Ninety-Nines Inc., an international organization of women pilots, representing all areas of aviation. One of the founding members, Amelia Earhart, promoted this new phenomenon by repeating her mantra, "Fly for the fun of it!"

Women definitely were flying out of the box.

More and more women cut their hair and shortened their skirts. Economic times boomed and women wanted to be part of it. They were taking jobs in schools, in retail stores, and in offices. Until then — the decade known as "The Roaring Twenties" — a single woman might open a millinery shop, a cafe, or a beauty shop, and still be considered respectable. But during the 1920s, spurred on by the right to vote, women moved *en force* into the world previously occupied by men. Oh, they were supervised by men — after all, men were the power people, the hiring people — but women were turning up, newly visible in the male world.

Dan was promoted to principal late in the school year, and on June 11, 1928, he and Dora were married in a small ceremony with just a few of their families present. That fall, he was asked to head the growing Arkansaw School System, a combined school of first through twelfth graders.

Dora continued to work regular shifts until Ginger was moved into a supervisor's job in Durand. With the duo split up, Dora-the-wife stepped down and agreed to help out as a relief operator. She didn't know the other operators; most were neighbor girls all grown up. At twenty-eight, Dora felt old and out of touch.

Dan was very supportive of his new wife. She could work… or not. It was Dora who wanted more time to roam about with her camera. She took pictures for the *Arkansaw Journal* occasionally, and a few friends asked her to photograph their weddings and their children at Christmastime.

Still, something was missing. The thought crossed her mind once that she ought to complete her schooling — but how would it look for the principal's wife to be sitting in a class with teenagers?

It was then that Dan offered to coach her and give her high school tests that would earn her a diploma. "We can do this at home and you'll still be able to graduate," he told her. On their first wedding anniversary, Pandora, very large with child, accepted her graduation certificate in a private ceremony conducted at the Chesterfield home. They took the prize to Dora's family home to share the good news.

"Off for the summer now, are ye?" Fayette commented as the couple arrived at the front door. "Ye like this principal's job?" he asked. "Full principal now. Yer the boss, the head cheese, the whole shootin' shebang? And ye got wimmin working for ye."

"Yup! Three new women teachers last year. Men seem to be moving away from teaching."

"Still, you're limited, Dan," Dora commented as she settled uncomfortably into the porch swing, "with that silly rule against hiring married women because they might get pregnant." Her voice turned sarcastic, "And we can't have... *woman with child*... in the classroom, can we!"

Breaking the silence that followed, Fayette went on, "Ain't it fun tellin' all those wimmin what to do?"

"Sorta. Actually, they tell me what to do. How could you expect one man to hold out when confronted by all those women?"

"But yer the boss."

"And the women run the place, Pa," Dora cut in. "Don't you understand? It's the *wimmin* who do all the work. Dan just collects the credit and a big paycheck."

"Which you don't mind," Dan added.

"Now, that's just not... quite... oh, I see. You're joshin' me."

Pandora and her father laughed their hearty Irish laughs. Except Fayette failed to see the truth behind the wisecracks.

"My paycheck is bigger so I can support my family... my growing family," Dan countered. He could read his wife's expression. "The women are teaching because it's their mission. Most of them teach until they get married, then they raise their children. Women don't spend their lives teaching."

"Still claim it ain't right for wimmin to work," Fayette added. "Just ain't right."

"If things get much tighter on this farm, Dad, you may have to eat those words and put Ma out to work," Dora teased.

"No way!" her father bristled. "Never. Times ain't that tough and they won't get that tough — ever."

But times were getting tougher throughout the country, and the squeeze would hit Arkansaw soon.

Pandora's first daughter was born in July, right in the midst of haying. Dora was working in the beastly hot kitchen, cooking meals for threshers when she felt the first contraction. Iris kept an eye on her sister that morning as Dora, green from the smell of food, dished up plates of eggs and sausages.

Dan had combined a flying trip to Madison with a statewide principal's conference. By evening, Dora lay in the sweltering hospital room in Durand, only a slight breeze stirring as the sun lowered to the horizon. Fayette had driven his daughter there, bumping across the hard clay road as Dora pressed her feet hard against the floorboards to soften the ride.

Bonnie Jean Chesterfield was born at three a.m., the coolest part of the night, a healthy baby at eight pounds, four ounces. She squalled only a few minutes before finding the heat too oppressive to continue, suckled briefly, then slept until the sun was high in the sky.

Ginger telephoned the news to Dan who sent a telegram to the hospital. "Happy Birthday, Bonnie Jo. Your daddy will see you soon."

"Exactly ten words." Iris re-read the yellow Western Union telegram. "Didn't you tell him you wanted to name a girl Bonnie *Jean*?"

"He probably just forgot. Men don't pay attention to things like that."

Dora's little sister had taken the day off from feeding threshers to spend with her new niece at the Durand hospital. "I wonder if he'll fly back today or wait until the weekend."

"I'd bet on the weekend. This conference is important to his work. It may even lead to another promotion, to a larger school. Who knows? I may be moving away soon."

By the weekend, Dora had returned with Bonnie Jean to her parents' farm in Arkansaw and was again helping feed the threshers. *Another week and they'll be gone*, she thought. *Then maybe we can get back to normal around here, and Dan and I can return home.*

Normal was the smell of fresh bread baking in the kitchen. No sweaty field hands. No smell of grease, no fried potatoes, no fried ham, no fried chicken and gravy. In summer, greasy smells tended to linger in the kitchen. *Normal* in summer included the heavenly aroma of potato salad and deviled eggs and fresh vegetables right from the garden and berries from the field and lemonade.

Iris strolled onto the front porch chewing on a green apple, shaking salt on it from time to time. "Ooh, I'd love one of those," cooed Dora. "But Baby wouldn't appreciate it, I'm sure. I keep forgetting I'm feeding two of us."

"I'm not going to have children. None."

"Not even one? Look at that face, Iris, and tell me you don't want one like her." She placed her hand on Bonnie's oak cradle and gave it a rock.

"Nope. Going to be a career woman, like you were before… well, you know."

"Before I fell in love? Got married? Started my family? What?"

"You know. Aren't you the one who preached about women having the right to follow their own dreams? Have careers? Become President? Well… maybe not President… but something more than just a wife and mother." Iris tried to hold her tongue, but she had to add, "Did you give up your dreams?"

"Oh sis, I haven't given up my dreams. I've added to them. Don't you see? Women can have careers and be married too. Look at me. Nothing says I can't take her with me to work. The new girl takes her child to the telephone office from time to time."

"But Dora. They don't pay you like they'd pay a man to do that work."

"Telephone men don't do switchboard work. They're out in the field, connecting new lines and stuff."

"And look at the money they make. I'll bet you could connect those lines just as well as they do."

"Sure I could. But…"

"Why don't you then? I can see you shinnying up a telephone pole!" The sisters laughed loudly enough to interrupt the baby's dreams. She stirred and the two lowered their voices.

"Maybe you're right, Iris. It does seem like men do the better-paid work. Look at Dan; principal of a school full of women teachers who don't get anything near his take-home pay."

"Except the science teacher; he's a man."

"You're right. Yeah! But that shouldn't stop you from having a family if you want. Life is too short to live it alone."

"We'll see." Iris shook her short-cropped head and went to the kitchen for another apple.

"By the way, sis, I've never heard how you got Ma to let you cut your hair?"

"Didn't ask her," came the voice from the kitchen.

"But didn't she complain?"

"Sure, but what good did it do when the deed was already done." Iris reappeared at the door. "She called me a senseless flapper, a wild woman, a loose woman, a... let me see, what else... oh yes, a jezebel."

The two young women giggled again and Bonnie Jean flailed her arms as she stirred. "Let's hope this little one doesn't have to worry about whether or not to cut her hair."

"Or what kind of dress to wear. Did I show you that new yellow fringed dress I made? Ma thought it was the top of an outfit until I told her it's the whole dress. She nearly fainted."

"Iris Rosella! You have to remember that Ma is old-fashioned. Or hadn't you noticed she still wears her skirts down to her ankles?"

"I know. Maybe I shouldn't tease her so, but she has to learn that times have changed. Besides, with the depression, it's time to save fabric."

The two sisters nearly doubled over with that idea, bringing Bonnie Jean fully awake. "No time for sitting around. Time for my daughter's feeding." Dora picked up her baby, pulled back her bodice and began to rock gently, half-singing along with the squeaking porch floorboard as the baby began to tug at her breast. Iris sat quietly chewing the tangy apple and reconsidered her choice of words about "never having children".

Dan returned over the weekend with news he'd been offered a new job as principal of a larger school, at Cherry City in the eastern part of the state. He also had been encouraged to think about returning to college. Since he had graduated with only a three-year teaching degree, he needed a four-year degree to continue in the administration field — in line for a superintendent's job or even a teaching job at the University.

"But Cherry City. That's so far from here."

"We can always fly home. The plane will carry a couple of passengers," he winked at his wife, "no matter how many children we have."

"Still, we'll have to watch our pennies. Times are getting tighter and now we'll have to pay more rent, I imagine."

"Not a problem. My salary will cover it. Almost like pennies from heaven," he paraphrased a popular song, "we'll just keep our umbrellas upside down."

The decade had offered a major change in women. As if let loose of their senses, many jumped on table tops to shimmy in their short dresses and short hair and drink homemade gin from coffee cups and smoke cigarets and… (mostly the wild city girls).

Still, many women grasped the opportunity to show their abilities in other fields, contributing greatly to areas of government, finance, public health, sports, the arts, social justice, and aviation.

This was the time that Pandora most loved to refer to as the decade the lid came off the box. Women were peeking out no longer; they had flown to the outside.

With the signing of the 19th Amendment, women poured into the streets to celebrate. After the initial excitement, many of them returned to their homes and mommyhood. Women who were widowed or divorced set up their own small businesses. (Although few were divorced because it was legally difficult and financially expensive, as well as socially abhorrent.) More and more women were turning to the "acceptable" positions opening to them, including nursing, teaching, typing, and clerking — none of which would ever make them rich.

Still, there were courageous, ambitious women bold enough to delve into the world inhabited mostly by men.

Pennies — and dimes and dollars — fell over the nation during the Roaring Twenties, before the supply dried up and blew away with November's falling leaves in 1929. And all the umbrellas would soon be turned upside down, empty.

Pandora's Notes of the 19-twenties

ALICE ROBERTSON (R-OK) became the second woman elected to Congress (following **JEANNETTE RANKIN**) and the first to chair the U.S. House of Representatives (1921).

WINNIFRED HUCK (R-IL) and **MAE NOLAN** (I-CA) won special elections to Congress the same year (1921).

REBECCA LATIMER FELTON (D-GA), an author, lecturer, reformer and leader, served just one day in the U.S. Senate at the age of 87. She was the first woman Senator and the oldest ever sworn in (November 22, 1922). She was honored as a Georgia Woman of Achievement in 1997.

ELIZABETH SHACKLEFORD, the first woman in Washington State to champion causes for minorities and disadvantaged people, was admitted to the State Bar (1922).

JANE LEE, Chinese activist, joined Mills College, San Francisco, as translator and journalist, and found jobs for Chinese women (1922).

BLANCHE FUNK MILLER became the first Justice of the Peace in Tacoma WA, running on the campaign slogan, "At least one judge should be a woman". She later instituted a domestic relations court (1923).

ALICE PAUL, suffragist and leader of the movement that resulted in the 19th Amendment that gave women the right to vote (1920), wrote the Equal Rights Amendment that was introduced in Congress by two male Representatives in 1923. Although re-introduced in Congress every year afterwards, the Amendment remains unratified.

After the U.S. Supreme Court upheld THE 19TH AMENDMENT to the Constitution, guaranteeing women the right to vote (1922), it struck down minimum wage laws for women, calling the measure unconstitutional (1923).

VIOLETTE NEATLY ANDERSON, of Chicago, became the first black woman to practice law before the U.S. Supreme Court (1926). She was also the first black woman to practice law in Illinois.

ADELAIDE JOHNSON sculpted the Suffrage Monument depicting SUSAN B. ANTHONY, ELIZABETH CADY STANTON, and LUCRETIA MOTT. It was dedicated in February 1921 at the U.S. Capitol.

The Women's Bond Club was founded by Wall Street pioneers BETTY COOK, MARY RIIS, and LOUISE WATSON, for women working in the financial industry (1921).

BETTY CROCKER made her first appearance on baking products (1921).

M. CAREY THOMAS opened a summer school at Bryn Mawr (women's college) for women in industry (1921).

The first MISS AMERICA PAGEANT attracted oglers to Atlantic City (1921). The winner was 16-year-old MARGARET GORMAN of Washington, DC, whose measurements were 30-25-32. She stood 5'1", weighed 108 pounds, and bore a striking resemblance to the popular screen actress of the era, MARY PICKFORD.

BESSIE SMITH signed a contract with Columbia (recording studio) to make "race records". Her recordings helped rescue Columbia from failure (1923).

MARY PICKFORD, super star of silent moving pictures, founded United Artists Pictures (1920), and later the Academy of Motion Picture Arts and Sciences.

LOIS WEBER was signed as film director with Famous Players-Lasky Productions (Paramount Pictures) at a salary that made her one of the highest paid directors of the day ($50,000 plus one-third of film profits) (1920).

IDA HUSTED HARPER published six volumes of *History of Women Suffrage* to document the suffragist effort (1922).

Writer **EMILY POST** published what would become a definitive book, *Etiquette* (1922).

CHRISTAL QUINTASKET, of the Okanagan people, authored the first novel written by a Native American. *Mourning Dove* featured an American Indian female as the central character (1927).

ANTHROPOLOGIST MARGARET MEAD published her social research in *Coming of Age in Samoa* (1928).

Author **EDITH WHARTON** won a Pulitzer Prize for her book *The Age of Innocence* (1920).

EDNA ST. VINCENT MILLAY won the Pulitzer Prize for Poetry for "The Ballad of the Harp-Weaver" (1923).

ZONA GALE became the first woman to win the Pulitzer Prize for Drama, with her play, "Miss Lulu Bett" (1920).

LILLIAN BERTHA JONES HORACE, pioneering educator and writer from Texas, was one of the first southern black woman novelists, publishing *The Diary of Lillian B. Horace* in the mid-1920s.

ANITA LOOS wrote more than 150 screenplays, but is best known for the comedic wit and observation displayed in "Gentlemen Prefer Blondes" (1925) and its companion "But Gentlemen Marry Brunettes" (1928).

REGINA ANDERSON helped found Harlem's Negro Experimental Theater (1929).

DOROTHY DETZER, a worker at Hull House, served as national secretary of the Women's International League for Peace and Freedom where she became known as the "Lady Lobbyist" in Congress (1924).

RUTH BUNZEL, anthropologist, studied art and culture of southwest Indian women, and learned the Zuni language and pottery (1924).

ALICE MCLELLAN BIRNEY, noted for encouraging mothers to take an active role in public education, founded the National Congress of Parents and Teachers (1924).

SELENA SLOAN BUTLER founded the National Congress of Colored Parents and Teachers, focusing on segregated schools in the South (1927).

SALLY GERBER is the reason for creating Gerber baby foods. A sickly child at birth, she is the reason her mother, **DOROTHY GERBER**, founded Gerber baby foods. Dorothy suggested ways to strain and preserve food for babies to her husband who operated a canning company (1927).

ANN TURNER COOK is the baby whose picture was painted in a contest to name the Gerber baby. She was compensated with "a small amount" (1928).

DOROTHY HOPE SMITH, the artist who drew the famous Gerber baby picture, received only a few hundred dollars for her work (1928).

IDA ROSENTHAL, a Russian Jewish dressmaker in Manhattan, designed the first *Maidenform* bra (1922).

LILIAN JEANNETTE RICE, a pioneering master architect and city planner, designed a number of buildings on the National Register of Historic Places (1920s).

KATHARINE BLODGETT was the first woman to earn a Ph.D. in physics from Cambridge University. She improved wartime gas masks by inventing invisible glass (nonreflective) and other military patents (1926).

LOU HENRY HOOVER became the first First Lady to speak over the radio, make speeches on her own, and create controversy with such actions as inviting the first black man to tea at the White House. She also played a major role in developing the Girl Scouts and expanding the Amateur Athletic Union to include women.

NELLIE TAYLOE ROSS was inaugurated as the first woman governor in U.S. history (1925) and the only woman governor of Wyoming to date.

LIZZIE MURPHY was the first woman to play professional baseball, moving up from the semi-pro Boston All Stars to play for the Boston Red Sox in the American League All-Stars game (1922) and then to play in the National League All-Star game (1928), becoming the first person of any gender to play for both All-Star teams. She played first base and was widely known as "Spike" and "Queen of Baseball".

GERTRUDE EDERLE, just 19 years old, was the first woman to swim the English Channel (1926). Only five men had accomplished this feat before her.

SONJA HENIE, from Norway, debuted as an Olympic figure skater at the age of 11, in the first Winter Games (1924). She won the gold medal in 1928, 1932, and 1936, before retiring from competitive skating to become a U.S. film star.

PHOEBE ANN MOSES (ANNIE OAKLEY) retired (1922) at age 62 after a 47-year performance career as a sharpshooter, mostly with Buffalo Bill's Wild West show.

HARRIET STRATEMEYER ADAMS, a juvenile mystery novelist, wrote many of the Nancy Drew series (as **CAROLYN KEENE**) and a few in the Hardy Boys series (as Franklin W. Dixon). She and **HER SISTER EDNA** controlled the Stratemeyer Syndicate — too late for Pandora's childhood, but in time to entertain her daughters.

BESSIE COLEMAN, the first black woman in the world to earn a pilot's license, was a barnstorming aviator who performed daredevil tricks. She was the first black pilot in America to stage a public flight (1922).

FLORENCE LOWE (PANCHO) BARNES received her pilot's license after only six hours of flight training. She would break speed records in races, establish a union for stunt pilots, and test planes for military flight, all while snubbing her nose at society. She later built the Happy Bottom Riding Club in the desert, where she entertained friends, including Hollywood celebrities and many well-known aviators (1928).

Women pilots participated in the first **WOMEN'S AIR DERBY**, a major cross-country race for women pilots of the Ninety-Nines (1929).

A new age for women had begun in this decade that followed the establishment of the rights of women to vote.

1930-1939

PANDORA at 30

Hello. My name is Pandora. I am a woman and I function as well as any man. Still, I am held "in my place" by convention. "A woman is supposed to do... and be..." and I'm sick of it. There is so much I want to do in this world. I am married with a child, and my husband likes to think of me "at home". On the other hand, he seems supportive of my efforts to get more education. I'd call him two-faced, but I love him too much.

Times did get tougher, and inverted umbrellas were no help. Even in Arkansaw, the Great Depression of the 1930s took its toll, perhaps later than the urban centers, but eventually. Prices at Hartung's Mercantile zoomed skyward. Prices paid to farmers for milk and eggs and other produce went the other way, causing farmers financial problems. President Hoover tried to keep the country's head above water, but the waves in the rural areas began to lap higher and higher as the decade progressed.

At the close of the school year in 1931, Dora, Dan, and Bonnie Jean moved to Cherry City, then added another daughter to the family less than a year later, named Helen Madelaine and nick-named Hattie. To help the family's wavering finances, Dan began to drive Dora's old Model-T, fast becoming a relic. The Bell Telephone logo had long been rubbed off, and the engine chugged harder with each hill it climbed. Mostly Dan walked to school, saving the car for family excursions into the country on weekends.

Twice Dora walked down to the Cherry City telephone office to apply for work. But hiring was frozen because of the Depression. Besides, she'd have to hire someone to stay with her daughters if she went back to work; she knew a woman's salary wasn't enough to make that a choice. She raised the subject to Dan once and was so overcome by his abrupt rejection of the idea that she never raised it again.

"No wife of mine is going to work. I'd never have a chance at a superintendent's job if you did. No. No. No!"

The next year, Dora received a call to go home as soon as possible. Her father was ailing and not likely to last long. Dan managed to scrape up train fare and she left for Arkansaw. She was too late; Fayette had died the previous night in his sleep, snoring one minute, then silent the next. Dora stayed to help her mother cope with the family members who came to help out. Some of Fayette's first family showed up — Grace and Billie and Andrew. Adam couldn't leave his farm, and Lynna, the youngest, was living in California.

"There's a will… of sorts," Mary Belle told the children. "Fayette wants Andrew to take over the farm."

"Andrew?" Grace nudged her younger brother.

"I heard."

"Well?"

"Gee, Mary Belle. I don't know."

"What you got going on that's more important? You have some big job somewhere that we don't know about?"

Andrew's own farm had been foreclosed, and this proud man, nearing 40, was close to becoming the town's next handyman — like the men who circulated throughout the neighboring farms offering to do odd jobs in return for a day's pay.

"Please, Andrew… your dad wanted you to." Mary Belle took his hand and looked into her step-son's eyes.

After a moment, Andrew looked back and smiled. "Okay. But you have to stay put — right here. You'll always have a home."

Dora took another two days to catch up with her family before becoming lonesome for her own children. The train ride home seemed longer than before, giving her a chance to think more about how she was going to make her mark in the world. She'd never do it in a telephone office. There had to be something else. Teaching perhaps. But then she'd have to go to college. *Maybe I could become a writer. I could write at home and not have to leave the girls. Maybe… someday.*

By the mid-thirties, Dan decided to return to college himself. "We can move in with my folks in River Falls and I can attend the state college there," he suggested one afternoon in the spring of 1936. "I can get my degree in less than a year; Mom can take care of the girls; Bonnie can attend the Normal School, and you can work at the telephone office."

"Really? Do you mean it?" Dora heard only the last part about going back to work. She hadn't thought much about the trials of living with in-laws at the time they moved, right after school ended in June. Dan caught a few credits during the summer term and enrolled full-time in the fall.

"I've got the classes I wanted," said Dan just before Labor Day. "Being so close to the school, we can sell the old jalopy. I can walk."

"But the telephone office is across town. I'll still need a car," Dora countered.

"You can manage."

"But it's a crank car; there aren't many left on the road. And it's sooo old! It won't bring much."

"It still runs, doesn't it?"

"Sometimes… but…"

"Baby, we need the money. You'll be okay. The snow never gets too deep here anyway."

Dora needn't have worried about selling the car. No one had money to buy it. Nor did she need to worry about walking to work in the snow. There were no jobs, not at the telephone company, not in the retail stores, not in the cafes, not in the offices. The few jobs available went to men who had families to support.

Dan kept the old rattletrap and sold his plane instead to an old flying buddy. Times were rough. Men walked the street — even in River

Falls — without jobs, offering their skills as handymen. Men often appeared at the Chesterfield's back door asking for a sandwich, something to eat, or a handout of clothing. Her mother-in-law shooed them away with a rude slam of the door. But if Dora answered, she'd find a sandwich or piece of cake, something to put into their growling stomachs.

Once she gave away a pair of Dan's old work gloves, figuring he no longer would be involved tinkering with engines or gardens or household repairs. Dan hit the roof, but quickly softened to his wife's explanation: "That poor man's hands weren't used to chopping wood, and he could use the gloves better than you."

Dora managed to keep peace between the two families, wedged as they were into the tiny house. She and Dan and the children kept to their rooms on the second floor — the attic cleared of storage boxes and cobwebs. At first Dora tried to help in the kitchen, but quickly learned to keep out. She ate whatever her mother-in-law prepared, and fixed food separately for her daughters.

On most days, Dan's father disappeared right after breakfast and spent the day visiting with his old cronies before returning for supper. The elder Mr. Chesterfield took occasional odd carpentry jobs around town, but mostly he relied on a state welfare check and his new Social Security check that arrived regularly each month. The catch was that he had to sign over ownership of the house he had built with his own hands, since the new "welfare" program didn't allow people to own their homes. While he enjoyed the leisure of the financially secure, he harbored guilt about not earning his way.

Dora's girls drove him up the walls with their squeals and laughter and loud talk. "Can't you hush them kids up?" he'd ask Dan angrily, preferring to talk with his son rather than his daughter-in-law. "They screech around here all day long."

"Actually, they play mostly outdoors, Dad," Dora countered quietly. "And they take naps in the afternoon. You just catch them at their best." She smiled, hoping to pacify the old man.

"Children should be seen and not heard," he grumped, grabbing the water pail and walking out the back door. Dora could hear the old man mumbling to himself as he pumped a fresh pail of drinking water. Dan's folks didn't have indoor plumbing, so there was constant traffic — to the pump to replenish the indoor water pails and to the outhouse.

Somehow they got through the ungraciously severe winter, but spring arrived late. The extended Chesterfield family was grouching at each other by Easter as new snow covered the roads to church. It wasn't until late May that the sun melted away the last remnants of winter and the children could play outside, tossing a ball over the outhouse that was sweetened with a confusion of lilac bushes thick with blossoms.

"Dora, how would you like to move to Milwaukee?" Dan asked one sunny spring day when he found Dora alone. The house had been thrown open and Mother Chesterfield was outside pounding at dusty carpets thrown over the clothesline. Spring housecleaning was her way of working off the turmoil of her winter guests.

"Milwaukee?" Dora repeated.

"Yes, Milwaukee. I've been offered a job with the University's new Agriculture Extension Department. The pay is more than I've ever seen in teaching, and the girls would go to good schools, and we'd have all the fun of living in a city." Clearly Dan was excited over the prospect.

"Milwaukee. Sounds big. Just the name sounds big. Would I be able to find a job there? River Falls is big enough for a small college, but Milwaukee... that's a metropolis!"

"You wouldn't have to. I'll be making good pay. You can join church clubs and go to theaters and women's clubs and garden clubs and..."

"Is that what you'd do if you were me?"

"I don't know. Isn't that what women do? Mom said that's what she'd do if she were to move there."

"You talked to your mother about this? Before me?" Dora turned away so Dan couldn't see the hurt. Still she was thinking about the freedom of the city, the opportunities for her daughters, the possibilities of college for herself. Finally she said, "Well, uh, okay... if you think this is a good move."

"Dora, Pandora, my pet. You know I think of the whole family." He put his arms around his wife and hugged her tightly. "And hey, we'll be able to afford a new car. Won't that be dandy?"

"Yeah, dandy," she murmured into her husband's jacket. She was still stewing about Dan's mother hearing about his plans first.

Dora pulled back and looked up at her husband. "Agriculture? I thought you were heading toward superintendent of education. Why would you want to leave education? What about your aviation business? What happened…?"

"I *will be* in education, sweetheart. I had been thinking about returning to farming, on a farm like the one where I grew up. It's that class I took last term that turned me towards this new job. The Extension Department is something new — like taking the classroom to farmers. I can do that. At least my professors said I could. That's what I was checking out when I flew down to Madison three weeks ago."

"And you waited until now to tell me about this?"

"I didn't think you'd be interested. Earning the bread is my business; baking bread is yours. I stay out of the kitchen, you stay…"

That's all it took to turn Pandora's temperament from *hurt, listening wife* to *raging hoyden*. She pulled away from Dan, set her hands on her hips, and stared at his eyes for a moment before she exploded, "Baking… bread… my… business…? Do you think I want to spend the rest of my life baking bread and cleaning house? You encouraged me to think about college. Well this settles it. Yes, we'll move to Milwaukee. Yes, you will take this fancy new job. And yes, I will be going to college. They do have colleges in Milwaukee, don't they?"

"Uh… yes… several, but…"

"But nothing. Your wife is going to college. Get used to it."

By this time, Hattie had wakened from her nap and was crying for attention, and Bonnie had wandered into the room, staying well out of sight. When Dan's mother came through the back door holding the carpet beater, Dora looked ready for action.

"It's all right, Ma," Dora assured her. "We're just discussing our careers."

The move took place immediately after graduation. The young Chesterfields bought a new 1938 Chevrolet car as a graduation present to themselves right after Dan received his diploma. Dan had to buy it on the installment plan since it cost over $700 and most of their savings had been spent during the school year. Dan's new job provided the credit they needed, and off they drove to Milwaukee.

Dora was still unpacking boxes when school started just after Labor Day. Excited at being in the big city, she coached the girls. "Keep to yourself. Don't talk to strangers. Come right home after school. Memorize our address." They'd have to wait for a telephone number to memorize; the family had been put on a waiting list. "You can learn about buses and trolleys," Dora told Bonnie Jean, nearly nine years old. She had taken her daughters aside to prepare them for life in the big city. "That's the way folks get around in the city. And you might see colored people. I'm told some of them live in Milwaukee."

"What kind of colors, Mama?"

"Gee, I'm not sure. I'm told there are black people and brown people..."

"And red Indians," Bonnie offered. "I'll be looking for them — all the colored people."

The world again was rumbling with the sounds of war. Dan's position in the field of agriculture, his age — he was nearly 44 — and his status as a family man would keep him out of a military draft that was sure to come. Moreover, Dora could see job opportunities for herself if a war did start and the men went off to fight it. Maybe she could get one of those telephone installation jobs that paid more than operating a switchboard.

Dan had been reading about the potential of a new insecticide called DDT. Billed as a miracle chemical, it was considered the answer to meager crops. Now with the increased demands of war, farmers could increase their production and their income without investing in more land or seed. He spent his summers earning extra income at a near-by airport, training pilots, and servicing planes.

During the summer of 1939, Dan went to the Milwaukee County airfield with a new idea. He had discovered ways to spread the miracle chemical by airplane, and he had found a partner, Harold Pedersen.

The two formed a private business as crop dusters. Using Pedersen's plane, they spent the summer dusting vegetable and corn crops throughout southern Wisconsin and northern Illinois.

Dora, who had never known anyone of a culture other than French and Irish and a few Germans, recognized the opportunity to stretch her mind. She now lived in a German neighborhood with foreign-sounding neighbors and sent her children to school with Jewish children. She felt very sophisticated, worldly, and tried hard to hide her small-town background by asking neighbors about their families "in the old country" and seeking their recipes. She had discovered a library close by and dragged all kinds of books home to tease her curious mind.

What was it Ma used to say? "Curiosity killed the cat?" *Well curiosity opens doors. Curiosity seeks truth. Curiosity opened Pandora's box. Maybe curiosity will open my world.*

Pandora's Notes of the 19-thirties

Women in the 1930s took advantage of their newly won status as voting citizens. They flew planes, claimed political office, took home Nobel prizes, and exhibited their art work.

AMELIA EARHART flew solo across the Atlantic from Newfoundland to Ireland in just 15 hours (1932). She followed that by making the first solo flight from Hawaii to North America in 1935. Two years later, in an attempt to fly around the world, Earhart's plane was lost near Howland Island in the Pacific Ocean and never heard from again.

MAXINE DUNLAP became the first American woman to earn a glider pilot license (1931).

JEANETTE PICCARD, an American adventurer, set an altitude record for female balloonists when she ascended 57,579 feet (1934).

HATTIE WYATT CARAWAY (D-AR) was the first woman elected to the U.S. Senate (1931), the first woman to chair a Senate committee, and the first to serve as the Senate's presiding officer (1932). She served until 1944.

RUTH BRYAN OWEN, the first woman to represent the U.S. as a foreign minister, was appointed envoy to Denmark (1933).

LILLIAN GILBRETH received the Society of Industrial Engineers (all-male) Award for her work in motion study (1931), and continued to make contributions in the field following the death of her husband — all while raising 12 children. (Think *Cheaper By the Dozen*.)

JACKIE ORMES is considered the first African American female cartoonist (1937). Her characters and promotional dolls were the first not depicted as "mammy" or "pickaninny".

JANE ADDAMS, well-known in her field of social reform, was awarded the Nobel Peace Prize for her dedicated work at Hull House in Chicago (1931).

Two novelists turned out classics and were named Nobel Prize winners in the field of literature: **MARGARET MITCHELL** (*Gone With the Wind*, 1936) and **PEARL BUCK** (*The Good Earth*, 1938).

LAURA INGALLS WILDER published *The Little House in the Woods* (1932), the first of the "Little House" books that have never been out of print since.

DOROTHY THOMPSON claimed journalistic prowess for an interview with Adolph Hitler (1931).

An aging artist, **ANNA MARY ROBERTSON MOSES (GRANDMA MOSES),** 79, exhibited her paintings at the Museum of Modern Art in New York (1939). She continued to paint until her death in 1961 at age 101.

AUGUSTA SAVAGE opened the Savage Studio Arts and Crafts in New York, the largest art center in the country at the time (1932).

LAURA GILPIN, photographer, acclaimed for mastery of a platinum printing process, and her early work with autochromes of still-life and portraits of Native Americans, was elected an Associate of the Royal Photographic Society of Great Britain (1930).

KAREN HORNEY, noted psychoanalyst, challenged women toward classical Freudianism with her book, *New Ways in Psychoanalysis*, in which she debunked the idea that women were dysfunctional versions of men (1939).

MAY EDWARD CHINN was the first black woman doctor in Harlem and studied cytological methods for cancer detection, using the Pap smear (1936).

The first American woman to be beatified as a saint was **MOTHER FRANCES XAVIER CABRINI** (1938).

DR. DOROTHY H. ANDERSON was the first physician to recognize cystic fibrosis as a disease and, together with her research team, created the first tests to diagnose it. She presented the results of her medical research at a meeting of the American Pediatric Association (1938).

MARY MCLEOD BETHUNE was named as Minority Affairs Advisor by President Roosevelt and created the National Council of Negro Women (1935).

MARIAN ANDERSON sang an Easter Sunday concert before a crowd of 75,000 at the Lincoln Memorial after being denied permission to sing at a Daughters of the American Revolution (DAR) Hall. Eleanor Roosevelt resigned from the DAR in protest of their refusal (1939).

FLORENCE PRICE won the Wanamaker Prize (1932) and became the first black woman composer to have her work played by a major symphony, The Chicago Symphony Orchestra (1933).

BILLIE HOLIDAY recorded her timeless ballads with Teddy Wilson (1935).

SANDY OESTREICH, feminist, nurse, author, wife, mom, activist, champion and Equal Rights Amendment firebrand, was born (1935). She grew up to become an activist for hospital nursing issues, vice mayor of North Reddington Beach, FL and the steam behind bugging the Florida legislature to ratify the Equal Rights Amendment.

JUSTINE POLIER fought for the rights of the poor, especially education for black students, as the first woman Domestic Relations Court Judge, New York's Workmen's Compensation Division (1935).

JANE MATILDA BOLIN, the first black woman judge, was appointed justice of the Domestic Relations Court of New York (1939).

HATTIE MCDANIEL became the first African American to win an Oscar for Best Supporting Actress, in "Gone With the Wind" (1939).

Congress enacted the **SOCIAL SECURITY ACT** (1935), with provisions for dependent women and children.

Federal Courts ruled the **COMSTOCK LAW** definition of "obscenity" cannot include birth control (1936).

JULIA GODMAN RUUTTILA, union recruiter, activist, and labor journalist, raised community support for the CIO International Woodworkers of America during an 8-1/2 month lockout (1937).

FRANCES PERKINS, Secretary of Labor and the first woman appointed to the U.S. Cabinet (1933), created **THE FAIR LABOR STANDARDS ACT** (1938).

GEORGIA NEESE CLARK was the first woman to be confirmed as Treasurer of the United States (1939).

RUTH WAKEFIELD, a dietitian and food lecturer, and co-owner of the Toll House Inn in Whitman MA, invented the famous chocolate chip cookie (1938).

LETTIE PATE WHITEHEAD became the first American woman to serve as a director of a major corporation, Coca-Cola Company (1934).

Lots of little girls born in the 1930s were named Shirley or Eleanor, after two famous females. **SHIRLEY TEMPLE (BLACK)** entered movies at the age of three and became the darling of the screen throughout the 1930s and '40s. She later served as U.S. Ambassador until 1989. **ELEANOR ROOSEVELT** made her mark by supporting women, thus bringing to life the role of First Lady (beginning in 1933) and transforming that position forever.

OSA HELEN LEIGHTY JOHNSON, deemed "the greatest woman explorer and big-game hunter" in the 1920s and '30s was chosen to lead an expedition to Africa to film safari scenes for the movie, "Stanley and Livingstone", earning the distinction as "the first woman ever to take the entire responsibility of an African expedition" (1939).

DOROTHY ARZNER, a pioneer in the film industry, was the only female film director in the 1930s. She rigged the first boom microphone and is credited with its invention.

HELEN WILLS MOODY, professional tennis player when women rarely made that claim, retired in 1938 from competition after setting a record for eight Wimbledon singles titles that stood until 1990.

JACKIE MITCHELL, just 17, became the second woman (after Lizzie Murphy in 1928) to play baseball in the all-male minor leagues (1931). She pitched an exhibition game in Chattanooga TN against the New York Yankees and struck out both Babe Ruth and Lou Gehrig. The next day her contract was voided by the baseball commissioner, who claimed baseball was too strenuous for women. (That ban was not overturned until 1992.)

1940-1949

PANDORA at 40

Hello. My name is Pandora. Clearly, we're headed for another war. I've almost forgotten the pronouns "I" and "me", lost to "we" and "us". Our little family has grown to four; Dan's work is iffy; the war may take him away from us; and... yes... I... am still without a college education. Whatever happened to that little girl's dream of "a career"?

By late summer 1941, Dora had become active in her church, singing in the choir and attending Ladies Aid teas. She continued to haunt the library to learn about the world. *How I wish Miss Horne were here to show me the best books to read.*

Meanwhile, the Chesterfield-Pedersen Dusting Company had earned enough to buy a second plane. By fall the following year, they had acquired four more planes and six pilot-mechanics. Dan seriously considered giving up his University Extension job and devoting all his time to the business.

The company was about to open a branch operation in Iowa when Pearl Harbor was bombed on December 7, 1941, and the world changed — again.

"Dora, I can't just sit here thinking about improving crops and dairy production while the world falls to pieces."

"Aren't both those industries feeding our boys in the service?"

"Yes, but..."

"Please Dan. You have a family, remember? You're doing work that you do well, and it will help the war effort. Besides..."

"I know, but I feel so useless. I'm a healthy man who knows how to fly. And I'm good at it."

By the end of May 1942, when the sun returned after its winter retreat, Dan became restless again, looking more and more into the clouds. The draft had been invoked and several of the young men who had been teachers with him in northern Wisconsin came through Milwaukee, headed for Army and Navy training bases. One of the men who had barnstormed with him for two summers was about the same age as Dan.

"You miss the flying, don't you?" Dora asked her husband one morning at breakfast.

"What makes you ask that?"

"You tossed all night after you talked with your old flying buddy yesterday. I think you were flying through a storm or doing loop-the-loops or something. Are you still thinking about going back to flying?"

Dan didn't answer right away, but the nostalgia that flew across his eyes told his wife what she wanted to know. At last he told Dora about his visit with the 47-year-old barnstormer. They're going to let him fly some of the planes left from the last war. And they're building new ones. They need men to fly them."

"But you're draft exempt, aren't you?"

"I've been classified B-3 for the time being. That means I'm involved in agriculture and I'm over the age they're taking." He looked around the table at his daughters who tried to look as if they weren't listening, then added, "…for the time being."

"Will they bomb us, Mommy?" Bonnie asked her mother that night at bedtime.

"I don't think you have to worry about that, sweetheart." Dora tried to sound reassuring.

"But the kids at school say the bombers can fly right over the North Pole and bomb our factories."

"Now why would they want to bomb our factories? They're breweries." Dora tried to laugh it off. But she knew they were training pilots at Billy

Mitchell Field. She also knew that Dan had gone out there several times, trying to enlist in the National Guard.

Even in Milwaukee, far inland, the scare of bombs compelled citizens to honor blackouts, rig bomb shelters, and instigate bomb drills at school. Pandora received a note from the school principal explaining that the school was designated a neighborhood shelter. It never occurred to anyone that the children alone would fill the basement. What if the neighborhood adults tried to cram in there too?

Dora's older brothers were too old for the draft, but Apollo, the youngest, was 38 and still single. *If only he'd get married*, Dora thought, but she never said it. That would be unpatriotic if it was only to avoid the draft. Besides, he was helping Andrew on the farm, which might qualify him for exemption.

Pandora was never a good cook outside of the basics. As a young girl, she preferred hanging around her father in the barns or roaming the fields behind the house or sitting on the woodpile contemplating the clouds. In fact, she was nearly dangerous in the kitchen, always slicing her fingers along with the tomatoes, burning food on the hot side of the wood stove, leaving pies in the oven too long (although it probably helped to soften the tough crusts she rolled out). Her longest stints in the kitchen were at haying time — and she hated it.

Now here came another war and store shelves began to clear almost as quickly as men were shipped overseas. No longer could she buy simple staples like sugar, coffee, tea, and meat. Worst of all was the lack of chocolate, coconut, pineapple, vanilla, cinnamon, and other spices that came from the besieged tropical Pacific. Dora had a sweet tooth that would have to wait until after the war — after the *duration* — whenever that would come.

Determined to learn to cook "nutritiously", she sought help with booklets from Dan's Extension office and books she dragged home from the library. She replaced meat with macaroni, and rice with potatoes. She used sweet vegetables in cakes (her carrot cake was actually passable without frosting), and she collected stacks of recipes for vegetable casseroles. Her family ate healthy food, even when it tasted like Bossy's hide.

"What a waste," Dora said to Dan one evening as they sat reading the newspaper after a grand supper of macaroni, bean and tomato casserole, with sugarless pudding. "Look at today's list of casualties. Nearly fills a whole column."

"Likely to fill more columns before this is over," Dan mumbled. He wasn't sure if he had the guts to join up and head overseas. Still, it was on his mind, and he felt he ought to — patriotic duty and all that. But he didn't mention anything to Dora. If the time came, it would come.

The time came in late 1943. A whispered promise of an invasion of Europe was to begin with heavy aerial bombardment. Planes and pilots were at a premium. The war was destroying pilots from both America and England at a frightening rate.

Dan had completed the autumn crop dusting when he made his decision. "Look at the casualties tonight!" He waved the Sunday newspaper as he and Dora waited for the Charlie McCarthy radio show to begin. "I remember you said the list would get longer and you were right. Almost a half page of names. And the type gets smaller. Wonder if they don't want us to read it."

When Dora didn't respond, he added quietly, "They've made another call for pilots. I've decided to sign up."

Dora gasped, but didn't move. She took a deep breath before lowering the paper and looking at her husband. "Dan, you're nearly fifty! There must be younger men..."

"No Dora. There aren't. Too many of them are in that list you're reading. They need more pilots, and I'm well trained. Besides, I'm only forty-eight."

"Have you already...?" She didn't want to finish the question.

"Yes. I handed in my resignation at the office and... I leave Tuesday by train for Texas where I'll train on army planes for three or four weeks."

Dora took another deep breath before, "Then?"

"Probably England. That's where most of the bombing squadrons are based. I don't know, and they won't tell me."

"How are we going to tell the girls?"

"Can you?"

"Oh Dan. This is something they have to hear from you. They'll have questions that I can't answer. Like *why*?"

"I'll tell them tomorrow after school." Dora walked over to sit on her husband's lap. Her tears flowed softly as she hugged him, but he didn't hear them.

"I told the guys after we finished work Friday; I think two of them may come with me. Harold knows he's too old. The others may join us later, and Harold will handle the business the best he can for the duration."

"Damn the duration," Dora whispered into her husband's shoulder.

Dora waited just one week after Dan left before she looked for a job. She didn't have to look far. The Kilbourn Exchange office right in her neighborhood needed a long distance operator. The last one had left to join her husband at a training base in Florida. Sure, she had to learn how to operate new equipment, but she caught on easily. Once you learn the basics of something, the bells and whistles become added attractions.

Dora worked daytime hours while the girls were in school. She added the chore of packing lunches, since the girls no longer could come home at noon. And she grew to enjoy the daily whirlwind of "Where's my jacket?" "What did you make for lunch?" "Can I wear my new shoes?" The answer to the last question was, "No, they'll have to last for the duration." Shoe leather was rationed too.

The busy-ness of the telephone office kept Dora's mind from fretting over Dan's absence. She came to enjoy the daily chatter with the other women, the brief shopping trips during breaks, and the weekly cash envelope she took home. She didn't have to spend much of what Dan sent home and was building up a substantial savings account — her own money.

"Mom, why do you work?" Bonnie looked up from her notebook one evening. "Cookie says mothers are supposed to be home."

"Well, this is wartime. You'll have to tell Cookie about it. Maybe she doesn't know." At the end of the day, Dora could be very sarcastic. "Sorry dear, that isn't what you wanted to hear. I work because I feel good having important work to do. Sitting around the house knitting isn't my idea of *important*."

"But Cookie's mother knits sweaters and watch caps for soldiers. That's important."

"Yes, I guess it is. But did you ever see anything that I knitted?"

Bonnie giggled as she flipped her pencil back and forth idly, then returned to writing an essay about China. After a moment she looked up again. "Oh I get it. We do the things we do best."

"That sounds about right to me." Dora smiled. Some teenagers can be very smart some of the time.

Dan and his crop dusting crew stayed together and ended up not in England running bombing raids, but in North Africa covering the Italian invasion. After France and Italy were returned safely to their owners, Dan's squadron was transferred to the South Pacific. V-E Day came just before Dan's fiftieth birthday.

Dora saved all his letters, folding them neatly and returning them to their envelopes before adding them to the packet she kept tied with ribbon. Dan and his crew had just begun to ferry planes to Honolulu when word came of the end of the war in the Pacific. Two atomic bombs dropped over Japanese cities resulted in a peace treaty, signed aboard the USS Missouri in August 1945. "The duration" of World War II was over.

Pandora expected Dan home within a few days. After two weeks without any mail from him, she was beginning to worry when she received only a brief letter. About all Dan said was that he and his crew were stuck in Honolulu, that returning wounded vets took priority and filled the planes headed for the mainland. Oh yes, and he loved her and looked forward to returning to his family.

Weeks went by, with only a few short impersonal letters. *Why doesn't he use his time to write longer letters?* Dora wondered. *And why doesn't he volunteer to pilot one of those returning planes?*

Still, she regularly posted letters to him, just as she did throughout the war. It began to look as if he'd miss Thanksgiving and maybe even Christmas. Something else must be keeping him away.

Returning heroes were met with open arms by their families and loved ones, paraded down the streets in open cars, showered with flowers and speeches and decorated with medals. A grateful government had legislated the means for veterans to go to college, buy homes, finance new businesses, and cover themselves with insurance, even before the war was ended. Why couldn't that benevolent government bring her husband home?

A week after Thanksgiving, Dora returned from work to find the front door ajar. In the parlor, Bonnie Jean and Hattie sat on their father's knees. They barely looked up as Dora reached out her welcome-home arms.

"Dan! You're home." When he stood up, the girls continued to cling to his arms as he looked at his wife across the room. She looked... younger than he remembered, than her picture he carried in his wallet.

"Dan!" she repeated, then threw her arms around him.

"Hey! I'm under here," he yelled, trying to extricate himself.

Dora stepped back. "Girls, you've had your turns. Would you go fix some sandwiches and make some coffee, please. Let me welcome my husband home... please."

The girls let go reluctantly and backed out of the room, still looking at their father.

"They've missed you," Dora began. "Almost as much as I have. Welcome home, darling." She wrapped her arms around his neck again and barely noticed that he hadn't shaved recently, and his beard was growing in gray. His hairline too had pulled back, with more gray slipping through. And his uniform was as rumpled and soiled as his long flight could make it. She had never seen him this disheveled.

His kiss felt different... it had been a long time. Dora didn't know this man who now embraced her and held her tightly. Had they become strangers?

"Sit down here, sweetheart," Dan said, pointing to the sofa. "We have some catching up to do."

Dan talked on about his new assignment at Billy Mitchell Field while he awaited discharge papers, how warm it was in Hawaii, and how restless he had become waiting to get home. Dora listened. She wanted so much to tell him about her job and how she had kept things together while he was gone, how she was very proud of the way she had made do with the shortages, and how she kept up the letter writing, even when she was dog tired after a day's long shift.

Pandora was sure the old feelings would return, as soon as they got reacquainted. But something had definitely shifted; something had come between them. Perhaps it was only time, but still she wondered.

After Dan described Hawaii's beauty, he switched to North Africa, how hot and dry it was, then Italy and the raids his plane had made to soften up the invasion. He was about to launch into a story about flying into Rome when his daughters returned with Spam sandwiches, potato salad, and coffee.

"Oh, just what I've looked forward to," Dan raved. "Did you make that potato salad yourself?"

"No," Bonnie Jean admitted. "Mom made it for us yesterday."

Dora sat back and watched as Dan eagerly dug into the snack. He didn't look at her. Dora was not dull; she knew something wasn't right, but how would she get it out of him? *Maybe later, when the girls have gone to bed*, she promised herself.

When bedtime came, Dan looked frantic. "Would you mind if I slept on the sofa?" he asked. "I'm not sure I could sleep in a soft bed. Can you give me some time?" He looked towards her, forlorn, lost, confused.

"What's really the matter, Dan?"

"Nothing. I mean… nothing."

"C'mon. This is your wife here. I know you too well. Something is haywire, and it's not the texture of the bed. I've missed you so much and looked forward to this day. Now you say you want to sleep down here? What's happened to my fly guy?" She waited.

After a long silence, he took her hand, still unable to look into her eyes. "Dora…"

More silence. "My darling Dora, I've… oh god, how can I hurt you? And I know this will."

Dora froze, her spine feeling a shiver from one end to the other. "Holy cow, Dan, what in the world… just tell me. I'm stronger than you think. Did you catch some dreadful disease in the Pacific? I heard lots about malaria and quinine and…"

"Hush. No, I didn't catch anything. I'm very healthy. It's just that…" Dan put both hands around his head and began to sway.

"For God's sake, Dan. Tell me what happened."

"Okay. But first, I'm sorry, so very sorry. I fell for… no, that's not right. I've had an affair… there was this girl… oh god, how can I…?"

As Dora's head felt the relief that he wasn't sick, her heart filled with the tears she kept trying to hide. She wasn't going to be a *cry baby*, like they used to call her as a kid. Calmly, with as much composure as she could manage, she whispered, "We can work this out. You're home now. That's all that matters. You're healthy, and now you're safe."

She stood up and walked to the bedroom, every step feeling as if she was fighting that sinking mud hole all those years ago. Inside her room… their room… she threw herself onto the bed and sobbed. She cried until no more tears came, then she slept a cruel nightmarish sleep.

Dan was gone when she came downstairs the next morning. The emptiness she felt grew emptier. Will he come back… ever? What will I do if he doesn't? The last few years were compacted into a forever that lay ahead.

But he did come back. Two days later, Dan returned to Dora, shaved, cleaned up, and apologetic. They talked through the night and agreed they could get past this. They didn't want to divorce; they'd stay together "for their daughters". They rationalized that they were among the lucky ones, the couples whose love was strong enough to withstand mistakes. At the very least, they were one of few couples who were both alive after a dreadful separation.

Somehow, the Chesterfield family survived the 1945 Christmas holidays and Pandora's 46th birthday.

Dan invested part of his military back pay in a small airport — a short landing strip just north of Milwaukee in what folks then called the *boondocks.*

They didn't remain boondocks for long. Other servicemen chose construction as their investments in the future and set about to build houses on all the land that ringed the airport. It wasn't long before Dan, Dora, Bonnie, and Hattie moved into one of them, a small three-bedroom house that looked as though it needed a picket fence. They settled for a Sears wire fence instead and began to plant flowers and shrubs to hide it.

The family had just nailed a sign over the mailbox that identified theirs as "The Chesterfield Home" when Dora received her pay in an envelope that contained a pink slip.

"They said that a returning serviceman needed my job," she wailed at Dan. "Just like that. I'm fired."

"They're only doing what's right, supporting all the men who fought the war for us so we could have this home, our freedom…"

"Oh please don't sound like a war propaganda machine. I have children to feed. You men are showered with all kinds of severance benefits. And what do we women receive? Orders to go home!"

"But that's what I'm for," Dan patted his wife's shoulder. He always felt so helpless when she cried, like he was to blame and there was nothing he could do to help. That day, he felt protective and back in control, the control he had lost when he came home with his confession to find his wife happily drawing a regular paycheck, appearing not to need him. Now she did.

"You men just don't appreciate us. I had to take over your duties around here. Other women ferried your airplanes, and thousands of nurses tended wounds in your military hospitals around the world. Now we're all looking for work. It isn't fair."

Dan placed both arms around his wife's shaking shoulders and tried to soothe her with, "That's all right, dear. Daddy's home now. I'll protect…" But he got no further.

"Ohh men!" Dora wailed as she broke away from him and stormed out of the kitchen and into the bedroom, slamming the door behind her.

"She really liked working," Bonnie said softly. "Mama liked the telephone office."

"I know, baby. She'll be all right in a few days when she sees how much work there is to do in our new home."

"But Daddy, it's not fair that women can't…"

"You're beginning to sound like your mother, kitten. It may not be fair, but that's the way it is. Men do the work; women keep the house."

"Oh, Daddy!"

Following Dan's return, his partner Harold asked to move his half of the business down south and begin dusting cotton crops in Mississippi. Because Dan had used his accumulated pay to buy the airfield, he had to take out a government loan to restore his own crop dusting business, which he re-named *Chester Field Dusting*. Only this time he planned to keep his feet out of the airplanes.

Plans went awry after the first of the year when Harold asked Dan to help him out Down South for a few weeks. Dan accepted eagerly, saying he was giving Dora a chance to mull over her options.

She mulled all right, recalling how much she had enjoyed writing "Head of Household" on the income tax forms she had to fill out during Dan's absence. She liked being in charge, receiving a regular paycheck, and being responsible for herself and her daughters. If Dan decided to stay away, she'd get by. Something was broken between them that could never be completely fixed.

Pandora sulked around the new home before she took any interest in decorating it. About the same time she found new supplies of sugar and chocolate and vanilla returning to the grocery store, and she took up baking, determined to conquer the kitchen. As meat returned to the stores, her menus expanded to include entire meals, prepared with thought and a great deal of cutting and slicing. She found recipes in the magazines she purchased at the checkout counter of the new super market; she couldn't wait to get home to try them. She bought a new sewing machine and discovered she had a knack for copying dresses she found pictured in those magazines.

In other words, Pandora Nelle Chesterfield, like so many wives of returning servicemen, attacked homemaking as a full-time job worthy of her complete attention and energy. She was determined to "make a good home" for her family.

No one noticed that she no longer pulled out her watercolors to paint in silence for hours at a time. No one noticed that she never touched the new piano that she bought with her savings. No one noticed that she only aimed her camera on holidays.

Pandora's Notes of the 19-forties

Until the middle of the 20th century, women as a group were squelched, controlled, and ignored. The only women recognized by mid-century, albeit briefly in Bonnie Jean's history books, were QUEEN ELIZABETH I, CATHERINE THE GREAT, QUEEN ISABELLA, SUSAN B. ANTHONY, CARRIE NATION, MARIE CURIE, AMELIA EARHART, ISADORA DUNCAN, SCHEHERAZADE, and EVE.

During the war years, women stepped up and took the places of men who were away fighting the enemy. Like women of the ages, they shouldered responsibilities. Leading the way were the British princesses, ELIZABETH and her sister MARGARET ROSE, who joined the Women's Auxiliary Territorial Service, a motorized unit that repaired vehicles for the military.

Ever since December 7, 1941, American women actively participated in the war — both on the homefront and within the military, even if they were kept away from the frontlines of battle ("for their own protection").

CAPTAIN ANNIE FOX was the first woman to receive a Purple Heart (1942), awarded for her service while under attack at Pearl Harbor on that fateful Sunday.

In 1942, women joined the military. **JACQUELINE "JACKIE" COCHRAN** and **NANCY HARKNESS LOVE** created the **WASP (WOMEN AIRFORCE SERVICE PILOTS)**; Cochran was its first commander. These pilots ferried bombers and fighter planes to the troops, towed targets for airmen to practice on during training, and served as instrument instructors.

Other U.S. women joined the newly formed **WAAC (WOMEN'S AUXILIARY ARMY CORPS)**, designed by a bunch of male bureaucrats; the first director was **OVETA CULP HOBBY**, a prominent society woman from Texas (1942). Their ranks increased to 32,000 before 1945.

MARY A. HALLAREN was a member of the first officer training class in the WAAC (1942) and assigned as battalion commander in England. She later worked on legislation to make WAAC a permanent part of the regular Army and Reserves (1948).

MILDRED MCAFEE, president of Wellesley College and the first female commissioned officer in the history of the U.S. Navy (1942), was named the first director of the **WAVES (WOMEN ACCEPTED FOR VOLUNTEER EMERGENCY SERVICE)**.

Women were also accepted into armies in civilian roles, such as aviators, nurses, clerks, and instructors; others took jobs in munitions and military equipment factories to build guns and planes and submarines.

"ROSIE THE RIVETER" grew into the symbol for women who took over the jobs of departing soldiers. Women became taxi drivers, bartenders, band leaders, stockbrokers, baseball and football players, builders, farmers, trades people, and factory workers. "Rosie" appeared on the cover of the *Saturday Evening Post* in May 1943, making the name "Rosie" a symbol of American women in the war industry.

ROSE HICKEY, with her partner, set riveting records working on planes in Tarrytown NY, and **ROSE MONROE**, from Michigan, made a film to sell war bonds.

SYBIL LEWIS was one of a few African American women who drove rivets for Lockheed Aircraft in California.

HEDY LAMARR (HEDWIG EVA MARIA KIESLER), film actor and inventor, received a patent for her method to detect and jam radio-guided torpedos (1942), which aided the Allies during WWII, paving the way for "frequency hopping", used by cellular phones and other technology.

"Pinup girls" became a familiar term as women posed in bathing suits to "keep up the morale of servicemen". **BETTY GRABLE** and **RITA HAYWORTH**, film actresses, probably were the most famous. Their photos often hung in barracks alongside a photo of the serviceman's wife (1940s).

The **USO (UNITED SERVICE ORGANIZATIONS)** was founded in October 1941 by a group of service organizations. During the war, numerous movie stars and entertainers joined Bob Hope's Camp Show Tours overseas to entertain troops, beginning with **FRANCES LANGFORD, DORIS DAY, DOLORES HOPE, DOROTHY LAMOUR,** and the **ANDREWS SISTERS**.

The **ANDREWS SISTERS — PATTI, MAXINE, AND LAVERNE —** sang the world through WWII with their vivacious singing style.

When women began to wear slacks during WWII, they were harassed with accusations such as "If you're going to wear men's pants, expect to be treated like a man." Clothing designer **VERA MAXWELL** is credited with designing sportswear that permitted women greater freedom of motion (1947).

At the close of the war, women's military organizations were disbanded and the women in them were summarily dismissed, receiving no benefits, no discharge pay, and little acknowledgment for their bravery. While some women replaced their uniforms, head scarves, and factory jumpers with dust bonnets and aprons, many women found "their places" in politics and government, literature, sports, and the arts, as they worked to stay "out of the box".

YVONNE CLAEYS BRILL, pioneer rocket scientist, worked on the first designs for an American satellite (mid-1940s). She went on to invent a propulsion system to keep communication satellites in their orbits in 1983.

EUGENIA GORECKI, a design engineer who escaped from Poland before the war, was hired as the first and only woman at the Ford Motor Company in the 1940s.

IRENE MORGAN KIRKALDY, a black worker in a plant making WWII bombers, defied a bus driver in Virginia when she was told to give up her seat to a white person. NAACP Attorney Thurgood Marshall won her case in the Supreme Court on grounds of promoting and protecting national travel (1944). She was consequently awarded the Freedom Medal by President Clinton.

ELEANOR ROOSEVELT, the President's widow, was appointed as a U.S. delegate to the newly formed United Nations (1945).

RUTH BRYAN OWEN, the first woman from the Deep South (Florida) to be elected to the House of Representatives, was named to assist in drafting the United Nations Charter (1945) and appointed as alternate delegate to the UN (1949).

ALICE DUNNIGAN was the first black journalist accredited to cover Congress and the White House, Supreme Court, and State Department (1947), the only journalist of color to travel with President Truman on his train (1948).

EMILY GREENE BALCH, co-founder of the Women's Intl. League for Peace and Freedom, was awarded the Nobel Peace Prize (1946).

ETHEL PERCY ANDRUS, PHD, a teacher and the first woman high school principal in California, founded the National Retired Teachers Association (1944).

DR. FRANCES L. WILLOUGHBY became the first woman doctor in the *regular* U.S. Navy — *regular* meaning "all-male" (1948).

ELIZABETH KENNY, an Australian nurse, brought her unorthodox treatment for polio patients to the U.S. and set up clinics around the country (1942).

MARTHA ELIOT, pediatrician, the only woman to sign the constitution of the new World Health Organization (1947), helped dependent and crippled children through the 1935 Social Security Act.

Margaret Chase Smith (R-MN) was elected to the House of Representatives in 1940 and became the first woman to serve in both the House and Senate (1949).

Hattie Wyatt Caraway (D-AR) became the first woman legislator to co-sponsor the Equal Rights Amendment (1943).

Ruth Muskrat (Bronson) made it her life work to bridge the gap between Indians and Whites, beginning with her book *Indians Are People Too* (1944).

Maria Tallchief, from Oklahoma, became the first Native American to dance in the New York City Ballet (1948).

Sylvia Porter, financial columnist since 1936, helped design Series E Savings Bonds (1940). First published as S. F. Porter to hide her gender, she was granted floor access at the New York Stock Exchange in 1942.

The **New York Stock Exchange** listed 67 women in firms accredited for floor trading (1949), in contrast to 12 in 1929.

Evelyn Boyd Granville (Smith College) and **Marjorie Lee Browne** (University of Michigan) became the first African American women to earn doctorates in mathematics (1949).

Muriel Apfelberg Brownstein (Monchy) took saxophone lessons alongside Stan Getz, but couldn't find work in a jazz band "because she was a woman"; she started her own band in college during WWII (1944), then was married. At the age of 56, she earned a Ph.D. from Temple University in Education and became a beloved high school science teacher. Her daughter, **RUBY BROWN**, carries on her mother's love of jazz; she's general manager of a jazz radio station, and noted jazz radio host.

In sports, the **ALL-AMERICAN GIRLS PROFESSIONAL BASEBALL LEAGUE** gave more than 600 women an opportunity to play professional baseball (1943-1954). It was created and managed by men to replace "real baseball" (all-male) until the war ended.

BABE DIDRIKSON ZAHARIAS was voted the outstanding woman athlete of the 20th century shortly after founding the Professional Ladies Golf Association (PLGA) (1949).

ESTHER WILLIAMS, U.S. freestyle champion and Olympic contender, popularized water ballet through her MGM movies in the 1940s, and is credited with founding competitive synchronized swimming.

A Russian immigrant named **AYN RAND** became a best-selling author in the '40s with her publication of *The Fountainhead* (1943) and *Atlas Shrugged* (1957), her last novel. She since has become an "institution for objectivism" and literary discussion.

1950-1959

PANDORA at 50

Hello. My name is Pandora and I'm 50 years old! Halfway to the goal I set as a child. When I reached twenty, I was sure my life would be over by this time. I seem to have settled for being "just a housewife", while I hear about women who have lives of interest and value. Oh yes, I know! I've raised future good citizens. But what am I doing — about a career for me?

Just when Dora figured she had become the essential homemaker, Dan brought home a new invention, a new kind of box called a television set, opening up a wide new world to her, a world she could now see for herself. Here was proof of the possibility not only to hear people from far away, but to see them too — and Dora was fascinated by it. *How Pa would have marveled at this successor to his ray-dee-oh!*

She'd turn on the set and watch the color patterns on the screen until the Arthur Godfrey show came on; she had listened to him for years over the radio; now she could see him. Then came Bishop Sheen with his saintly worldly advice on life. In the evenings, the GE Theater opened her to live drama, and to Milton Berle with his antics and zany outfits that earned him the title of Mr. Television. (All men, or had you noticed? Dora did.)

Sitting in front of that box, she became completely absorbed with the people who were talking directly to her. Here was another magic box, the answer to the radio box that offered its magic thirty years earlier, full of new ideas and new people. Here was a box that provided a view of the world and everything in it, that provided laughter, tears, philosophy, drama, advice, celebrities, even dance shows for youngsters. Of course *her* daughters were too old for such teenage nonsense. Bonnie was at college, staying with her grandfather in River Falls, and Hattie was in love.

While watching a gardening show, Dora was reminded of the scent of lilacs, like the ones around her father-in-law's house, like the ones her own father added to Grandmother Rosella's yard. The spring lilacs always reminded Pandora that life could be renewed. She turned off the television, threw a sweater around her shoulders and dashed off to buy six lilac plants.

"What do you want me to be?" a serious Bonnie asked her mother a few weeks after high school graduation.

"You have to follow your dreams, Bonnie," Dora told her. "You have to give yourself enough education to know what opportunities are out there." *Did I really say that? I haven't lived it, how can I suggest it to my daughter?*

"I know, but what do *you* want me to be?"

Dora sat back next to her daughter and asked, "If I said I wanted you to drive a truck or run a dairy farm or clerk in a dress shop or fly an airplane, would that affect your choice?"

"Probably not."

"What do *you* want to do with your life?"

"That's just it. I'm not sure, and I don't want to commit to something for a lifetime, in case I don't like it. Maybe I'd like college… I like school… and then, afterwards, maybe I can decide."

"Sounds good. You don't have to make lifetime choices; you can always change your mind. I'm just glad you aren't determined to get married right away. I want you to have a chance at a career. It never hurts a woman to have something to fall back on if… when…"

"Muh-ther," Bonnie Jean wailed in the same key her mother used to wail at Mary Belle. "I'm going to have a career, a real career. I know that. I'm not going to get married — ever."

"Now don't make frivolous statements. You'll change your mind one day, when the right man comes along."

"No. I thought Rick was the right man, but he isn't. I mean, we just didn't... you know... he can be such a dense... he just doesn't send me."

"Oh!" Dora seemed stumped. She knew that Bonnie and Rick had become "an item" in school, *steadies*, but she hadn't heard about a split up. "Have you told him?"

"Not yet. I figure that when... if... I go away to college he'll get the idea."

"Bonnie, that's not fair to him. You have to tell him how you feel."

"Mother! I can't talk to you about this. You're my mother."

Bonnie returned to her homework and Dora's mind asked, *What do you want to be, Miss Pandora? Where is your career? Your heart?*

The year after Bonnie left for college, left Rick to pine away, and left her family to fill in the missing place at the table, Helen Madelaine Chesterfield announced her engagement to Rutherford B. Lawson, the boy next door, literally... next door.

"Ford and I have been dating for months," Hattie announced one morning. "We've decided to get married when he graduates from college."

"But he's so much older than you," Dora pointed out.

"Not really, only four years. He'll be graduating soon."

"You're not even out of high school. Don't you want to go to college?"

"No, not really. I want to marry Ford and have babies, lots of them, like Grandma. I don't want to waste any more time in school than I have to. I hate it."

"Bonnie always liked school. What happened to you?"

"I'm not Bonnie. I never have been. You always think Bonnie is everything and I ought to be like her, but I'm not. I'm me, Helen Madelaine Chesterfield. And me, Hattie, wants to get married and have children."

Dora poured another cup of coffee and sat with her hands in her lap, waiting for both the coffee and her insides to cool.

"Well then, I guess we ought to plan a wedding." *Ye gods, I sound exactly like Mamá.*

Hattie jumped up, nearly upsetting the table as she reached to hug her mother. "Now I can show you. See? I have a ring." She pulled the band out of her pocket and fit it onto her finger. "He gave it to me last night; isn't it beautiful?"

Dora hid her disappointment and grabbed her daughter's hand. "Yes, it's beautiful. So are you — a beautiful daughter who will give me beautiful grandchildren." Mother and daughter wrapped their arms around each other and Dora rocked her *little girl* — perhaps for the last time. Hattie had grown up, and Dora hadn't noticed.

Empty Nest Syndrome, they called it — that time when the last Child has left home and Husband is busy with his job and Wife is left with a big empty house — reduced from a full-time job of homemaking to a part-time job of waiting on Husband.

After the flurry of Hattie's wedding, Dora got caught up in the upcoming elections, fascinated with the "egghead" Adlai Stevenson, but entranced by the handsome General Dwight Eisenhower.

When both candidates placed education at the top of the nation's priority list, Pandora decided her new direction. Her only education after eighth grade was the two years at Business School and Dan's coaching toward her high school diploma. *My word, that was a long time ago. I wonder if I'd even be able to study, much less pass a course. I'm fifty-two years old, for crying out loud!* "Wait, Pandora Nelle, you can't quit. You have a long way to go and much to do," came a childlike response from nowhere. She buckled; *I'm going to try.*

"I'm going back to school," she announced one summer evening to Dan as they weeded the flower beds.

"Why?" was Dan's response. "Why on earth would you want to go through all that when you don't have to?"

"I don't know; it sounds like fun."

"Fun? College is not fun. It's hard work," he said, remembering his own college days.

"Bonnie says she's having fun. You have fun with your work. Why can't I?"

"Because you're my wife. I take care of you. You don't want for anything. You have a nice house; your closets are full; you have everything you…"

"Why? I'll tell you. It's because I *am* your wife. Because I *do* have a house full of things. Because *you* have been taking care of me. Now I want to take care of myself, to develop me, to find out what else I can do besides keep house and run a telephone switchboard."

Dan couldn't top that, and Dora trooped down to the Milwaukee campus of the University of Wisconsin the next day to register for fall classes. They didn't even ask to see her high school diploma, which she conveniently failed to mention. On the way home she picked up the braatwursts and chips for the Fourth of July picnic.

Hattie and Ford were coming over from their new home in New Glarus; Bonnie was already home for the summer break and working at a local drive-in movie. Dora's old friend Ginger, from the telephone office days in Arkansaw, had phoned to tell Dora she had moved nearby and wanted to see her and Dan. She accepted the invitation to the picnic, and would bring her husband Phil and their son Grant.

"That makes eight by my count." Dora was figuring out the size of the potato salad. "Is that right, Dan?"

"You're the college student," Dan muttered in one of his moods.

"Come on, Dan. We're having a party. Cheer up. I promise I won't get smarter than you, nor will I earn more money than you — when I get my job."

Dan stood up without a word and left the room. Dora watched him walk about the backyard, kicking at dandelions in the lawn and swiping at tree limbs as he passed. *Guess I shouldn't tease him like that.*

Dan and Dora had been married for 24 years, a marriage that had survived good times and bad, crowding and separation, straying husband and bored wife. Their major achievements: they had raised two children they were proud of. They had a nice home, were comfortable by 1950 standards, and they still could manage an evening out once in a while.

Of late, with the children gone, their focus returned to themselves, but something had shifted. They began to prod each other, looking to stir the embers to see if any sparks were left. The more they poked, the more they bruised each other rather than stirred sparks. Too much had changed, perhaps beginning with Dan's absence during the war, or perhaps with Dora's restlessness.

Dora watched from the kitchen window. Was Dan afraid that he was losing her, again? Was he bored with her? Was he looking for something she couldn't provide? What had gone wrong? Yes, she had noticed the distance growing over the last few months. Dan kicked another dandelion, decapitating it and sending white feathery seeds into the air.

Attendance for the Fourth of July picnic in their backyard mushroomed after Dan flew to Arkansaw and returned with Mary Belle, Iris with her new husband Toby Tortelli, and Billie without her old husband.

Dora was particularly excited to see Ginger again. She had missed her friend's wedding and only heard about the birth of their son after his first birthday. Now the boy was a teenager.

"Ginger, are you happy?" Dora asked when the two friends found a moment together.

"What a question? Why do you ask? Are you?"

"I've always believed women weren't supposed to be happy, you know that."

"Yes, I remember. All that women's suffrage stuff. But look how much women have changed since then. We're over the hill, in our fifties now." She paused and looked skyward. "If we ain't happy now, there may not be time to figure it out. Does that make sense?"

"Not sure, Gingersnap! I've decided I have another half century to figure it out, but I'm still unsure. I know something's missing. Something isn't..."

"Gee, I haven't heard *Gingersnap* in ages." She put her arms around her friend. "Dora, I think you've already figured out this happiness thing. You're so smart. Look around you. Your family together, good friends, and good food in your own lovely home. What more could you ask for?"

"A husband who truly loves me."

"C'mon, Pandora Nelle. Your Dan is perfect for you. He seems..."

"What he seems is one thing, but he... how do they say it... strayed while he was in the Army."

"What do you mean… strayed?"

"From what he's said, she was a nurse; he had been away from home a long time; she was young and pretty and… well, you fill in the blanks."

"Oh no, not your Dan. Not that guy out there hovering over the hot barbecue grill."

"The very same. We've drawn some lines, made some rules, but things will never be the same again."

Dora so wanted to share her college and career plans, but decided not to. She abruptly closed the conversation. "You seem happy too, Ginger. Your Grant is a good-looking polite young man and your husband is a doll. Hold them close."

The Fourth of July picnic 1952 was a celebration that Dora would long remember.

A month later, Dan took one of the company planes up for a flight test, replacing one of the mechanics — the first time he ever flew a plane he hadn't worked on himself. It failed and crashed at the edge of the airport, narrowly missing a new development of homes. Those who watched in horror reported that Dan purposely flew the plane into the ground to avoid hitting the homes. Only the tower heard the curses as the motor failed, and then his heart.

Dora's life crashed that day too. Bonnie and Hattie rushed to their mother's side and tried to deflect some of the pain. Andrew and Laura drove down with Mary Belle, Billie, and Iris. They all tried to calm Pandora, but she would not be consoled.

"I killed him. I never forgave him. I told him I wanted to go back to school. He took that as rejection of him. I know it. He wasn't happy… with me."

"Mom, you know that isn't true. You saw how happy he was at the party on the Fourth, how he took over the barbecue, set off the fireworks. He was the life of the party. I've never seen him happier." Bonnie said the words, but she had sensed something different about her father all through the day. She even asked herself why Dad had invited the whole family, especially Grandma, for the celebration.

"Why don't you come live at our place, Mom?" Hattie offered. "We have plenty of room. You would have the place to yourself for a while. Ford and I have decided to travel before beginning our family. Europe is gathering itself back to life and countries are begging for tourists. Come on, Mom, get rid of this big old house and come live at ours."

"Or you can come back to Arkansaw and live with Andrew and me... and Billie," Mary Belle added. "It will be like old times to have my girls back on the farm."

But Pandora would not be coaxed. She had done much soul searching over the past years. She listened to all the talk, then decided in the end to continue life as she had planned it. She would stay in the house, go to college, pursue the dreams that were hers alone. It was time for herself. She had hoped that Dan would share her plan, but now his death seemed to underline that internal sense that her own time had come.

When the house was quiet again, Dora recalled Ginger's suggestion. "Write out your feelings. Put down on paper the things that bother you, those that upset you, and those that make you feel good and keep you sane." She sat down with pencil and paper and began to write. She intended to describe her marriage and how it ended. Another idea popped into her head.

"All marriages end." She said it out loud as she stood up and began to pace, back and forth, dictating to the air as her mind whirled. "All marriages end! That has to be true. As all lives end, so do the lives of wedded bliss. How? Sometimes in death, yes, as two of my own loves have ended," she said, remembering dear Leo. "Some marriages end in divorce, rather like mine almost did. And sometimes...," she paused to think. "Sometimes they end in desertion; one partner walks out on the other — perhaps even subconsciously abandoning a marriage while sticking around in body only."

Pandora sat down again and began to write. The words poured out of her head as she filled page after page.

One day, as a psychologist, she would understand how writing out one's woes often clarifies a situation thought insoluble. By the time summer decided to cool off, she had covered a couple hundred pages. "I wrote a book!" she yelled after placing the final period to the last sentence. "I wrote a book!" (Pandora never published this book, *All Marriages End in D.*)

Welcome to the Class of '56 read the sign over the registration tables. Dora stood in line, registered for classes and bought her books — a process that took her most of the day. She returned home eagerly to scan the books before wondering what she had gotten herself into. She had chosen a class in writing, but discovered it required a class in freshman composition that she would have to finish first. Her other class choices were history, anthropology, French (she knew a bit already from listening to Mary Belle and Fayette when they didn't want the children to understand), and... she couldn't remember the other. *Oh yes, psychology. I'm over fifty and I'm studying psychology. What am I thinking?*

If there were doubts on registration day, they were doubled after the first day of classes. She drove home slowly, her mind reeling with the new subjects, the new ideas. She reeled more at the realization of how young were the people around her, even the instructors.

Evenings alone became almost unbearable. *My darling Dan, what did I do to you? How will I live without you here to set me straight? Why didn't I...* and the tears would start. Most nights she sat up studying late so she didn't have to think any more. But that wasn't any help either. She missed her husband. She wondered too if she had started her classes too soon after Dan's death.

"I'm not sure if I belong in this class," she murmured to her psychology instructor in mid-November.

"Why not, Mrs. Chesterfield?"

"I'm not used to studying. I don't know if I can keep up. I don't believe I've thought this much or used my brain this hard... ever. I'm going to have to drop this class and concentrate on the others."

"I'm sorry to hear that," the instructor responded properly. He knew that class size was connected to paycheck size. "Can I give you any encouragement to stick it out?"

"I'm afraid not. I've already talked to my counselor who sent me here to have you sign this withdrawal slip."

The instructor signed, and Dora fairly skipped away from psychology, replacing the credits with a course in oil painting. She began to use the painting "homework" to ease her into sleep at night. She had found a way to express the deep feelings of loss and grief, which helped to relax her mind in the other classes.

"You're doing well, ma'am," came the voice over her shoulder. "You paint well. I wouldn't be surprised if you'd pull an A in this course."

"Thank you," said Dora without looking up. She assumed it was the instructor who had spoken to her.

"I probably won't get much above a C," the voice continued.

Then Pandora looked up — into the biggest brownest most sparkling eyes she had ever seen. Under them was a very dramatic substantial nose and under that a smiling mouth. "Oh!" was all she could manage.

Brown Eyes appeared to be about Dora's age, a few gray hairs showing behind the high forehead, and a chubby body that belied a love for ice cream. He hovered over Dora as he continued to discuss her work. "Your paint strokes tell me you have painted before... the colors are magnificent... I particularly like the way you arranged the background... the depth..."

"Excuse me," Dora found her voice. "I'm trying to work here. Would you mind...?" She turned back to her easel, flipping her ponytail behind her. She already had begun to help her hair keep its light brown tone with a monthly color treatment, and she tied up the ponytail when she noticed other students with them. She wore a paint-stained smock over her dress and sported a smudge of green paint on her cheek. Immediately, her paint brush smeared the paint in the wrong place and she swore under her breath as she tried to fix it.

"Confab? May I join in?" inquired the instructor of the two older members of his class.

"Sorry," said Brown Eyes as he shuffled off to his easel.

"You can get that smear off with a dab of this." The instructor pulled a small bottle from his pocket and handed it to Dora. "See, just a little dab'll do ya. Now let it dry before painting over."

"Thanks. That man wasn't bothering me much. I don't want to get him in trouble."

"Wendell Westcott? He's been in my class so long he's like an assistant. But he does like to offer his opinions."

"I don't mind, really." Dora looked across the room to catch Wendell Westcott smiling at her. "What do *you* think…" she asked the instructor, "… of my work?"

"He's right. You have had experience, haven't you? What we'll do here is show you how to harness your talent and express yourself rather than copy some other painter. You must have spent time in the galleries. What I'd like to see more in your own work is… you."

"How can I learn that?"

"It's not something you learn. It's something you feel. Tap into yourself, what's inside you."

"I've never thought about that before… what's inside me."

"Perhaps the time is now." The instructor left Dora to mull over another very disturbing idea. What indeed lay inside her that needed letting out? Perhaps she should have stuck with psychology.

Dora looked forward to the art classes. Wendell had moved his easel closer to hers and they had moved themselves away from the younger students. Wen invited Dora to share ice cream and coffee after class late one fall day. The Indian Summer sun warmed the patio enough for them to sit outside.

"Whatever brings you back to college at your age?" Dora asked.

"May I ask the same of you?"

"But it's different for a woman. My family is gone; I'm alone, with nothing else to do. I'm… looking for myself… no, that doesn't sound right… I'm taking time to find myself… no, that's worse." Dora took a deep breath. "I don't know why I'm here. I guess I just needed to do something for me."

"And your husband?"

"He died last summer… a plane crash."

"I'm sorry."

"Yes, we had a good life together. I miss him." Her voice drifted off.

"Well, I'm here because my wife kicked me out of the house. I retired early and I guess I was driving her crazy at home. So I came back to school. Since math and engineering were my life, I opted for the opposite — art. I've always enjoyed good art; I collect it. The idea of creating it simply sounded groovy… as my kids say. And here I am." Wendell sat back, holding the ice cream dish in one hand and spooning out the last bits with the other.

"You have children?"

"Yes, three — two boys and a girl."

"Grand kids?"

"As a matter of fact, I'm a new grandfather. Oh God, I'm feeling my age today."

"How lucky for you — your first?"

"Yes, and probably the last with my daughter. She wanted just one child and this one is a daughter. But hey, maybe I'll paint a picture of her… one day."

"Or maybe your sons will give you grandchildren. Women don't have children all by themselves," she teased.

"If they ever settle down. One is in Korea with the Army and the other is going for a doctorate in Art Admin. Both of them would rather play than work.

"But one is following your interest in art."

"Would you believe… he can't draw a straight line?"

"I used to paint. Watercolors. When I was a girl," Dora offered. "I did it just for fun. I didn't know people did this for a living, or tried to make a living at it. All I knew was that I loved painting pictures of our farm, my sisters and brothers, my folks, but especially my kittens. We had loads of cats. I think I painted every one of them at one time or another."

Wendell threw back his head and let out a hefty laugh. "Painted cats. I can see them now: here's blue kitty, red cat, yellow puss-puss."

"I didn't mean I… painted *them*… I mean, I painted… oh, you're teasing me."

"I like you, Dora… I'm sorry, you never told me your last name."

"Chesterfield, like the cigaret, only I don't smoke… much."

"I enjoy talking with you, Mrs. Chesterfield. May we do this again tomorrow?"

"I… er… of course. Does your wife paint too?"

"No she doesn't. She suffered a stroke two years ago and she's bedridden. We have a nurse to care for her."

"I'm so sorry. I didn't mean…" What did she mean? Even Dora wasn't sure… then.

At Christmas, Wendell presented Dora with a portrait of herself that he had painted. And Dora parted with an early watercolor of one of her cats. They had become friends, close enough so that Dora was invited to the Westcott home for a New Years party.

HAPPY NEW YEAR, read the banner over the fireplace. A dozen or so friends milled about as Wendell introduced Dora to his wife Joan. The two women found immediate food for discussion: Wendell, his painting, the difficulties of raising a family — Dora's and Mrs. Westcott's. Funny, Dora always thought of her as Mrs. Westcott, not Joan.

Dora mingled with the other guests and at midnight cheered in the new year with "Auld Lang Syne" and a glass of champagne. Wendell, standing near the bay window behind his wife, raised his glass to her and she returned the toast to… him. A few minutes later he sat down beside her on the sofa and asked about her plans for the new year.

"First I'm celebrating my birthday. Tomorrow, well actually it's today… now. I was born on the cusp of the new century."

"Well, happy birthday. Hey folks, this is Dora's birthday." They sang the song to her, tipping up another champagne toast. "I'll bet you go through this every New Years Eve."

"Yes, but never with so many smiling faces around me. Thank you, Wen."

By spring, Wendell and Dora were considered *an item* at school, although few gossiped about them; they just accepted the closeness of the "cute old couple". In fact, the art students started to refer to them as "Georgia and Albert". For indeed, Dora and Wendell had fallen in love, even if they weren't exactly aware of it themselves. They never would have worded their relationship any way but "friends, just friends, good friends".

Here was this charming man who was sweeping Dora off her feet, luring her with promises of trustworthiness and loyalty, all the while keeping their trysts secret from his wife. Poor house-ridden Joan had Wendell to lie next to each night, but she couldn't hold him in her arms in the way the lonely Dora held his attention during the day.

When Bonnie called to ask about the Fourth of July family picnic, Dora couldn't bear to consider it. Only last year Dan was barbecuing braats and laughing and… here, in front of her. She couldn't think of another holiday without him. But Bonnie came anyway. So did Hattie and Ford. Ginger called to cheer up her friend on that sad day.

Wendell telephoned too, to tell Dora he had decided to leave Joan, that he wanted Dora to live with him and paint with him the rest of their lives.

"You're out of your mind, Wen. You can't do that to Mrs.… Joan, or your kids."

"Dora, I can't stand to live this two-faced life anymore. I want to choose and I've chosen you. I think Joan will understand. I want us to live together."

"No, Wendell. We've been… friends, maybe too good of friends, and maybe it's time we stopped seeing each other."

"Dora, you can't mean that. You can't…"

"Yes, Wen, my dear friend. That is exactly what I mean. I've been thinking about it for some time and you just helped me put it into words. Perhaps I should have seen it in my painting, but we have to stop whatever is going on between us."

"Do-ra." Her name sounded like a plea from a weary heart. "Oh Do-ra." And he hung up.

With classes ended for the summer, Dora had moved her easel and paints home into a spare bedroom. She sat, looking deeply into the picture she was working on. There it was, that speck of something she had been looking for, that speck of something she instantly recognized as… herself. Blue and green and yellow and beautiful and scarred and aching and sad and frightened and delirious and old and young and… everlasting. The picture itself was a little girl sitting on a woodpile holding a kitten. Why hadn't she seen it before? There was the little girl purring into her kitten's ear, "I'm going to live to be a hunnert years old and do big things in the world."

"I'm halfway there," said Dora to the picture. "Halfway there and I haven't lost her yet, that determined little me. I haven't lost her yet."

"But I haven't done big things in this world either," she reminded herself, recalling the milestones. *A job as a telephone operator: connecting people. My love for picturing life: paintings and photographs. People I love: Dan, Leo, Ginger, my big old family, my lovely daughters. What could possibly be the big things I'm to do in this world?* She had forgotten the completed book manuscript.

By the time Pandora earned her bachelor's degree, she had taken the Introduction to Psychology class she eschewed in her first semester and shifted her major to behavioral science. What she learned in her second year was that Wendell had been typical of the frightened man who needs a woman to take care of him, rather than the other way around. Perhaps that was what had attracted her. After all, Dora had grown up with men wanting to take care of her. Wendell was a man who needed a woman. When he lost Dora, the dutiful husband returned to Joan.

What seemed obvious to Dora — and the *latest finding* in the psycho world — was that men are cared for by their mothers until they find wives to continue the caring… and finally daughters. Dora's experience bore out the theory. Her father left his mother's home to marry his first wife, then immediately sought a replacement in his second wife. When Mary Belle became so blind she couldn't do the caring anymore, Fayette had turned to Billie. When she left to seek her fortune in California, Iris had taken over. And when Iris Rosella left to be married, old Fayette died.

Come to think of it, Pandora's brothers followed the same pattern; they lived at home until they married, and when their wives were gone, they depended on daughters.

Even Dan had lived at home until he married Dora. Men are like that, Dora concluded. Not a very professional conclusion, but one she observed almost without deviation — *empirical*, the psychologists call it. *Men claim to be self-sufficient and capable of running things, but they can't even feed themselves.*

"Men are afraid of women," Dora suggested to her instructor once in class.

"That may very well be," the instructor agreed, "but we haven't had a man admit that as yet."

"Nor a woman with enough gumption to say it aloud either. Do you agree, Miss Tambarri?" Dora asked. "As a woman and as a psychologist, do you agree?"

"What I think or not think isn't relevant to what you're suggesting, Mrs. Chesterfield. Only what *you* think, what you discover through research, or what you discern from empirical data."

Miss Tambarri never knew it, but with those words she had given Pandora more fuel for the fire that was building inside her than she had ever known before. "I have thoughts that count, opinions that matter, ideas that are *relevant*," Dora told her mirror that evening. "I am a person who has something to say. Enough of something to write that book," she remembered. "What an empowering notion!"

What Dora was missing was specific knowledge of how to write. That freshman class in composition helped, but perhaps there was more she could learn. She asked around campus and quickly attached herself to the

Milwaukee Writing Society. She regularly attended the meetings and delved ambitiously into the writing assignments.

Late in the 1950s, Dora lost the income from Dan's crop dusting business. In the flush of soaring stocks, high interest, and flourishing business, Dan's successors found a willing buyer for the company and they retired. Dora received a sizeable share of the sale and invested it in chemical stocks immediately. She had decided to support herself, earn her own income and, make it or not, she would live completely on her own.

Many other empowering notions were arising from the *Kinsey Report on Male Sexuality* and the newer *Kinsey Report on Female Sexuality* of 1953, studied in Dora's psych classes. The reports sparked new magazines for men, such as *Playboy,* and the revival of the old *Esquire.*

Perhaps for the first time, people talked out loud about *sex.* Even that new television box offered such discussions on what came to be called "talk shows". Psychologists were discussing human sexuality — in public — brainy people like Dr. Joyce Brothers and who's that new one? Dear Abby. What popped out of the academic Kinsey box about human sexuality was an entirely new world of ideas for women, especially for Dora.

Both Bonnie and Hattie shuddered over their mother's late-arriving education and were ready to pick her up when she fell. Both were surprised when Pandora graduated *cum laude* with the class of '56 and obtained a teaching job while working on her Master's Degree. She then obtained a position with an experimental mental health clinic and planned to earn a Ph.D.

The end of the decade found Dora polishing her Masters thesis: *Are Men Automatic Leaders of Today's Society?* Once in touch with the world, Pandora Nelle Whaley Chesterfield had begun to record women as they crawled, jumped, climbed, skipped, and flew out of boxes across the country.

Pandora's Notes of the 19-fifties

After the war, women were expected to climb back into their boxes and bottles and bustles. Well, not bustles, but peplums — a fashion statement that resembled the bustle. The women refused.

As if it were just discovered, *Sex* became a subject for discussion, mostly hidden in the acceptable guise of academia. Women were scratching at the remaining chains that bound them.

Pauline Esther Phillips, known as **Abigail Van Buren** and the "pioneering queen of salty advice", published her first "Dear Abby" column (1956).

Dr. Joyce Brothers, psychologist, began a television show offering advice on love, marriage, sex, and childrearing. She went on to become a syndicated columnist, author, actor, and popular TV celebrity, opening doors for other therapists (1958).

Margaret Chase Smith, senator from Maine, delivered a rousing speech on the Senate floor (1950) titled "A Declaration of Conscience", aimed at the activities of Senator Joseph McCarthy and his demonic search for Communists through the House Un-American Activities Committee.

Two years later Playwright **Lillian Hellman** testified before that committee, one of few women called.

Revolutionary **Rosa Parks'** arrest following her refusal to give up her bus seat in Montgomery AL (1955) heralded the oncoming strife over civil rights in the South. Dora couldn't imagine the cause of the furor. She had never been in The South, nor had she seen anyone with skin darker than hers after a summer in the sun — except on TV.

JUANITA HALL won the Tony Award for her role of Bloody Mary in "South Pacific" — the first African American to do so (1950).

ALTHEA GIBSON broke the color barrier in professional tennis by playing at the Forest Hills Country Club in the U.S. Open national championships in Augusta GA (1950). She became the first black woman to win a Wimbledon title in women's singles (1957).

Literature acknowledged the work of **GWENDOLYN BROOKS**, the first black woman to receive the Pulitzer Prize, for *Annie Allen*, a book of poetry (1950). She later was named Consultant in Poetry for the Library of Congress, and Poet Laureate in 1985.

The Pulitzer Prize in 1951 went to poet **MARIANNE MOORE** for *Collected Poems of 1951*, which also earned her the National Book Award and the Bollingen Prize.

LORRAINE HANSBERRY'S play, *A Raisin in the Sun*, opened on Broadway, furthering her family's battle against racial segregation in Chicago (1959).

MARIAN ANDERSON became the first black woman to sing at the Metropolitan Opera (1955).

LOUISE ARNER BOYD, at age 68, became the first woman to fly over the North Pole (1955). An Arctic explorer in 1926, her scientific and surveying findings in Greenland, sponsored by the American Geographical Society, proved of great importance to the U.S. War Department during WWII.

ETHEL PERCY ANDRUS, PhD, a retired educator, founded the American Association of Retired Persons (AARP) at the age of 74 (1958).

TENLEY ALBRIGHT became the first American woman to win the World Figure Skating championship (1953). She went on to pick up a gold medal in the 1956 Olympics, and later became a surgeon at Harvard Medical School.

HELEN THOMAS became the first woman member of the National Press Club (1959), leading the way for future women journalists.

NORMA SKLAREK became the first black woman licensed as an architect (1954).

The **REV. MARGARET TOWNER** became the first woman ordained a minister in the Presbyterian Church (1956).

LILIA ST. JOHN was the first black woman to pass the New York Stock Exchange exam (1953).

JOSEPHINE BAY, president of A. M. Kidder, became the first woman to hold a member seat in the NYSE (1956).

MARY ROEBLING became the first woman director of a stock exchange — the American Stock Exchange (1958); she already was chair*man* of the board of the Trenton NJ Trust Company, and described as "the top *man* of one of New Jersey's largest banks".

MARION DONOVAN invented the disposable diaper (1951), a precursor of *Pampers*, among the 20 patents she registered in her lifetime.

RUTH BENERITO, a physical chemist, took charge of the cotton chemicals laboratory at the USDA's Southern Regional Research Center in New Orleans, where she helped the cotton industry compete with new synthetic fibers by discovering a method to create wrinkle-resistant cotton (1958).

PATRICIA SHERMAN, with Sam Smith at 3M, found a successful application for the fluorochemical polymers they discovered in 1956 — *Scotchgard*.

BETTE NESMITH GRAHAM provided the world with liquid paper for use with electric typewriters (1958). Her refined product, *Liquid Paper™*, was patented and trademarked that same year.

DR. TEMPLE GRANDIN, professor of Animal Sciences at Colorado State, used insights gained from autism and behavioral science principles to invent systems to control animals, eliminating excess force (1959). Her systems remain in use in livestock handling around the world.

ROSALIND FRANKLIN was a scientist on whose work the discovery of the structure of DNA was built, although primary credit was taken by her two male colleagues (1953). Following her death in 1958, Franklin was commemorated as a brilliant scientist and "a warm, vibrant woman"; her name appears on three Cambridge University buildings.

ROXEY O'NEAL BOLTON, known as Florida's Pioneer Feminist and Founding Mother of Florida NOW, helped organize the Democratic Women's Clubs, and served as charter president of the Dade County chapter of NOW (1957). She later founded the first women's rescue shelter in Florida (1972), and the first Rape Treatment Center in the country, in Miami (1974).

Seven women from Illinois founded **LA LECHE LEAGUE**, further causing concern over what was being labeled "the beginning of the sexual revolution". The founders were **MARIAN TOMPSON, MARY**

WHITE, MARY ANN CAHILL, EDWINA FROEHLICH, MARY ANN KERWIN, VIOLA LENNON, and **BETTY WAGNER** (1956).

Another woman prominent in the sexual revolution was **MARILYN MONROE** who startled the nation's mores with her role in *Gentlemen Prefer Blondes* (1952).

FRANCES LANGFORD, popular singer with the USO during WWII (1940s), returned to entertain troops in Korea (1953). She also wrote the "Purple Heart" column for Hearst newspapers, recounting bravery of the troops.

RUTH HANDLER, a co-founder of Mattel Inc., designed the *Barbie doll* (1959). Considered an insult by many feminists, the doll with life-like breasts was claimed to have led girls to better understanding of sexuality. Handler, a survivor of breast cancer, originally invented Barbie Millicent Roberts as a grown-up three-dimensional doll for girls to use to act out their fantasies.

KATHERINE MCCORMICK, biologist and women's rights activist, financed research of "The Pill" (1953). As a parting shot at the revolutionary first half-century, "The Pill", approved in 1957 only for severe menstrual disorders, was finally approved as a contraceptive by the U.S. Food and Drug Administration (1960). This tiny tablet would become the key that unlocked the sexual revolution that was already stirring.

1960-1969

PANDORA at 60

Hello. My name is Pandora. I feel I am closing in on what I came
to do — although I'm unsure exactly what that could be. With my
new college degree, I feel ready to look at possibilities. The world is
changing, getting smaller. I want to see more of it.

"Pandora Nelle Whaley Chesterfield, doctorate in behavioral science," called
out the president of the University of Wisconsin. Dora walked proudly
to the podium and accepted her honor stole, turned to the audience and
absorbed the applause. She could see her daughters, Bonnie and Hattie;
her sisters Iris, Billie, and Grace; her brothers Andrew, in a wheelchair, and
Apollo. And amid her family sat their mother Mary Belle, her beaming face
outshining them all. Not only did she have a daughter who finished college,
she had a daughter who would be known as *doctor*. What she would give to
see that girl's face clearly right now. No, she wasn't a *girl*, she was a *woman*.

"Mama, let me show you the certificate. I'll read it to you." Dr.
Chesterfield stood beside her mother at the celebration in the University
Garden and extended the document to her mother as she recited the words.
Mary Belle held it, then fingered the honor scarf and the gown it covered.
At last they all sat down with glasses of punch, plates of finger sandwiches,
and cookies.

Dora had already opened a small office of her own near campus. Most
of her clients started work with her at school and wanted to continue.
On weekends, Dr. Chesterfield conducted Gestalt retreats that were well

attended. Dora was attracting attention from the world of psychology. Not only had her thesis been published, it had been picked up by Harper & Row and distributed across the country as a book, although the title had been changed to: *Women's Work: Keep Men Happy.*

At the next meeting of the writers group, she was approached. "Come on, Ms.… excuse me, Doctor Dora, you're a professional writer now. We insist you lead the writers; perhaps you can nudge us into writing well enough to be published too."

Dora fell for the schmooze and accepted. "For your next assignment," she began, "write in 500 words or less all the reasons you are a writer."

The results astonished the new leader. "I've read all your work. At this meeting, I want you to read aloud what you wrote — and listen to what others have written." The exercise astonished everyone. Every single writer, but two, expressed reasons for writing as "unavoidable". Each confessed they "had to write". The two holdouts admitted they wrote to become rich and famous. Neither attended more than a couple meetings after that.

"You see, writing is a part of who you are," Dora continued after a break. "I tried out this exercise on myself and learned exactly what you did; I have to write or I won't be me."

Dora continued to write articles that appeared in many of the popular magazines, especially those grocery store magazines that Dora once depended on for recipes. Her writing style was easy to read — and to understand. She knew her audience, housewives.

The articles reflected her original thesis, boldly asking such questions as: "Without Women, Where Would Men Be?" and "Is Marriage a Form of Brainwashing?"

The latter came out as a follow-up to reports of *brainwashing*, a new term, introduced in connection with the Cold War focus on Communism. In her articles, she reviewed the traditional rites of marriage, comparing them to the brainwashing technique: isolation of the bride, covering her head, trimming her hair and decorating her, then divesting her identity by tossing away her flowers, removing her garter, and the final ignominy, taking away her name.

Fellow writers in her group also found magazines to publish their short stories and articles. One, a woman older than Dora who wrote a charming story about her yellow roses, managed to attract attention of an editor looking for a gardening columnist.

"Maybe this is what I'm meant to do," Dora told a colleague at the University after one of the meetings. "I get such a kick out of watching their faces when they tell me their good news."

"Sounds as if you've found a niche," the colleague responded. "Wish I knew what I'm doing here on earth."

All Dora could think of was, *Doctor, cure thyself,* but she didn't say it aloud.

In 1961, the marvels of television were bringing the world even closer together. Dora anxiously watched reports that filtered in from Miami as the disastrous Bay of Pigs invasion unfolded in Cuba.

Always a baseball fan, she followed the new Milwaukee Braves during their initial years, and watched Roger Maris on the day he hit his 61st home run, breaking Babe Ruth's old record. Why do men so vehemently refuse to share the baseball plum with their sisters? Remembering her experiences in grade school, she knew that women can throw and hit a baseball as well as men. Her hopes had been raised during The War with the organization of the Girls Pro Baseball League.

Mostly what she saw were men still trying to set off another war, if not in Cuba, then in that distant Asian place called Viet Nam.

Pandora's article, titled "Men Hold All the Cards", appeared in *Esquire Magazine* just before she was invited to attend a seminar led by Fritz Perls himself in California. This was a dream come true, and she jumped at the chance to fly to Berkeley during the summer of 1962. There she witnessed the famous Perls "hot seat" and languished in the California sun with psychology peers who seemed to understand what she talked about.

The following year, Dr. Chesterfield found herself among 300 academic women invited to an International Women's Conference in Crete. What became her introduction to worldwide women's issues also brought connections with women participating in important and exciting activities in places she had never known existed outside of magazines and television.

The trip gave Dora time to review the matriarchal past of Crete as well as seek the Greek goddesses in and around Athens and at Delphi, including her namesake. How she wished Mary Belle could roam with her amid the ruins associated with the namesakes of her cats… and her children.

Dr. Chesterfield was particularly awed by the growing number of women active both in academics and psychotherapy. Had the world changed so much since she entered college back in 1952? Still, those same university women quietly explained how they were denied tenure and were still receiving smaller salaries than their male counterparts.

Among the glories of Greece, her favorite was the astonishing Delphi, with its oracle honoring the innate powers of women. "We are all goddesses," she remarked to a traveling companion on the bus returning to Athens.

"Goddesses yes, but we still scrub floors," was her companion's response.

Betty Friedan's *The Feminine Mystique* was shaking up the world of women in 1963, and further encouraging Dora's work. Everything Friedan wrote supported Dora's views, which were confirmed during her conference in Greece. Until she read Friedan, Dora had been unsure of the veracity and the strength of what she was saying. The notion that women could form their own opinions — opinions that were worthwhile — remained a stumbling block for her. She had traveled a long way from Arkansaw, both physically and emotionally, and still she harbored doubts.

When Dr. Chesterfield was asked to join the faculty at Santa Clara College in San Jose, Hattie fussed at the idea of her mother leaving Milwaukee. Still, Dora accepted without a second thought, sensing the freedom of ideas that flowed in California. Bonnie was more supportive, offering, "You'll love the region around San Francisco. It seems to buzz with new thought, new ideas, new ways of perceiving."

"What will become of your writers?" Hattie asked. "You know they depend on you; you've said as much."

"Perhaps I've finished what I needed to do here, my darling daughter. The group will go on without me, which may be a good idea. Change and shaking up is always good for creativity."

"Oh Mama, don't..." Hattie began, then caught the look from her sister. "...don't forget to write," she finished lamely.

Pandora Nelle, Doctor of Psychology, published author, and scared little girl with a mission, was off to the West Coast and new adventures.

Barely settled into her tiny stucco apartment, Dora picked up on a California theme and wrote *The Twenty Year Itch*, a book about the aggressive male tendency to work off accumulated testosterone steam by going to war every couple of decades: the Civil War (1860s), followed by the Spanish American War (1890s), followed by World War I (1915), World War II (1940s), and now, after almost two decades of peace, the country was poking at Viet Nam and Russia.

The book was published immediately and held third place on the *New York Times* Nonfiction Bestseller List for eight weeks, just behind Charles Schulz's *Happiness is a Warm Puppy* and Rachel Carson's *Silent Spring*. Dora received piles of mail — some supportive and some derisive — and she was invited to appear on the big television talk show, the popular afternoon Mike Douglas Show, her favorite.

Dora had chosen to write by using her initials and Dan's name: P. N. W. Chesterfield. This offered a pseudo identity, which could be construed either as male or female, a ruse used by many women authors in order to get published. She avoided using the offbeat name Pandora under the advice of her agent, who remained entirely befuddled by the name thing.

Television in the 1960s offered instant fame for anyone appearing on it, especially for someone daring to question the "way things are", in order to promote confrontation. Dora concluded that she'd insist on being called *Dr. Chesterfield* on television or choose a more familiar first name. Perhaps, she thought, *Dora Chesterfield* would work. Still, what about her own family identity — her brothers and sisters and all her long-time friends who knew her as Dora Whaley? Perhaps this was the time to retrieve her family name; other women were doing that in the tumultuous days of the '60s.

The Twenty Year Itch was discounted by men as the author's envy of men who went to war. Borrowing from the Spanish, the word *macho* came into use to differentiate between men who would fight for their beliefs and men who were considered *wimps*. When it was discovered that Dr. Chesterfield was a woman (she couldn't hide that on television, could she?), she was accused of being a man-hater, mentally ill, of being a cynical old woman who needed a man to clue her in, and a "wizened bitch who wished she were a man". That last one came from an aggressive balding man in the center of the Mike Douglas audience.

"If war is such a great idea, why are women excluded?" Dora had asked.

Her critic returned, "Would ya go if called?"

"Would you?" Dora countered.

"We're both too old, aren't we?" he muttered and sat down.

Never one to miss making a point, Dora grabbed the opportunity and, facing the audience, asked, "Are there any women here who would hesitate to pick up a gun and go to war if you were called?"

The resounding applause with accompanying "No!" easily answered the question.

Following her first television appearance, Dora was deluged with requests from media representatives. Her pointed criticism presented with a calm, motherly approach begged confrontation and drew attention. She chose a graduate student from her new college to represent her and handle bookings — a choice that turned out to be a mistake. She was touted at her next appearance as "the psycho-grandma who put down men". Dora quickly replaced the student with a more seasoned representative.

Dora pulled off appearances as guest lecturer and as television and radio guest, euphemizing her "criticism" by asking questions that encouraged rational thought. All offered with a quiet smile. She *was* into her sixties, after all. Who would describe a woman old enough to be their mother as a *wizened bitch*? She knew her subject well, quoted backup statistics easily, and received support of her premises from women around the country. Still, in the back of her stomach remained the questions: *could I be wrong? do I envy men? or worse, am I really a man-hater?*

Her own answer: she probably did envy men. After all, hadn't she longed to do the kinds of work they do? (install telephones, fly airplanes), enjoy the privileges they enjoy? (hold public office, earn top pay, sit in a chair while her meals are prepared), have the fun that men have (play baseball and music in public)? Envy them? probably; hate them? No, at least not the ones she knew.

As for being wrong? She concluded that this was the natural effect of *doing something*. "People who never risk, who never do anything, should not criticize," she repeated, almost as a mantra. She believed she was right or she wouldn't be expressing her opinions, would she?

Dora sat at her typewriter one Friday afternoon in November 1963, working on another theory article, "Men Hold All the Cards", likening the status of women to a poker game. She leaned back in her chair and stared across the campus noticing the bare trees against the overcast sky. The college had provided her with an office to enhance her connection with academics and to make her frequent appearances more convenient.

A scrambling of students drew her attention, waving their arms wildly, crying, aimlessly walking in circles. Something was wrong. At the same time she heard a commotion outside her office door and went to investigate.

"The President's been shot! President Kennedy's been shot!" Dora heard the words and, at first, thought someone was making a bad joke. She followed her colleagues to the television set in the break room and watched in horror at an unraveling world.

The nation and the world mourned for weeks, months, disbelieving what had happened. The era of innocence had died — the magical world of Camelot that had embraced the Kennedys in the White House had come to an abrupt and tragic end.

The unraveled world remained shaken, as if the floor had been pulled away, everyone dangling over an abyss that grew wider and deeper with time. Dora's theory about men's testosterone let loose in ten-to-twenty-year cycles appeared to be developing into another war, a suicidal war. The remainder of the decade only added fuel to her perception.

Dora's health took a turn as she approached her 65th birthday. Something about that dreadful date — "retirement time" — weakened her determination to live "a hunnert years". Would she have to retire and risk losing promised tenure? Was her career finished almost before it began? The stress brought about a shortness of breath that doctors diagnosed as a form of asthma.

"You'll have to quit smoking," she was told, "and start taking better care of yourself. You could stand to lose a few pounds."

"Ah vanity," she professed. "You men just have to have your women skinny."

"Not that, my dear…"

"Don't you 'dear' me! I'm a grown woman, not a little girl."

"Sorry, Doc-tor Chesterfield," the man emphasized. "Your body is trying to fight for you, but you need to make some adjustments to help it."

Dora had smoked on and off since her telephone office days during The Great War. She never gave it much thought. Everybody smoked. She could remember a couple times when she and Dan swore off cigarets, but it never lasted. One or the other would light up again.

"What is your recommendation, doctor?"

"Find a gym and start exercising, something regular."

"I've always wanted to learn to swim. Is that good?"

"The best exercise ever, next to just plain walking. Your body will have to learn to breathe all over again."

After only a few weeks of daily swimming, a determined Dora had stopped using the asthma medication. She didn't need it anymore. What's more, she was getting a kick out of swimming. The more she learned, the more her body relaxed. A friendly instructor had shown her what to do and she did it, splashing and kicking her way around the pool.

Besides, by swimming laps mindlessly, she came up with more ideas for her students and for her own writing projects.

The world in the mid-'60s continued to fall apart. During a weekend retreat, Dora led a group discussion about the strange dichotomy that had been produced by world events — America's entry into the Vietnam debacle. (Yes, the spelling had changed, and no, it was not a declared "war".) Flower children and their raging peers roamed the streets passively, soon to be followed by guns and terror tactics.

The study group of 26 men and women, college students and adults, sat in a meeting room discussing revolution, outright aggression, and peace. "Your dichotomy doesn't seem strange at all to me," responded a slightly balding man wearing a garish flowered shirt. "Seems to fit the times."

"How so?" Dora asked.

"Antithesis. Pure and simple. Where you have black, you find white. Where you have height, you have depth. Where you have violence, you also have peace. Pure and simple."

"Life is seldom simple, Mr...." she waited for him to fill in the blank.

"Howard. Just Howard. You'd never pronounce the rest."

"Life *is* seldom simple, Howard," she repeated. "There are too many layers of wants and needs, goals and expectations, experience and..."

"Hooey! Why do you brain squeezers have to make all those layers so complicated?"

"Not complicated, just..." Dora was stumbling over her words. "Just..."

"Try simple. Why make it complicated when it doesn't have to be?"

"But how does that explain the hippies and peaceniks wandering about the countryside while terrorists shoot at our leaders?"

"Antithesis, as I said. Opposites. Peaceniks and warniks."

"What, no in-between? No undecideds? No neutrals?" Dora spoke directly to him, fascinated with this simple idea coming from a self-assured man.

"Sure there's in-between. But you weren't asking about them."

The group laughed, and Dora became aware of where she was and how strained the dialog had become. "Let's take a ten-minute break," she said and bent over to shuffle her notes.

"Sorry I disrupted things." Howard approached and held out his hand for forgiveness. "I was about to fall asleep and needed to talk."

"I'm sorry I'm boring you, Mr.... er... Howard." Dora didn't look up.

"Can I get you a soda? or a cup of coffee?"

"No thanks. I drink neither carbonated beverages nor caffeine."

"Whew! Uh, they have nice herbal tea."

"No thank you." Dora's voice sounded stern and final.

"Sorry I bothered," he said and turned away.

"Wait," Dora called out. "I'm sorry. I didn't mean to snap. I was trying to make a point about male aggression back there, and you took the wind out of my theory. Perhaps I ought to give your perception more attention."

"Sure, we can *discuss* it," he began. "Uh… perhaps we could have dinner this evening and…" He left the sentence unfinished.

"No, I don't think so. I have a meeting to attend."

"Tomorrow evening then."

"I have a very long day tomorrow; I may be tired."

"I may be dead. Would you join me for breakfast… tomorrow?"

"No, I…" but Dora had run out of reasons. "Oh, all right. Breakfast tomorrow."

In the morning, Pandora rose early and found herself taking extra care choosing her clothes. Retreat goers dress casually, but instructors dress up. That day, Dora chose a casual cotton short-sleeved sweater and a pair of slacks. She applied a small amount of lipstick and brushed mascara on her eyelashes. She didn't usually wear makeup and it was making her self-conscious. "Good god, I'm 65! I'm not going to a party, just breakfast. And I don't even have a class until this afternoon." Still, she didn't remove the makeup and went down to breakfast with mascara on her lashes and anticipation in her footsteps.

"Good morning, Dr. Chesterfield," Howard greeted her. "You're looking fetching."

Dora ignored the remark. "Good morning, Mr.... Howard." They walked to the food line and ordered omelets.

"Let's sit over by the window," Howard suggested. "We can talk there."

"Please call me…" she thought a second about Pandora, then said, "… Dora."

Breakfast turned into lunch and continued later as dinner before the two talked themselves out of breath. In between he sat in on her afternoon workshop, they attended a seminar, and even listened to a lecture on ESP.

Their conversation continued as if there were no interruptions. She learned that he had spent his life as an auto mechanic and had his own shop. She learned to pronounce his full name, Howard Cyzmanski. He learned her first name was Pandora and that she was intent on living a hundred years and making a mark on the world.

"You have to use it — for your next book. Just sign your name, *Pandora*. No last name, no explanation. Just *Pandora*."

"Simple, huh? At least you are consistent."

"I'm serious. Lots of people use just one name."

"You mean, like Cher? and Euclid?"

"Well, yes, but also like Shakespeare and Garbo and Bing."

"Bing? I thought he used his full name."

"You know what I mean. You have a unique name. I don't know anyone else named Pandora, except the goddess herself. Do you?"

"No, I can't say I do. I always felt self-conscious, like people expected me to open a box or something."

"Actually it was a jar, an urn."

"What?"

"A jar. Pandora opened a jar, not a box. And I suspect that what she released weren't the evils of the world, but perhaps the fears of the world."

"Now there's a thought. Are you sure? About the jar?"

"Look up mythology in its native Greek. Look at the art of the era. You'll see depictions of women *with* jars and *on* jars, not boxes. People in those days didn't have box factories; they made pots out of clay. It only stands to reason that Pandora lifted the stopper of a jar. Although it really doesn't matter; she let those fears escape."

"I'd prefer to think of what she released as Truth. She released Truth on the world, which opened eyes and changed lives. Evils, even fears if faced truthfully, can be much more dangerous — more threatening."

"Isn't fear the consequence of truth?"

"You don't quit, do you? But you may have something there. Truth, once exposed, cannot be denied and therefore may be feared."

"Ooh, you are deep." The two of them smiled at the depth of their conversation.

Dora closed her eyes and saw the picture in front of her — plain as could be: Pandora opened the lid of the forbidden vessel (jar or box didn't matter) and exposed the world to Truth, which included the fears that men had long tried to suppress, and which could be considered evil. Women are powerful. Women have stamina, energy, and talents to match men, which in turn scares men to death.

She had learned in Crete how women once held positions of honor in society and contributed their life-giving and life-sustaining powers to the world, all the while holding men accountable for their own areas of responsibility. *The goddess stories that abound in early Greek history point to women's honorable state! Why haven't I seen this clearly before?*

She opened her eyes and took Howard's hand. "Thank you."

"You're welcome, but I'm not sure for what."

"You have helped me clarify some ideas that were right in front of me. I couldn't see them… until now. Thank you. By the way, how do you know so much about mythology and Greek? Do you speak it?"

"A little. I took a trip to Greece during the war and couldn't get it out of my system. So I took some classes, you know, a little art, a lot of history. And you?"

"I attended an inspirational conference in Crete recently. That's where I learned about a balanced culture that existed thousands of years ago in that part of the world. The women stood side-by-side with men in all areas of government, art, business, and society."

"Yes, I know about the Minoan culture that was replaced about 1500 BC by some unexplained event. Don't you wish that egalitarian culture could be revived?"

"I'm impressed. You seem to love learning."

"Oh yes. The more the merrier. That's why I'm here. When I stop learning, I'll know I'm dead!"

Howard returned to his home in Sacramento and Dora returned to her school to begin her new book. In this one, she decided, she would concentrate on women and how they think, rather than trying to reason away men's behavior. Howard had suggested she had become an apologist for women. Now it was time to become the spokeswoman for women.

The new book would take off the gloves and make comparisons of marriage to the brainwashing that was reportedly happening as a tool of the Cold War. Where she had only grazed the subject in an earlier article, she attacked the institution of marriage as *old-fashioned* and *out of touch*. *Is Marriage a Form of Brainwashing?* was published in 1968. She dedicated the book to her step-sisters, Grace, who had died only a few months earlier, and Lynna, who was killed in an auto crash in 1962. Grace had been Dora's mentor as she grew into womanhood and became a strong supporter of feminism during the last decade of her life.

However much Dora wanted to focus on women, the decade of the sixties had turned violent. She worked each intense episode into the reasoning behind her theories. Men were trying to stuff women back into the bottle (she had settled on combining *urn* and *jar* into *bottle*) by increasing the pressure on society. Men were angry with women who wouldn't stay "in their places". Male anger was behind the killing, the police brutality, mob violence, assassinations, and terror that enveloped the country. Men rumbled and raged; women cried, declaring they weren't going to climb back into that bottle.

Women were coming *out* for good throughout the world, on their own terms. All the witch hunts, raping, pillaging, and roaring that men had used over the ages to control women no longer worked to stuff them back inside. Was Pandora realizing her destiny? It was up to her to write about these wonderful women who were drawing themselves out of confinement for good.

Pandora had noticed and recorded the great progress of women for the past six decades — her whole life thus far. *This indeed could be the century*

*for women to take their rightful place alongside men. Maybe this is what will
make my mark in this world and make my hunnert years worth the living.*

Howard was not out of Dora's life. They talked often by telephone,
sometimes long into the night. He came to San Jose several times, learning
more about her and how to share himself with her. He finally told her about
his marriage that had ended in a mess. He admitted to Dora how wrong he
had been. After reading Dora's book about brainwashing, he realized how
isolated his wife must have felt in the big suburban ranch house where he
kept her.

Still, he had been so drained by the war — he served as a mechanic with
the Merchant Marines in the South Pacific in WWII — that he used his
veteran's benefits to buy a garage for his own business and a big house for her.
After their daughter Holly was out of school, his wife lost her reason for being,
became fidgety and disagreeable, then fell into a bottle of scotch and never
came out. She died just before their granddaughter Amelia was born in 1953.

That wicked year 1968 brought a different surprise to Dora. As the
world disintegrated into fear and death, Dora and Howard discovered a
strong bond of love and respect between them, and Howard suggested
marriage. Dora turned him down. She didn't want to move to Sacramento
and he didn't want to live in San Jose. They agreed they might share their
lives in other ways and not change anything for the moment.

It didn't take Howard long to change his mind and move his garage
business to San Jose; Dora received a job offer from Berkeley, adding
another element to their plans. Dora hesitated, witnessing the uprisings
and rebellions taking place at the volatile campus following assassinations
of Martin Luther King Jr. and Robert Kennedy. The war in Vietnam and
the expanded Civil Rights Act Title VII drew the attention and rage of
extremists. Opposition arose to establishing a study course that included
a series of lectures by Angela Davis, a spokeswoman for the notorious
Black Panthers and leader of the U.S. Communist Party. Sit-ins and
demonstrations disrupted classrooms.

Berkeley had been targeted as a rallying point for political and social upheaval. And all because Congress had declared all U.S. citizens to be equal — at least in theory, but hardly recognized by everyone as fact. Even Santa Clara felt the rage.

Fueling some of that rage were the lectures given by Davis. Dora couldn't help but be impressed by the zeal of this activist who spoke out on behalf of blacks, women, and prisoners of all kinds.

The only bright spot that Dora could see in her own school was a new attitude toward women students. Following a "lock-out" in women's dormitories, the school opted not to punish the women who returned after a prescribed time. Instead, a new policy allowed women to visit in men's dorm rooms — with the doors kept ajar.

Howard and Dora decided that Berkeley wasn't right for them and chose as a workable alternative the purchase of a small house in San Jose, where they moved in together. As if to emphasize their feeling of family, Howard's granddaughter turned up unexpectedly on their doorstep the next summer.

Amelia, her long hair flying in the wind and her eyes glassy from drugs and lack of sleep, arrived very early one Sunday morning. Dora and Howard had slept in and took their time starting the day. By the time they got to the kitchen, Amelia had fallen asleep on a patio chair.

"Don't wake her," Howard put his fingers to his lips. "I want to call her mother first." He went inside and dialed his daughter.

"Holly? It's Dad. Do you know where Amelia is?"

"No," came the response. "Isn't she in school? Why are you calling?"

"She's here. Just turned up. I haven't talked to her yet; she's sleeping. What do you want me to do?"

"I don't know, Dad. She's such a mess. We don't talk anymore. I'm the wicked mother; you know how that is."

"Will you mind if we keep her here for a time? We have plenty of room."

"Won't Dora object?"

"I don't think so, but I'll ask."

Howard turned to see Dora nodding. He hugged her, told his daughter not to worry, and went to the patio where his granddaughter slouched in deep sleep.

When Amelia woke in mid-afternoon, she shuffled into the kitchen, rubbing her eyes. "What's up?" she asked.

"Looks like you are," Howard replied. "Coffee? Are you hungry?"

"Oh yeah. That'll be good." She sat down as Dora opened the refrigerator and pulled out some eggs.

"So tell your old grandpa what you're doing here?"

"I needed someplace that wasn't home. Mom is going to kill me."

"Naw, she says we can keep you for a bit. So what about school?"

"I quit! I just walked away from that old boarding school and headed here. You're the one person who understands me, Granddad." The girl smiled as sweetly as she could beneath her red eyes; she pulled a cigaret pack from her pocket.

"Well yes, maybe I do get you, and I love you. But..."

"There's always a 'but'!"

"But, I don't like this drug business, nor the cigarets."

"Grandpa, I can't help it. I need something to keep me from jumping into traffic or off a bridge or something."

"That bad, huh?"

"Okay, you two. Enough talk for now. Here's your breakfast, Amelia." Dora set down the plate and whisked away the cigarets all with one movement.

"Hey, I need those."

"Not here, not with me in the house. I've just been treated for lung disease because I *needed* cigarets once."

Amelia looked at her plate glumly, then picked up a fork and shoveled food into her mouth hungrily.

By the next morning, Howard had made it clear that if Amelia was to stay with them — and she appeared to want to — she'd have to lose the bad habits. Surprisingly, Amelia agreed.

Howard quickly sent his granddaughter into a rehab facility, then watched over her recovery at home. With loving care from both her grandfather and Dora, the young woman gradually returned to her old self.

Over that summer, the three shared the awed gasps of the world as they watched Neil Armstrong kick up the dust of the moon and later as they watched the coverage of the young people plodding through the mud at Woodstock.

One afternoon, Amelia appeared to be pacing nervously, enough for Dora to notice. She grabbed a pen and yellow pad and handed them to Amelia. "Here," said Dora, "write down all the ways you like yourself."

"But... I don't... I..."

"No buts, remember? Just write. I'll give you ten minutes. Write as quickly as you can; don't think about grammar or punctuation or spelling. Just put your pen on the paper and write. And keep writing until I tell you to stop."

The surprised Amelia obeyed without question. She picked up the pen and sat down at the kitchen table and began to write. Dora watched the clock. After ten minutes, she said, "Okay, you can stop now."

Amelia drew a long breath and shook her writing hand. "Geez, that was a funny feeling. I kinda enjoyed it."

"All right. Now read what you wrote."

"Out loud?"

"Yes, read to me."

Amelia drew another long breath and began. What Dora heard were the words of a child recognizing she was growing into a woman and scared to pieces about what others thought of her. At the same time, Amelia wrote about how good she felt when she didn't care what others thought. *Typical teenager*, thought Dora.

The psychologist later repeated to Howard how the exercise explained what was going on inside his granddaughter's head. "She wants to finish high school, that's apparent. And, she likes to write."

"Amazing. You are really good at what you do. Maybe we'll come out of this on top after all."

Amelia did enter a public high school in the fall and quickly discovered the joy of pursuing her dream to write. "They actually have a course in screenwriting," she told Dora. "All Mother wanted was for me to bone up my secretarial skills and 'get a job'." She started with writing a school play, then penned an episode of the TV show, "I Dream of Jeannie". Weeks later she received a letter telling her what a fine script she had written, but unfortunately, the series was about to end.

Dora, on the other hand, inspired by Amelia's determination to follow her own life, wanted to write about it. "I can see me at her age," she told Howard.

"And do you see you at your age now?"

"Yes. I'm spending too much time in faculty meetings and doing paper work. I need more freedom to work with clients and write my books."

"Have you thought of dumping the academics and opening your own office again?"

"Well, yes, at odd hours of the night and when I've had too much wine."

"What do the experts in your field suggest? Do your own thing?"

Dora blushed. Howard had spent his life with engines and auto chassis, which filled his heart with simple truths. Why hadn't she seen this one as easily as he did?

They received word late one afternoon in April that Mary Belle had passed away at the Durand Nursing Home. She was 86 years old. Pandora took a few days to fly back to Arkansaw alone. Andrew didn't travel with his wheelchair, nor did Iris, and Billie was god-knows-where. Jason, Grace, and Lynna had died. The only siblings to join her were Selene, who closed her Durand business for the day, and Apollo, who took time off from spring planting. Pandora felt alone in her grief.

At the end of the school year she *retired*, handing in her resignation and refusing to discuss or even care about tenure; by mid-June she had opened a new office in downtown San Jose. The distance from her home gave her the professionalism and the privacy she needed to muse and wander around her world, searching for Truth.

Having an office away from home made coming home at the end
of the day more pleasant. Usually Howard and Amelia had prepared a
meal and met Dora at the door with a glass of wine and a home-cooked
meal.

Life was looking up. Could it get any better?

Or worse?

The weird dichotomy of the '60s brought an end to the serendipity of
the Camelot years and the onset of a dreadful Asian war, flower children
and protest mobs, assassinations and love-ins, hordes of demonstrating
students and the police who beat them back. Dora was clearly aware of the
pressure intensified by men as they raged and fought each other. Women
cried, but they wouldn't climb back into the jar. They were out to stay, no
matter how men continued to rape and pillage and roar.

As the chaos swirled about her, Pandora sat down to begin her new
book — one that was to pull together her views that had built up over
decades of observing women and men as they inter-relate. She sat down at
her new electric typewriter and typed the words, "Why Men Hate Women."
Below it, she wrote: "© Copyright 1969 by Pandora".

Pandora's Notes of the 19-sixties

Bolstered by **TITLE VII OF THE CIVIL RIGHTS ACT** (1964)
that prohibited discrimination of individuals in employment
because of gender, the nation's women, awakened to their rights,
stirred, and acted. With "The Pill" returning control of their
bodies (1960), all manner of opportunities occurred to women.
The *American Women* report, delivered by the President's
Commission on the Status of Women, sparked similar reports in
state organizations and eventually served as a turning point in the
women's movement.

An address by Rep. **MARTHA GRIFFITHS** (D-MI) is credited for the inclusion of civil rights for women in Title VII (1964).

Congress passed the **EQUAL PAY ACT** (1963), which attempted to legislate women's salaries that lagged far behind men's salaries. Women accepted the encouragement and responded by increasing their drive toward equality and stature.

FRANKIE MUSE FREEMAN was the first woman named to the newly formed Commission on Civil Rights (1964).

The **VOTING RIGHTS ACT** outlawed discriminatory literacy tests that had been used to prevent blacks from voting. Finally, suffrage was being extended to black women (1965).

Four little girls were killed when the 16th Street Church in Birmingham AL was bombed by racists: **DENISE MCNAIR, CAROLE ROBERTSON, ADDIE MAE COLLINS**, and **CYNTHIA WESTON** (1963).

FRANCES OLDHAM KELSEY, pharmacologist and public health activist, during her first month at the Food and Drug Administration (1960), refused to approve release of thalidomide in the U.S. The drug later caused thousands of birth deformities in Europe. She was named chief of the Division of New Drugs, director of the Division of Scientific Investigations, and deputy for Scientific and Medical Affairs, Office of Compliance.

HATTIE ALEXANDER, microbiologist and pediatrician, became the first woman elected president of the American Pediatric Society (1964). She identified and studied antibiotic resistance caused by random genetic mutations in DNA.

The '60s that began with the revitalization of the White House by the new First Lady, **JACQUELINE KENNEDY**, also witnessed the tragedy that destroyed the aura of the Camelot years when her husband President John F. Kennedy was assassinated (1963).

The horror continued to haunt the decade with the assassinations of the husbands of **BETTY SHABAZZ,** (Malcolm X, 1964), **ETHEL KENNEDY** (Robert Kennedy, 1968), and **CORRETTA SCOTT KING** (Martin Luther King Jr., 1968).

CONSTANCE BAKER MOTLEY became the first black woman to be appointed a federal judge (1966).

PATSY TAKEMOTO MINK, of Hawaii, became the first Asian-American woman elected to Congress (1965). She served in the House of Representatives for 24 years.

Concern for the planet and its people spurred **RACHEL CARSON** to alert the public to the dangers of pesticides with her book, *Silent Spring* (1962).

JANE GOODALL, 26-year-old primatologist and conservationist, traveled to Tanzania to begin a lifelong career and become the world's leading authority on chimpanzees, protecting the wild animals of Gombe National Park (1960).

DOLORES HUERTA, a Chicano woman from California, founded the United Farm Workers Union (1962), promoting farm work for the many Mexicans working in agriculture.

ANNIE DODGE WAUNEKA, a member of the Navajo Tribal Council, was awarded the Presidential Medal of Freedom for her work on the tuberculosis epidemic that resulted in funding for child health programs from the Bureau of Indian Affairs (1963).

Belief drove **ANGELA DAVIS**, scholar, radical feminist, and social activist, to lecture and risk arrest on behalf of the oppressed. She was barred from teaching at the University of California, Los Angeles because of her association with the Communist Party (1969).

WILMA RUDOLPH won three Olympic gold medals and was named Athlete of the Year (1961).

HELEN KELLER, born unable to see or hear, received the Presidential Medal of Freedom (1965), along with four other extraordinary women. President Lyndon Johnson conferred the medal on **LYNN FONTANNE** and her husband Alfred Lunt, actors, for their contribution to stage and film; **DR. HELEN TAUSSIG**, founder of pediatric cardiology and the first woman president of the American Heart Association; **LEONTYNE PRICE**, amazing soprano who became one of the first black leading artists of the Metropolitan Opera; and **DR. LENA EDWARDS**, a black college-educated physician who treated poor immigrant factory workers in Jersey City, founded a maternity hospital, did missionary work with immigrant Texas farm workers, maintained a private practice where she advocated natural childbirth, and delivered more than 5,000 babies, all while raising her own six children.

FANNIE LOU HAMER founded the Mississippi Freedom Democratic Party, an organization of blacks who demanded to be seated during the Democratic National Convention in Atlantic City (1964).

SHIRLEY CHISHOLM was elected the first African American woman to Congress (D-NY) (1968), against overwhelming odds. By 1970, leadership was encouraged by the newly formed Coalition of 100 Black Women, in New York. Within ten years, the group had more than 7,000 members in 59 chapters in 22 states.

CARMEN DELGADO VOTAW, a Women's Rights Activist, served on the International Women's Year Committee with the first United Nations Conference on Women, promoting her ideals in the "Decade for Women": equality, development, and peace (1964). Her community development work helped women in both North America and Latin America.

In business, the Mary Kay Cosmetics Company was founded by **MARY KAY ASH** (1963), who gave away pink Cadillacs to top salespeople.

HELEN GURLEY BROWN took over as the first woman editor of the popular *Cosmopolitan* magazine (1965).

HARPER LEE received the Pulizer Prize for Fiction with her best-seller, *To Kill a Mockingbird* (1961).

SHIRLEY ANN GRAU received the Pulizer Prize for Fiction with her novel, *The Keepers of the House* (1965).

LOTTE KAHN published her book, *Women and Wall Street*, one of the first guides to investing directed at women (1963).

SANDRA STEVENS became the first woman to work on the floor of the Chicago Mercantile Exchange (1966).

MURIEL SIEBERT became the first woman to own a seat on the New York Stock Exchange (1967). In ten years, she became the first woman Superintendent of Banking in the NYSE.

ELIZABETH MONTGOMERY began a long run on television with "Bewitched", about witchcraft, the first series to star a woman (1964).

The following year, **BARBARA EDEN** launched "I Dream of Jeannie", playing a bewitching genie who devotes her *life* (she's 2000 years old) to her *master*, an astronaut. (You can bet that Pandora wrote several articles that year about those two shows.)

LUCILLE BALL, model, comedian, and film star, became the first woman to run a major television studio — Desilu, which produced many popular TV series (1962).

JULIA CHILD, master chef, dropped into American kitchens via television (1963).

In science, **JOCELYN BELL BURNELL** made the first discovery of a pulsar, a rapidly rotating neutron star (1967).

VIRGINIA JOHNSON co-published results of a study of human sexuality in an era when even talking about sex was taboo. Her book, *Human Sexual Response*, drew fire from the public by giving women permission to honor their own sexuality (1966).

DR. GRACE MURRAY HOPPER, who had worked on the first commercial computer, UNIVAC, developed the first user-friendly business computer software program, COBOL (Common Business-Oriented Language) (1961).

MARION RICE HART, bored with life in her 40s, took up sailing to exotic places, recording her travels in her memoir *You Call That Lady a Skipper?* She then learned to fly at 63, and recorded her exploits in *I Fly As I Please*. She became the oldest woman pilot to complete a transatlantic flight to Ireland, at the age of 70 (1962).

After witnessing the way women in Togo, West Africa, carried their babies, **ANN MOORE**, a Peace Corps nurse, designed the original soft baby carrier, the *Snugli* (1969), as well as other kinds of specialized carrying cases.

One overwhelming contribution to women, for women, and by a woman was the publication of **BETTY FRIEDAN'S** *The Feminine Mystique* (1963), which opened the eyes of many women confused about their feelings and their societal roles.

This was followed in 1966 with the founding of the **NATIONAL ORGANIZATION FOR WOMEN (NOW)** and a Mothers Day march of welfare mothers led by **CORETTA SCOTT KING** and **ETHEL KENNEDY** in Washington DC.

The first **WOMEN'S STUDIES BACHELOR'S DEGREE** was established at San Diego State University (1969).

MARISOL ESCOBAR, controversial sculptor who made social commentary with her work, unveiled her statue of Father Damien in the Hawaii State Capitol Building (1969). Her statues were also placed in the U.S. Capitol in Washington DC. Her work includes a re-creation of DaVinci's "The Last Supper" (1984).

To put a cap on the decade, **MS. FRIEDAN**, stepping down from leadership in NOW, called for a nationwide protest called the "**Women's Strike for Equality**" to celebrate the fiftieth anniversary of women's suffrage (1919-1969). "My word," cried Pandora. "Has it been fifty years? How quickly the years fly by!"

In New York, as Pandora remembered her parade in Menomonie, crowds of women dressed in white wore banners like their sister suffragists of 1919, and celebrated the anniversary by walking down Fifth Avenue, covering the streets from sidewalk to sidewalk (1969). Banners declared, "Don't Iron While the Strike is Hot", urging women across the nation to cover their typewriters, remove their aprons, turn off the coffeemakers, and refuse to work for an entire day. What was called the Second Phase of the Women's Movement was culminating in the beginning of the next stage of the battle for gender equality.

1970-1979

PANDORA at 70

Hello. My name is Pandora. Great heavens! I'm in my 70s. Whoever thought I'd make it this far? My health seems okay; I'm writing for myself; I have an understanding fella and a surrogate granddaughter. Can I do another thirty years to reach "a hunnert"?

Dora's new book was taking longer than she had thought. She stopped writing her "magnum opus" about women and power and re-read Friedan's book. She took time to develop new theories about men's need to control women throughout the ages, which required more research than she had considered at first.

How To Hide a Woman was the title of the opus that was to cover the entire scope of womankind, from the prehistoric days that ended their equal status to the present, some 3500 years later. She used chapter headings to show how to Paint a woman, Decorate her, Bind her body, Lace her up, Pin things to her, Hang things on her, Swathe her, Spray her, Hobble her, Cover her, Starve her, Sell her, and Remove her name.

She added units on how to anchor a woman at home, keep her financially dependent and away from men's business. She attacked men's competitive need for game playing (sports) and battles (war). She showed how women are expected to bow to a male god (religion) and how men deny a woman's right of ownership and inheritance (economics). She pointed out how women are eliminated from recognition in the arts and history — obliterated or ignored. Would you believe how often she discovered male artists who passed off a woman's music, painting, or sculpture as his own?

She spent years digging through libraries on trips to Europe and the Middle East. Amelia accompanied her on the trip to Cairo, an eye-opener for them both, especially concerning stolen art. Then in the early 1970s, Dora, Howard, and Amelia flew to China, following President Nixon's famous visit in 1972, where they discovered yet another ancient matriarchal society that had been buried under centuries of patriarchy.

"It would seem that men wanted to replace matriarchy rather than join it," Dora commented to Howard one day.

"Is it any worse to expect matriarchy to replace the patriarchs?" Howard countered.

"Of course not. Why not put them side by side — a kind of matri-patriarchy or humanarchy?"

"Now you're making up words."

Dora took another trip, alone, to revisit the ancient Minoan matriarchy on Crete and the mysteries it left behind. While in Greece she had a chance to pick up some extraordinary books about the mythical Pandora, as well as artifacts that she sent back to Howard — copies, of course.

Her opus aside, Dora published another work she had begun much earlier, entitled *Women Don't Count*. This book covered the missing data about women and the impact they make on history, medical research, census, and surveys, to the extent that women are also missing from the U.S. Constitution. Her premise lay in the fact that women were missing from the histories of government, the military, law, religion, and education for so many centuries that they were also missing from information sources. She likened it to a chapter in history about the statistics of women in professional baseball and football, adding, "Oh yes, there aren't any!"

She concluded her book with an exhortation to women to "stand up and be counted". She wrote, "women comprise the majority of the population; by rights we should have our say in what goes on — at the very least a say in what affects our bodies."

She disclosed the sham of The White Christian Male, that stereotypical WCM majority, by pointing out that Caucasians are a minority; Christians are a minority; and men are a minority. "So why do WCMs hold so much power?" she was asked during an interview.

"Because women let them," was her answer.

Women Don't Count didn't go over well with many women and with male critics who were beginning to catch on to how her powerful writing affected major political issues. But the newly emerging women's magazines loved it. *MS. Magazine* asked to print excerpts and then accepted a commentary that Dora wrote especially for the magazine. She signed this book *Dora Whaley* and accepted her place as a newly discovered authority on *feminism* — a completely new field of study.

Amelia registered at the University of Santa Clara and attended for two years before she dropped out and returned to her parents' home. At last, Dora and Howard were alone together — and Dora was in town.

Back from a trip to Chicago where she appeared on the Phil Donahue Show, Dora had barely unpacked before the news of Richard Nixon's resignation broke. The entire Watergate mess had filled the news for the two years since the 1972 break-in, but the last episode seemed to lie ahead. Dora watched all those men in the nation's capital scurrying about to cover their tracks and point fingers at each other, and she was filled with a rage she could no longer control.

"Why don't more women run for public office?" she wailed at Howard over dinner. "Why don't we fill Congress with women? We could do a much better job handling negotiations with Russia; we know what to do about our children's education; we know how to balance budgets; and we know what to do when somebody breaks the rules — as Nixon did."

"You're right, absolutely right." Howard knew when to agree with her. "I wonder too why more women don't get out there and run for office. You women have been able to vote for fifty years. About time you voted yourselves in."

Dora looked at him warily. Was he teasing her? He was right, but did he mean it?

"If fact," he continued, "I wonder why you don't run for office yourself. Nothing like starting at home."

"Howard. Now I know you're teasing. Who'd vote for an old crone like me?"

"The same people who vote for all the old coots in Congress! Age has nothing to do with it. If you qualify, you get elected."

"More likely, if you put on a good show, you get elected. Don't forget, we chose Mr. Nixon."

Howard's suggestion started Dora thinking about civic responsibility, but not through politics. She said once she'd like to be a lawyer. Perhaps now was the time; the Equal Rights Amendment was under debate and likely to pass. Wouldn't now be a good time to get the education she'd need to help women with court cases that were sure to ensue after equal rights for all became the law?

Guest appearances on major television shows demanded more travel, and Howard occasionally went with her, although his eyesight was becoming a problem. He soon decided to stay home. Besides, he didn't always disagree with Dora's opponents.

He asked again, "Why don't you stay home with me and enjoy our senior years?"

"I'm just getting started, Howard," she answered, raising her voice. "I'm just starting to do all the things I've been holding back all these years. I feel more and more like a Pandora coming out of her own jar, letting loose and feeling the exhilaration of freedom."

"You sound like those hippies during a sit-in. Are you picking up bad habits from the youngsters?"

"Not bad habits, but free habits." She fairly flung the words into the air, along with her arms. "Free at last, free at last," she shouted, gesturing.

"I'm losing my eyesight, not my hearing," Howard said, covering his ears.

The year of the nation's bicentennial was the year Dora enrolled in the law school at Berkeley. Her LSAT score made her a good candidate;

being a woman made her a better candidate as law schools concentrated on increasing their quotas of women.

"This will be great," she told Bonnie over the phone. The E.R.A. ratification will occur in three years, about the time I become a lawyer. I'll be right on top of the litigation that will certainly take place."

The world outside continued to rage. Students and others aimed their fury at the crisis in Vietnam, calling it a war that couldn't be won. Blacks rumbled in the ghettos about the injustice of racism. Radical feminists burned their bras in rebellion against years of being laced up. Long hair for men became a symbol of power. In a kind of backlash, women's long hair had become a symbol of submission, harking back to feudal times and the Renaissance.

Dora pursued her law studies and wrote for magazines, discovering that her *feminist name*, Dora Whaley, enabled her to take advantage of the whirlwind that flew across the country, surrounding the proposed amendment to the constitution — the one that reads:

> *Equality of rights under the law shall not be denied or abridged by the United States or by any state on account of sex. The Congress shall have the power to enforce, by appropriate legislation, the provisions of this article. This article shall take effect two years after the date of ratification.*

Alas, neither the ratification nor Dora's law career came to be. The 1978 date for ratification came and went without completion — fifty-two words that were ratified by thirty-five states. Only three more states could make it happen. United States women became the only women in a major country of the world to be excluded from their constitution.

Dora made it halfway through law school before the pressure got to her. In her seventies, she continued those grueling public appearances with her books, which reduced her writing time as well as her studying time. Then too there was Howard's eyesight, which was fading. Dora had seen to the care of her blind, aging mother for years. Now she had to deal with Howard's blindness.

To add to Dora's dilemmas, she found law professors and law students to be maddenly serious. The young ones tripped all over each other competing for rank and recognition. Even the few women tended to leave their humor at home. For Dora, rubbing shoulders with attorneys-to-be was more deadly than the pressure of her fame. This was a woman who enjoyed neither cutting competition nor overzealous dedication. Her attempts at humor with other students dropped flat, which led Dora to drop law studies — flat.

A fortunate opportunity soothed some of Dora's dismay over checking out of law school (she had never before quit anything she started). Dora Whaley was invited to appear on stage with her heroes, Gloria Steinem and Betty Friedan, for a seminar to support re-introduction of the E.R.A. in 1978. The occasion was recorded for history by PBS, and Dora and her family watched it for years afterward in re-runs.

She returned to writing and was nearly finished with *How To Hide a Woman*, when her heart rebelled. During a normal physical checkup, her heart disclosed a freaky leaky valve and she was immediately hospitalized. She hastily cancelled a trip to Los Angeles to appear on Regis Philbin's early morning show and checked into St. Clare's Hospital in San Francisco.

Howard and Amelia hovered over her as she came awake following the surgery. She ached everywhere until her eyes focused on them. "I'm alive. Maybe I'll make it to a hunnert after all," she said before sliding back into glorious sleep.

For weeks, Dora did little but sleep. Gradually, she picked up enough energy to talk to her lawyer about updating her will. She made notes for another book idea, even toyed with writing a novel — pure fiction that had little to do with her previous work. (That idea died before it gained any form at all.)

Dora lay back and let her loved ones wait on her, for a time, before she began to feel antsy and started to complain. "Complaining's good," she told Amelia. "I'm sick of being sick; sick of being babied; sick of being… out of it. Help me up. I'm going to the living room and sit in a chair, a real chair, and watch television, real television."

"But Dora, Granddad told me to watch over you and keep you safe."

"You're doing that, my sweet. Now help me up."

"But…"

"No buts, remember. I'm getting out of this bed. I feel good. I want to get back to living again. Besides, Doc says I need to exercise."

"Okay, you're the boss. Take my arm."

"Thank you. You're one great gal, you know? What are you doing these days, besides taking care of me?"

"I have a new beau."

"A beau? That's a strange word for a California girl."

"Dora! You know I'm trying to find out how you'd feel about me getting serious over a boy… actually, a real man."

"Ooh! Even better. Tell me about him."

The two had made it to the living room and Dora was settling into the big easy chair as Amelia talked about her new love interest. She crouched on the carpet at Dora's knees and explained how she had met Jeff at a coffee shop and how they immediately knew something was special between them. "We sat down and couldn't stop talking. He's a manager of his dad's hardware store, but he dabbles in film making. He's a writer, just like you, well maybe not just… but he's a good writer and has a script under consideration at this very minute. And…"

"Whoa. How long have you known him?"

"I guess I met him once before, but we didn't hit it off until that day…"

"Not so long, huh?"

"Does that matter? We've been out on a few dates while you were in the hospital, and now…"

"No, don't tell me…"

"Yes. We're thinking of getting married. With the world the way it is, this may not be the time to put things off."

"Well now…" Dora began, but she couldn't continue. Amelia was radiant, absolutely glowing as she talked about her Jeff. "Does your grandfather know?"

"Sorta. He's met Jeff, but he doesn't know what we're planning."

"Don't you think you ought to tell him? After all, you're over twenty-one; you're an adult; you're supposedly old enough to make your own decisions."

"I guess so."

The two sat motionless for a moment before Dora picked up the remote and snapped on the television. The subject was left lying on the carpet until Howard was included in the secret.

Howard took the news better than Amelia's mother did. Holly yelled over the phone, and scheduled a visit to San Jose. She arrived two days later and yelled some more, until she heard that Amelia was "with child", and then she caved.

The small family-only ceremony took place a month later and Amelia became Mrs. Jeffrey Gilden — until Dora took hold of her and insisted she keep her own name. The newlyweds headed to Los Angeles immediately to follow their mutual screenwriting dreams.

Amelia managed to hold off giving birth to their first-born until she and Jeff were in the middle of writing their first contract film.

"Dora," Jeff crowed over the phone. "Dora, it's…"

"Calm down, Jeff. Is Amelia…?"

"She's fine. No, she's terrific! I'm so happy I can hardly talk. We have a daughter, Dora… a daughter."

"Congratulations, Jeff. How is Amelia?"

"She's… uh… can I say *radiant*? She's still under the anesthetic, but she's smiling."

"That sounds exactly right. I'll tell Howard as soon as he gets home — which should be very soon. I think he'd like to come down there."

"Holly's here. We'd all like to have him join our celebration. You too."

Dora had barely hung up the phone when Howard walked in. She greeted him, "Hi, Great-grandpa!"

"What? No! She's had the baby. Gee, that does make me a great-grandpa, doesn't it." He grinned wickedly as he added, "and you a great-grandma!"

"Oh, well yes, I think I'd like that. They want you to come down to help celebrate."

"Wait! Boy or girl?"

"Girl, lucky them!"

Howard beamed as he tossed his cap across the room. "A great-granddaughter! Why am I not surprised?"

"Of course, my dear. You know how everything I touch turns into *girl*."

Howard reached out and hugged his Pandora. "I'll leave in the morning. Want to come along?"

"No thanks; I'll let you handle this."

When Howard returned a week later, his face looked ten years younger as he floated atop the clouds.

Pandora's Notes of the 19-seventies

The *Searing Seventies* got underway with the first edition of the new magazine for women — *Ms.* — a long time dream of **GLORIA STEINEM**. The success of the magazine led to the **Ms. FOUNDATION FOR WOMEN INC.**, providing grants for research projects, and its subsidiary, and the **FREE TO BE FOUNDATION**, founded by **MARLO THOMAS, PAT CARBINE, LETTY COTTIN POGREBIN,** and **GLORIA STEINEM** — to fund nonsexist programs for children (1973).

The **CIVIL RIGHTS ACT ADDED TITLE IX** to prohibit sex discrimination in federally funded education programs (1972). Hopes were high after Congress passed the **EQUAL RIGHTS AMENDMENT**, but were dashed when the bill fell short of ratification by three states (1975). Women tried to recoup by holding the gigantic "Year of the Woman Conference" in Houston in 1977, but ratification did not happen. The bill remains dormant.

The **Education Amendments to Title IX**, one of the most important legislative bills passed for women and girls since 1920, guaranteed equality for both females and males in almost all aspects of educational systems (1972).

The first **Women's Equality Day** — August 26 — was instituted by **Bella Abzug** and established by Presidential Proclamation (1971).

Shirley Chisholm (D-NY), the first black woman elected to Congress (1968), announced she would enter the Democratic Presidential primaries (1971). She received more than 150 delegate votes in the Democratic Convention (1972).

When **Barbara Jordan** (D-TX) was elected to Congress, she became the first African American woman from a southern state to be elected to the House (1970). She presented the keynote address at the Democratic Convention (1976).

Nancy Landon Kassebaum (R-KS) was elected to the Senate in 1978, the first woman to be elected to a full term without a husband having previously served.

Mary Bush Wilson was the first African American woman to chair the board of the NAACP (1975). The first chair was **Mary White Ovington**, a white woman.

Roe v. Wade, a Supreme Court decision, struck down laws that prohibited abortions (1973).

In the middle of the Roe v. Wade turmoil was **Alyce Faye Wattleton**, who became the first African American to be named president of the Planned Parenthood Federation. She also was the youngest and the first woman president since **Margaret Sanger** (1978).

Congress provided for the admission of women to **U.S. service academies** (1976).

Fifteen women of the House of Representatives formed the **Congressional Caucus for Women's Issues** (1977).

Marjory Stoneman Douglas, writer, suffragist, women's rights advocate, and environmentalist, created Friends of the Everglades, with a million acres in Florida established as the Marjory Stoneman Wilderness Area (1978). She died in 1998 at the age of 108 — having lived more than a *hunnert* years.

Maya Angelou, an entertainer who, at 17 became the first African American streetcar conductor, published her autobiography, *I Know Why the Caged Bird Sings* (1970). She would read her poem, "On the Pulse of the Morning", at the 1993 inauguration of President Clinton.

Cheryl Adrienne Brown, Miss New York, was the first black woman to enter the Miss America Pageant (1970).

Germaine Greer redefined the terms of feminism with her book *The Female Eunuch* (1971).

Erica Jong became famous with her first feminist novel, *Fear of Flying* (1973).

Eudora Welty received the Pulitzer Fiction prize for her novel, *The Optimist's Daughter* (1973).

HELEN REDDY hit the #1 spot on *Billboard's* Hot 100 listing with her recording, "I Am Woman", thus inspiring feminists all over the world (1972).

MARY TYLER MOORE began to produce numerous television shows with her company, MTM Enterprises (1970).

JULIA MILLER PHILLIPS was the first woman film producer to win an Academy Award for Best Picture — "The Sting" (1973).

In sweet victory, BILLIE JEAN KING boosted the image of women in sports by crushing an arrogant Bobby Riggs in a tennis battle of the sexes (1973).

LYNN GENESKO, a swimmer at the University of Miami, received the first athletic scholarship awarded to a woman (1973).

The first woman to qualify for and complete the Indy 500 was JANET GUTHRIE (1977).

MARY DECKER was the first woman to run a mile in 4:17:55 minutes, beating the record of 4:20 minutes (1980).

DIANE CRUMP became the first female jockey to ride in the Kentucky Derby (1970).

Feminist artist JUDY CHICAGO completed the "Dinner Party" (1979), a project she created "to end the ongoing cycle of omission of women from historical record". The work is permanently housed in the ELIZABETH A. SACKLER Center for Feminist Art in the Brooklyn Museum.

CLEMENTINE HUNTER, of Louisiana, was recognized for her work of colorful paintings with "Cane River Funeral" (1970) and "Saturday Night at the Honky Tonk" (1975).

IRIS RIVERA gained national attention when she refused to make coffee for her boss in 1977. A legal secretary in the Illinois Appellate Defender's office, she received a long memo of rules for secretaries: *arrive at work on time, make coffee, etc.* Iris challenged the order and was given notice she'd be fired. Other secretaries turned out for a lunchtime protest; Iris got her job back.

DIXY LEE RAY, marine biologist, served on the Atomic Energy Commission before being elected the first woman governor of the State of Washington (1976).

STEPHANIE KWOLEK, inventor, scientist, and DuPont chemist, discovered a liquid crystalline polymer that led to the invention of *Kevlar* (1971), a synthetic material five times as strong as steel, used in life vests, skiing and hiking equipment, and in bridge cables.

PATRICIA BILLINGS, a sculptor, produced *Geobond*, a non-toxic, indestructible, and fireproof plastic which became the first workable replacement for asbestos in the 1970s. She later received a patent for *CraftCote*".

BARBARA ASKINS, the first woman patenting alone, was named National Inventor of the Year (1978). Her discoveries with radioactive materials were expanded to improve X-ray technology and restore old photos.

DR. GIULIANA TESORO, an organic chemist and research professor at M.I.T., holds more than 125 patents related to organic compounds and flame resistant textile processing. She received the Achievement Award of the Society of Women Engineers (1978).

WENDY RUE founded the **NATIONAL ASSOCIATION FOR FEMALE EXECUTIVES** (NAFE), the largest organization for U.S. businesswomen (1972).

THE WOMEN'S BANK, the first nationally chartered bank established by women, opened in Denver (1978).

ERNESTA PROCOPE was the first black woman to own a financial business on Wall Street (1979).

BARBARA WALTERS became the first woman to co-anchor an evening news program on television, at ABC (1976).

JILL KER CONWAY became the first woman president of Smith College, an all-women's college (1975).

JUDY BLUME published her first of many novels for adolescents, *Are You There God? It's Me, Margaret* (1970).

CAPTAIN LORRAINE POTTER, a Baptist minister, became the first woman U.S. Air Force chaplain (1973).

ELIZABETH ANN SETON, founder of the first U.S. Order of the Sisters of Charity of St. Joseph, was canonized, becoming the first American-born saint (1975).

PAULI MURRAY was ordained as the first female African American Episcopal priest (1977).

SALLY JEAN PRIESAND was ordained the first woman rabbi in the U.S. (1972).

As women strove to claim their heritage, attempts to right oversights appeared. "Exoneration of **ANNE HUTCHINSON DAY**" (August 26, 1976) highlighted the woman banished by the Massachusetts General Court in 1637, an early American foremother.

LOUISE JOY BROWN was born — the first human to be born after conception by *in vitro* fertilization (test-tube baby) (1978).

BRIGADIER GENERAL ANNA MAE HAYS, chief of the Army Nurse Corps, was the first woman and the first nurse in military history to attain general officer rank, a year before she retired (1971). She was a white woman.

GENERAL HAZEL WINIFRED JOHNSON-BROWN, the first black woman to command the Army Nurse Corps, became the first to achieve the rank of U.S. Army general — 40 years after the first black man achieved that rank (1979).

The Bethune Museum and Archives was opened in Washington DC to honor **MARY MCLEOD BETHUNE** and serve as a center for black women's history (1979).

WOMEN'S HISTORY WEEK was first observed in Sonoma County, California in 1978, highlighted by the issuance of the first postage stamp honoring a black woman, **HARRIET TUBMAN**.

On July 2, 1979, the first woman ever to appear on U.S. currency, **SUSAN B. ANTHONY,** was honored with the release of the new dollar coin.

Remember the **WASPs** of World War II who were surreptitiously terminated in December 1944? While **WASP Director Jackie Cochrane** and others hoped to militarize and commission WASP pilots, the winding down of WWII reduced the need for women pilots. WASP members remained civil service employees — without the pay or benefits of male pilots while sharing the same risks. President Jimmy Carter signed legislation providing WASPs be granted veteran status, although with limited benefits (1977).

Ironically, 1977 was the same year the **Air Force Academy** graduated its first women pilots. Still, it took another two years for the WASPs to receive discharge certificates, and another five years before they were awarded World War II Victory Medals, and those with one year's service to receive the American Theater Campaign Medals. How slowly does justice move!

1980-1989

PANDORA at 80

Hello. My name is Pandora. I have to admit, I'm slowing down — not much, because I ain't finished yet. When I forget my age and concentrate on what I'm doing, I still feel 16, or maybe 25... okay, I'll settle for 40. I have my companion; I have my work — oh so much to do. With the blockade of the ERA, I feel it's up to me to keep pointing out the distances between rights of men and rights of women.

Dora finished her book, *How To Hide a Woman,* and sent it off to her agent. It became another instant bestseller.

The proud new parents, Amelia and Jeff, had successfully poured themselves into their work and obtained a contract to write scripts for a Los Angeles film production company. When they asked Dora for film rights to her book, an astonished great-grandmother discussed the pros and cons with her agent for a long time before agreeing. They all knew the film wouldn't follow the painstaking research that went into the manuscript. Remembering the movie, *Sex and the Single Girl* that followed the book by Helen Gurley Brown, Dora didn't want her work trivialized.

She needn't have worried. Amelia and Jeff produced a movie that fit the title. They wrote the script as a comedy, understanding that more truths are told with laughter than with tears.

When the movie version of *How To Hide a Woman* was released and reviewed as "a rollicking romantic comedy", Dora's fame regained its height — or so she thought. Again, she was sought after as a television guest. She especially enjoyed doing the Dinah Shore Show and appeared on Johnny Carson's late night show often enough to be considered a regular. She took advantage of the Los Angeles trips to visit her great-granddaughter.

"Why do men so enjoy talking about the ways they control women?" Dora asked Carson one night.

"Do we?" returned the surprised host.

"Obviously, or you wouldn't ask me back so much," Dora responded calmly.

"You don't have to accept, you know," Carson joked.

"Oh yes I do, if only to straighten out your misinformation."

A hastily called commercial break interrupted. Afterwards, Dora continued, "Look at the failed attempt to secure a simple 52-word Equal Rights Amendment. All it asks is to place women on an equal legal status with men. You men have turned it into a guilt trip about abortion. You've scared women into the fear of rape in order to keep them out of the military. You point fingers at mothers who want to pursue careers by throwing accusations at them for shirking their responsibility. You're still trying to push us back into the jar that the other Pandora opened."

"You don't push easily, Miz Pandora," Johnny began. Silence from the audience.

Carson waited too long for a laugh. No gag in more than three minutes. He couldn't resist. "Looks like we won't get either you or Jeannie back into the jar." The awaited laughter ended the segment — and Dora's career on late night television.

However, she had made her point, one that got women to thinking more about exactly where they belonged in this society. Just as it made a few men think long and hard about the way they viewed women: Mother Theresa or Madonna, saint or slut, perched on a pedestal or kneeling to clean toilets. Still, the men repeated their mantra: "you gotta love 'em!"

"Surface is all that matters," Dora grumbled. "Big business makes a statement and it's taken as truth. It's like watching the images on television and knowing that a bitter quarrel is going on in the Green Room."

"The green room?" asked Howard.

"You don't watch much television, do you? That's the place where celebrities wait to go on."

"Oh!" Howard tinkered with a wrench and a stubborn bolt. Dora stood behind him and continued her diatribe.

"Take your business, for example."

"What do you mean?"

"You hire a couple of mechanics on occasion and pay them union wages. You don't have to provide insurance for them or offer them any other perks. Still, you make enough to pay your bills and make a profit."

"Is profit bad?"

"No... but..."

"I'm missing your point."

"Well, what if you hired a woman mechanic, paid her top wages and added insurance and health benefits, provided daycare for her children, and..."

"Whoa! I'd be broke before I finished the first repair job. Daycare? For one employee? You're outta your mind."

"You see the dilemma? Nobody seems to care about providing assistance to women in the workplace."

"Maybe they don't belong there..." He stopped abruptly and turned to see the look on Dora's face. He quickly added, "Sorry."

"If men gave birth to children, you'd be damn sure you had daycare, wouldn't you? And pre-natal care... and..."

"Now there's a thought. Maybe we ought to insist on..."

"Don't make fun of me. This is serious. Women need to fulfill their potential, but they can't if they're tied down financially and have sole care of children too. It's a big wall."

"For sure." Howard knew when to back off.

But Dora wasn't finished. "There's much to do. Women of color need the same support that white women receive — black and Hispanic women. How many black women do you see in the upper echelons of business, government, even the arts? In fact, how many women… period? With college professors — men —pumping gas and sweeping out convenience stores to put bread on their tables, who do you think will be given that rare job? Women don't have a chance at a decent job these days." She was on a roll as she paced about the garage.

"Look at that godawful war — that wasn't even a declared war. We're trying to hide, even punish, those who fought it. Even if it was a losing battle, service women and men should be honored. And now the big white bosses are trying to push women back into their boxes… jars, and they're trying to make room in there for minority groups too."

"Can't say as I disagree, sweetheart." Howard pulled his head from under the hood of the car, wiped a greasy rag across his face and hands and grasped his wife's shoulders. "I love you, you crazy wild woman!" and he kissed her, leaving a smudge on her nose.

Howard fell asleep late one night a few weeks later and didn't wake up. His dreams may have been about his beloved Dora and Amelia on one of their treks through history. More likely, his head was listening to a rumbling, hissing, coughing car engine as he gripped a wrench in his hand. Dora placed his remains in a simple casket, photographed the simple headstone surrounded by spring flowers, and never returned to that place.

Another beginning, she thought, resting her head against the arm of Howard's favorite chair. *How many times have I started over? Something or someone is looking over me. By gosh, you know, I just might make that hundred mark. I've come this far; I ain't gonna stop now! Ask yourself the questions, Pandora, the important ones. Demand the answers, just like you do… did… from your clients. Are you doing what you most like to do? Are you living for today?*

She had to answer both yes and no — the same way that many of her clients did. *Now I see the reason. Not easy questions to answer.*

Question: *What am I doing with my time?*

Answer: *Writing. Well, I've written enough books. I'm not sure if I have another one in me. Too much time spent running around to talk about them. Did I ever believe I'd get tired of the celebrity book tours? Good grief. I've come to Peggy Lee's question:* Is that all there is?

Question: *What do you most want to do?*

Answer: *How many years have I spent trying to answer that one? Take pictures? Play music? Paint? Write? Play with my grandchildren... or great grandchildren?*

I miss talking to Howard. He'd know what I want to do. He always did. Keep it simple. Maybe it's time for me to quit. After eighty years, aren't you supposed to slow up, slow down, run down, quit? My body doesn't respond to adrenaline as it used to. Actually, it doesn't respond to very much.

Dora threw back her head and let out a hearty laugh. *Whew! Almost got me, didn't you. Old Time almost drew me in.* Aloud she added, "But I ain't agonna quit," sounding exactly like her father. "Maybe it's time for a new career, a new direction, a new interest." Aware she was talking out loud, she added softly, "Gawd, I'm getting ditsy."

Dora stole a cue from her psych training and asked herself one more question as she looked for clues: *what did you enjoy doing as a child?*

Answer: *Playing on Aunt Ede's piano, using the camera she gave me, making pictures with my watercolors. Gee, I haven't painted in a long time, not since...*

Wendell Westcott's face appeared just behind her shoulder. "Haven't painted much lately, have you, darling?" His familiar voice chided her. "Maybe you could work in a California sunset or two."

Dora rummaged around the storage closet looking for her watercolors. *That box there, it's demanding I open it.* She tugged at the two-foot-square box, finally pulling it free and nearly falling over in the process. Scrawled across the top were the letters: S-T-O-R-E for Posterity. She sat down on another box and smiled, "Oh dear. My time has come. This must be

Posterity." Then she laughed, out loud again and long. She knew what the box contained.

The day disappeared as she culled through the photographs, some old and chipped, in varying sizes and shapes, some nearly as old as herself, showing that strange little girl in ugly cotton stockings and wearing a crisp white dress (or was it orchid?). Hard to tell with black and white photos. There were smaller boxes filled with prints of herself with Ginger and their classmates at Business School. *Oh how I miss Ginger, and she's been gone... how many years?*

Another small box produced prints of Bonnie and Hattie dressed alike as they prepared for Sunday School on *Easter. I remember it well.* She could identify the cameras that took the pictures, from her old Kodak Junior pull-out to the wartime box camera, then the 1960's Instamatic and the strange faded color prints of the '70s. *Cameras have changed since Aunt Ede gave me that old Kodak. Where could it be? I don't remember giving it away.*

She found other sets of photos of her travels, wrapped in plastic and tied neatly with string. There were the packets from the trip to Cairo where she crawled inside a pyramid, the Spain trip to sunny Barcelona, the weeks in Greece and Crete, canal cruising in the Netherlands where she met the newly crowned Queen Beatrix at a cocktail party. And the many trips to Paris. *Ah Paris! Always felt like I belonged there.*

Here was a stack of photos of heavy construction equipment — a project that had caught her eye with the brightly colored red, blue, yellow, and lime green monster machines used to dig, fill, and roll earth wearily along Arkansaw streets when they put in the new sewer system a few years ago. *I remember thinking these machines looked like large insects. Mamá thought I was nuts.*

Here were the pictures from her first garden with Howard: sweet peas, nasturtiums, three gladioli arranged to look like a bouquet, and the violets she had pampered into a full bed, alongside photos of bright tomatoes, juicy strawberries, stately string beans, and pod peas — all portrayed as if they were heads of state. And another packet that displayed trees of russet and gold, showing off their gaudy autumn wardrobes.

To think that I didn't believe California had trees that turned colors in autumn. Pandora! Photographer of green beans, red maple trees, and yellow and chartreuse Caterpillars. Now there's a legacy! Still, they all came out of my small camera boxes. There must be something metaphoric there. Pandora and the boxes that reveal my life!

What to do with all the photographs! Dora heard the town clock strike eleven. *Didn't know my trip down memory lane would last so long.* She gently replaced the photographs in the box marked "For Posterity" and went to bed. Not time for posterity yet.

Around four the next morning she awakened from a deep sleep and *saw* the cover of a book entitled *Pandora's Boxes.* She knew this was a collection of her photographs that spanned her lifetime. Accompanying each group of photos was an essay full of comparative adjectives, bright similes, dancing verbs.

It took months to complete the book and another year to publish it, under the sole name Pandora. Her many fans pushed *Pandora's Boxes* to the top of the bestseller lists.

Once more Dora took to the publicity circuit, including several television talk shows and radio interviews with people eager to show off an old woman who is "still" moving. This time she felt she had come full circle and insisted on using the name Pandora Whaley.

Relaxed as she awaited one such show in the Green Room, her mind wandered. When a fluster of people entered, she looked straight into the face of Geraldine Ferraro who was running for Vice President of the United States — another *first* for a woman.

"You're… you…" Pandora stammered.

"Yup… me!" Ferraro returned, waving off her retinue. "And you are Dr. Chesterfield."

Pandora gulped. "You know me? Have we met?"

"Oh that's right. You prefer Pandora. I've read all your books, Pandora, and I've enjoyed every one."

"Oh, I'll bet not all, Ms. Ferraro. You see, I've published under several names and…"

"No, my friend, I know all your names. I made a point to find out everything about the woman who wrote that terrific book, *Is Marriage a Form of Brainwashing?* And I have read all your books, starting with *Are Men the Automatic Leaders of Today's Society?* I admire your style of writing and the provocative subjects you choose."

The amiable chatter continued between the two women. Once before the cameras, the host, Don Fields, attempted to get into the conversation with, "Have you ever thought of running for public office, Miss… Miz… Pandora… Miz Whaley?"

"Please just call me Pandora. And no, not exactly. My late husband and I discussed it once… briefly… but…"

"…he wasn't too excited about losing more of you to the media," cut in Ms. Ferraro.

"You know, don't you," Dora responded, turning toward Ferraro.

"Yes. The absence from the family, the imposition of the media, the lost time from yourself… it all takes its toll…."

"…very much like the mantle of a marriage: imposition of others and lost time for yourself?" Dora couldn't help but finish Ferraro's sentence.

"And you're half-way through the campaign," Fields nodded at Ferraro. "Is your family suffering?" The host was definitely trying to regain control of his show.

"Not suffering…" Ferraro began.

"But your husband is fighting the press, and your children are…", Fields cut in with another try.

"Can we talk about the issues of the election?" Ms. Ferraro smiled demurely. "I'd prefer to talk about the problems of this country as the Republicans try to tear apart all the help programs, daycare, assistance to single mothers, health care…." She turned abruptly to Dora and added, "…I see exactly why you centered on the *men's fear of women* thing. It's beginning to make sense." She smiled again at Fields as the audience applauded wildly.

Pandora's appearances continued to draw attention as she became bolder, attacking society's inequalities, a liberty she decided extended to elders. But soon the emphasis came to be less on her work and more on her age. Eighty-whatever seemed to scare young people into saying dumb things like the 20-something host who cooed, "Isn't it wonderful that someone as old as you can still work?"

Dora wanted badly to say something sarcastic about the wonder of a 20-something still talking like a 5-year-old, but she restrained herself.

She hoped for more when she was finally booked on the Spud Johnson Show in New York. The old-timer had received recognition once on "Saturday Night Live" for his impersonations, and Frank was feeling his age as he neared 65. He welcomed Pandora, remarking, "You're looking well for your age, Miss..."

That was as far as he got. "Just what do you mean?" she shot back.

"It's a compliment, darlin'." He leaned back, hoping the mostly female audience would respond. They didn't. "I mean, you are old enough to... what... be my mother! And you're still out there creating books."

"What would you have me create?" Dora shot back. "Wrinkles?" The audience laughed and Spud shuffled papers.

Dora grasped the opportunity and asked, "Next are you going to say this is 'pretty good for a woman'?"

Spud paused, a blank look on his tight Botoxed face.

"You see, Mr. Johnson, you're not looking at my books, my work. You're looking at me. You are seeing first a woman, then an old woman. And that's why women and older people are sloughed off as being incompetent, not quite as worthwhile as men and younger women. And you... *son*... will soon be among the elders, the discarded golden-agers, old fogies." The audience, most of whom matched Johnson's age, applauded.

"Unfortunately," she continued, "we live in a culture that considers its norm as young and male. You're lucky to hold the job you do. Now, let's look at my latest book as if I were a lad of twenty-five."

The wild applause lasted into the commercial break. The interview continued with the host reluctant to allow more than brief answers to the questions from the curious audience. The older women in the audience responded to Dora's words; they knew exactly what she meant about society discarding women at the first appearance of a wrinkle. And they recognized their own lives in her new photo book.

About half of the mail following each interview applauded Dora's views. The other half contained suggestions that she return to the kitchen or the rocking chair, with some bordering on pure cussing insults. One thing she knew is that older women are often invisible until they raise their voices; then they risk being called *crotchety hags* and worse. What encouraged Pandora were the women across the country who sympathized with her and urged her to continue to speak out.

She did. And often. For Dora had accepted her role as the wise woman with important opinions to share. "That happens to women past fifty," she told the next talk show host, Mark Janson. "The day I turned fifty, I remember looking into the mirror and telling myself that I no longer had to accept the views of others; I felt free at last to express myself. All my life I've leaned over backwards to expound the views of my father, my husband, my teachers, my bosses. It wasn't until I turned fifty that I felt I was old enough to have my own views, and speak them."

Applause. "Wow… Mrs…. er, Pandora…"

"Just Pandora. That's my name. I'm not a missus or a miss. I'm right-on-target Pandora Whaley." She wasn't going to let this young man steal her limelight. Not today.

"I was just saying that's a brave thing to do."

"Brave? How do you mean, brave?"

"Well… er… I, uh… meant, most older women would…" Janson stumbled.

"You see? You have grouped us all as 'older women' and you're trying to shove us into a neat little cubby hole. A box, perhaps? or a jar?" Pandora grinned at the embarrassed host. "Sorry, Mark, I didn't mean to shoot you down like that, but I'm tired, really tired of being disparaged, evaluated, and dismissed as *just a woman*, a *senior*, and especially an *old woman*."

"I didn't mean that," Janson apologized. "I'm sorry if you thought I was calling you an old woman."

"Aren't I? Old? Is that so bad?"

"Well, you don't look… old."

"Why is *old* such a difficult word to say? And how is a woman who keeps on living, who hasn't died yet, supposed to look?"

Once again the young man stammered as Pandora rushed in.

"How do you gauge a woman's age? By the number of wrinkles per square inch or the number of gray hairs? Why does getting old scare you so much? Even more to the point, what is wrong with becoming old? We're all doing it every day! And one day, you…?" But Dora didn't get to complete her rant. The host called for a commercial break to recompose. As the cameras turned off, the audience came alive with, "You tell 'im, Pandora" and "Way to go" and "Right on". Pandora sat quietly and smiled.

Other interviews began to go haywire in the same way — haywire for the beleaguered hosts who found difficulty dealing with this feisty matriarch. Each time she left a television studio, she felt an urge to return to her hotel room and call Howard. Wouldn't he enjoy this kind of flap?

Then the interview requests slowed to a trickle. It seems the young talk show hosts were getting the word about the feisty Pandora and opted out of the controversy, even though it could increase their ratings. By the mid-'80s, the subject of men from Mars and women from Venus was drawing the attention of the young, completely disclaiming any relationship with the division of power. "Let's make nice with *those women*", was the message coming from men. "Sure we're different, but let's celebrate the difference and appeal to *those women who feel comfortable in jars and boxes*."

Returning home without Howard became even more difficult for Pandora. The garden they had planted and Howard had tended became overgrown. She no longer found the stamina to keep it going. She traveled too much to keep up with the weeds. She knew she could hire a gardener, but then the fun would be gone. So she let her yard return to grass.

Disappointing for Dora was the 1984 election that kept Republican Ronald Reagan in the White House and sent Dora's friend, Gerry Ferraro, back to her family. Much of the earlier controversy had centered around the ethics of Ferraro's husband's business rather than on Gerry's ability to govern, which may have scared off women who could have run for office four years later.

Even when the stock market began bouncing madly up and down, Dora's investments seemed to be safe. During the downward jolt of 1987, she lost a few hundred dollars, but her over-all portfolio managed to stay balanced. She had found a capable young woman to handle her financial affairs, as she had sought capable young women to handle most of her personal needs. She saw a woman doctor, dentist, and lawyer. Even the pastor at her new church was a woman. Dora luxuriated in the knowledge that competent women were doing all manner of competent work these days. Wouldn't Mary Belle be amazed at today's world and its career women?

It was during one of her respites at home that she received a telephone call from the college. Would she consider teaching a course or two in Women's Studies for the newly formed Women's Department?

"You mean a real live class of students?" she asked.

"Yes, real students. You can use your books, develop your own curriculum, handle it any way you want."

"You'll want a syllabus. Who will give me your guidelines?"

"As I said, it's solely up to you to write the guidelines. This is a new department; we're still feeling our way."

A special class to study women! What an idea!

Dora's first class was packed with both women and men. The need for this kind of education was apparent. Young women wanted to learn about women's long fight to get the right to vote, as well as the lost battle to be included in the nation's constitution. The men confessed they thought it would be a good place to meet girls… before they began to take notice and understand the subject matter.

"Amazing!" Professor Whaley remarked to a colleague one day after class. "A young man asked a pertinent question today. He asked if my history was accurate. He doubted the facts."

"You must be making progress — getting through to their brains."

"Still, these kids have no idea what E.R.A. stands for."

"They will now," was the response.

By the end of the first month, Dora was bounding to work early and staying late in the afternoons. She scheduled seminars for weekends, her energy racing ahead of her ideas like a red carpet being unrolled. The more she did, the more she wanted to do.

On a whim, Dora reinstituted her writing groups. Several women in her classes expressed attempts to write books and stories featuring strong women.

"After I heard your lecture in class yesterday, I knew I wanted to write. But I think I'd like to write a novel; I have some ideas." Annette had just joined the group, but she was not a regular student. She had heard about the fabulous Pandora and snuck into the lecture hall as it filled.

After class, she approached the professor. "Er... uh... Ms.... Professor..."

"Yes, young lady. Just spit it out."

"Well... uh... I just love this class, about writing...."

"I wish there were groups like this when I started to write," Dora told the student.

"Well, Professor..."

"Come on, call me Pandora, or just Dora."

"Oh I couldn't..."

"Of course you can. Like this..." and Pandora smiled as she pronounced her name slowly.

Annette laughed and tried again, "Hi, Pandora. I'm Annette Gardner. How can I start writing... seriously?"

Dora in a playful mood couldn't pass up the straight line. "Put on a frown and pick up your pen," she suggested.

Annette laughed again and, after a moment, relaxed. The two discussed ways for Annette to launch a writing career.

After about a half hour, Dora gathered her notes together and prepared to leave. "I've not written much fiction myself, but it might be fun to get back to it. I'd like to see your work when you get it together."

"I'd be so…"

"Never mind. Just concentrate on writing your story your way."

Over the next few weeks, Annette turned out a few pages. The two women put their heads together and fashioned a rather promising story. Before the end of the spring term, Annette had submitted it to *Redbook* magazine and awaited a response. At the end of the term, she promised Professor Pandora to write when she received word. She didn't have to. Pandora picked up a copy of *Redbook* a few months later and read the story under the byline: *Annette Gardner.*

As word of Pandora's new women's studies program spread, requests poured in from colleges around the country asking how to set it up. She carefully selected an invitation to speak at graduation ceremonies at the University of Wisconsin in Madison in June, and took copies of the syllabus with her. She managed to slip in a week's visit with Hattie and Ford in Milwaukee, catching them just before they left on an African safari.

She later joined her daughter Bonnie to present a seminar in St. Louis and drop off another copy of the syllabus. Bonnie, now in her late fifties, was lobbying for a women's studies program at the college where she taught.

"Mom, you can't know how I've looked forward to this. Working side-by-side with you. You're famous, you know. Getting you here goes on my record as a big plus."

"I'm just as happy to work with you, my dear, the light of my life." Dora hugged her daughter, marveling at how much she resembled her grandmother, Mary Belle.

"I keep up with what you're doing by watching your television appearances. It's almost like sitting down to chat with you, but not quite." She returned the hug and added, "You can't know how much I miss you."

Dora heard the tears before she saw them. "Bonnie, Bonnie. This isn't like you. You're always so… so in control."

"Sorry, Mom. I may be pushing 60, but I still feel like a little girl sometimes."

"Don't we all! And I'm over… my goodness, is it 80 already?"

"I don't know how you do it. All this running around. You're supposed to have earned a rest. You're supposed to sit quietly, read, garden, paint pictures…"

"Who said? Come on now, you're beginning to sound like those foolish talk show people who regard me as a relic, an old woman, not as a writer or photographer or artist or mother or whatever, just an old woman. Maybe in the end, that's all we are."

"Don't talk like that. No mother of mine is going to quit before she quits."

"You sound like that baseball player named… oh, what's his name?"

"Berra, Mom. Yogi Berra. You keep thinking of me as a kid, and I'm close to being an old woman myself. But you're right. I still think of myself as a kid too. Maybe we ought to collaborate on a book about mothers and daughters and growing up."

That idea, casually flipped into the air, hung there for some weeks before the subject arose again. This time Dora heard a plaintive question from a student during class. "Why can't my mother and I treat each other as grownups? Whenever I go home, she treats me like an irresponsible kid, and I accept it."

The more Dora considered the question, the more she felt the need to address it in writing. One weekend, after grading papers and planning the following week's lectures, she opened a new file in her word processor and marked it "Daughter, Let Go of Your Mother". By Monday she had outlined a book and written three chapters. She waded through file boxes of client histories and discovered a wealth of case studies that fit the subject.

A call to her agent encouraged her to write a proposal and cross her fingers. Dora phoned Bonnie, who agreed to read the manuscript and comment. Before the year was out, the finished manuscript was on its way to the publisher. Soon after *Daughter, Let Go of Your Mother* was released, Dora received a call from her daughter.

"Mom, I have a new book outlined and ready to write," Bonnie told her over the phone. "I'm going to California next week for a symposium and I've arranged time to spend with you. Do you mind?"

"Mind? I'd be very *very* happy. But I'm not sure I have the stamina to do another book just yet."

"Not your worry. We'll talk when I see you."

Sightseeing took the better part of the first two days of Bonnie's visit, interspersed with comments about the mother-daughter issue and Dora's new book.

On the second afternoon, the two women sat in Pandora's sunroom. Bonnie began, "You wrote your book as an instruction for grown women — me? — on ways to deal with their mothers, accepting their mothers outside the parent role. Now, I want to write a book for mothers on ways to release their daughters, ways to drop their own roles as mothers. What do you think?"

"Sounds terrific. Why didn't I think of that? Of course. Yes, I'll admit it. I have as much trouble letting go of you, seeing you only as my daughter, as you have seeing me only as a mother. Yes, that'll make a great book. Can I tell my publisher?"

"There you go, Mom, doing it for me. Let me call the publisher. Let me write it. Let me see this project through, alone."

"I'm sure you can do it, I just thought…"

"I know. You thought you'd help your little girl." The two women looked at each other and, possibly for the first time, saw each other as two women, two mature women, two college professors. They both smiled.

Bonnie's book was published under the title, *Mother, Let Go of Your Daughter*. And it was Bonnie who suggested to her agent that the preface be written by the well-known Pandora and that she be invited to join Bonnie on a book tour. Pandora agreed, with the stipulation that their relationship be downplayed. "My god, they'll be talking only about us as mother and daughter. We've got to keep them focused on the books, both yours and mine."

"Deal!" agreed Bonnie.

Pandora's Notes of the 19-eighties

At the time **GERALDINE FERRARO** was making history as the first woman nominated for national office by a major party (1984), other women were also making their marks in U.S. government, and more were on their way.

SANDRA DAY O'CONNOR was appointed as the first woman associate justice to the U.S. Supreme Court (1981), where she served until 2006.

WILMA MANKILLER became the Deputy Chief of the Cherokee Nation in 1983, and elevated to Principal Chief in 1985, the first time a woman served in either position within a major Native American tribe.

ANGELA DAVIS ran for Vice President on the Communist Party ticket (1980).

EMILY'S LIST was founded to provide funds for pro-choice Democratic women running for Congress and governorships (1985). Founder **ELLEN MALCOLM** chose the acronym for "Early Money Is Like Yeast" (it raises dough).

Women became active in the area of outer space and technology. **ASTRONAUT SALLY RIDE**, from Kansas, took her first ride into space, the first woman to do so (June 1983).

The second U.S. woman in space, **JUDITH A. RESNIK**, engineer and NASA astronaut, was aboard the first flight of the space shuttle Discovery (August 1984). She died in 1986 when the space shuttle Challenger disintegrated during its launch.

Aboard the fateful Challenger was **CHRISTA McAULIFFE**, a teacher selected from more than 11,000 applicants to take part in NASA's first Teacher in Space project. She and the six other astronauts were awarded the Congressional Space Medal of Honor posthumously in 2004.

DR. KATHRYN D. SULLIVAN took a "walk" in space during an earlier Challenger flight, the first U.S. woman astronaut to do so (October 1984).

DR. ANNA L. FISHER, a physician on the shuttle Discovery, became the first American mother and third American woman to fly into space (November 1984).

THE AMERICAN ASSOCIATION OF UNIVERSITY WOMEN (AAUW) established the **JUDITH RESNIK** American Fellowship Endowment — a memorial to a fellow member who was among the astronauts killed in the 1986 Challenger space shuttle disaster (1987).

ELIZABETH ANDERSON HISHON, an Atlanta attorney, won a Supreme Court case that stated law firms may not discriminate on the basis of sex, race, religion or national origin, in deciding which lawyers to promote as partners (1982).

MAYA LIN, a 21-year-old Chinese-American architect, submitted the winning design for the Vietnam War Memorial in Washington DC (1982).

WILHELMINA COLE HOLLADAY created the National Museum of Women in the Arts to showcase long-neglected women artists (1987).

Congress passed a resolution designating March as **"Women's History Month"** (1987).

Alice Walker, acclaimed poet and essayist, civil rights and women's rights activist, and author won the Pulitzer Prize for Fiction for her novel, *The Color Purple* (1983).

Tony Morrison received the Pulitzer for Fiction with her novel, *Beloved* (1988).

Anne Tyler received the Pulitzer for Fiction for her novel, *Breathing Lessons* (1989).

Rear Admiral Grace Murray Hopper became the oldest officer still on active duty when she retired from the U.S. Navy (1986). She was a computer scientist who in 1961 invented the computer language COBOL.

Rachel Zimmerman, 12 years old, came up with the *Blissymbol Printer* (1984), a software program involving symbols to help people who have difficulty communicating.

Oprah Winfrey, the first African American woman to host a nationally-syndicated talk show, founded Harpo Productions to produce television shows and movies (1989).

Dr. Barbara McClintock received the Nobel Prize for Medicine for discovering mobile genetic elements (1983).

Gail Pankey became the first black woman member of the New York Stock Exchange (1981).

Evelyn Rodriguez became the first Hispanic woman to be accepted as a member of the NYSE (1984).

Doreen Mogavero opened the first fully woman-owned and operated brokerage on the NYSE floor (1989).

Sally Fox created a $10-million business by producing naturally colored cotton. She received Plant Variety Protection Certificates (the plant equivalent of patents) for her work (1989).

Jeanette Loeb was named partner at Goldman Sachs, the first woman partner (1986).

Aulana Peters, the first black SEC commissioner (1984), became the first black woman NYSE director (1989).

Carrie Saxon Perry was elected mayor of Hartford, Connecticut, becoming the first black mayor of a large American city (1987).

Aretha Franklin was admitted to the Rock and Roll Hall of Fame — the first woman so honored (1987).

Ellen Taaffe Zwilich is the first woman to win a Pulitzer Prize for Music (1983). Her "Symphony No. 1" brought her instantly into international focus.

Vanessa Williams was the first African American selected as Miss America. She resigned after a scandal involving nude photographs, to be succeeded by **Suzette Charles**, Miss New Jersey, the second African American Miss America (1984).

The first **NATIONAL WOMEN IN SPORTS DAY** was celebrated by Presidential Proclamation (1987).

FLORENCE GRIFFITH-JOYNER became the first American woman to win four medals in one Olympics (1988).

SUSAN BUTCHER won the first of three straight and four total Iditarod Trail Sled Dog Races in Alaska (1986).

That same year **DEBI THOMAS** became the first black woman to win the World Figure Skating Championship (1986).

DR. DONNA SHALALA was named Chancellor of the University of Wisconsin/Madison, becoming the first woman to lead a Big Ten school (1987).

LEONTINE T. C. KELLY became the first woman bishop of any major American religious denomination, the United Methodist Church (1984).

BARBARA HARRIS was elected as the first woman bishop of the Episcopal Church (1989).

ARDEN EVERSMEYER founded the Old Lesbian Oral Herstory Project in Houston TX to record lost stories of lesbians born early in the 20th century and labeled mentally ill, fired from jobs, rejected by families, abused, or murdered with impunity (1987).

The **NATIONAL COUNCIL OF WOMEN** celebrated its 100th anniversary — the oldest nonsectarian women's organization in the United States (1988).

1990-1999

PANDORA at 90

Hello. My name is Pandora. Who would have thought that I'd be undergoing a renaissance at this age! What joy I have in working with my daughter and other young women and finding ways to impress them with the work of all the women whose shoulders they stand on. I believe I'm happier than I have ever been in this long and wonderful life. (Ten years more to go!)

Dora strolled through her small home, the California sunlight filtering through new blinds, and the warmth filling the corners as the new day started. She never would cave in to air conditioning; her home was built to enjoy the breezes from the ocean and the surrounding trees that tossed back the heated rays of the sun.

"Cool," she said aloud, smiling at her choice of words. "I have a cool house." Then she added, "It's the cat's pajamas! I love it here. I have everything I need." Sounding more like a soliloquy, she actually was talking to her daughter Hattie who had flown out for her mother's 90th birthday.

"But Mom, Ford thinks you ought to at least consider moving in with us. What if you fell? What if you had a stroke? or got sick? or..."

"Died? Is that what you're worried about, Hattie? What if I died and you weren't around to blame yourself?" Dora and Hattie had never solved the mother-daughter thing. Hattie would always need her mother and Dora would always treat Hattie as a little girl.

"Don't talk that way, Mom. I don't want to hear you talk like that."

"Like what, my darling. Like I am going to die some day? I am, you know, and according to statistics, I'm way overdue."

"Mother, please! I don't know what I'd do if…"

"Hold on now, Hattie. There's no *if* about it. I am ninety years old. I *am* going to die. And you'll know what to do when that time comes."

Hattie grabbed her mother by the shoulders and clung to her passionately, like a little girl who had scraped her knee. "Oh Mom, I love you so." The two women stood holding each other, feeling the pain of loss even as they were found.

Dora in her nineties continued to pace her schedule to include visits with her daughters, Hattie in Milwaukee, and Bonnie, who had accepted a chair at Columbia University in New York. The daughters made trips to Dora's cozy home in San Jose as often as they could, but Ford and Hattie had both taken volunteer jobs with a nonprofit, and Bonnie's newfound freedom to write and publish kept her equally occupied.

Over the years, Dora, an active member of the American Association of University Women (AAUW), had focused on the group's increased efforts to promote the education of women. She often was asked to contribute to ongoing studies, particularly the recent report on sex bias in schools. When the report was released early in 1992, Dora flew to New York to take part in the presentation.

The subject dear to her heart explored findings that girls excelled in grade school, but fell behind when they reached early teens, failing markedly in math and science. The study showed that by the middle school years, girls were losing their self-confidence and that teachers were often responsible because of their tendency to respond more readily to questions and comments from boys.

Grants setting up programs created to restore self-esteem to teen-age girls began to appear. Too late for Amelia's oldest daughter, a program installed at their school in Encino turned out to be a life changing experience for July, her youngest.

"Grandma, I can't thank you enough for getting July into this program," Amelia said when she visited Dora three months after the project began.

"Almost as soon as her teachers began noticing her hand in the air, July started to plan her clothes, stand straighter, and complete her math homework first. She even let me cut her hair and tame it — at last." Amelia hugged her grandmother.

Amelia and Dora had kept track of each other after Howard died. Amelia, the mother of two — 18-year-old Marie and 12-year-old July — easily acknowledged Pandora as "grandmother". Amelia remained active in Jeff's film production company that was slowly gaining the respect of the movie business, even though he no longer was around. Following a notorious involvement with a Hollywood actress, Jeff was kicked out and Amelia took over. Dora only learned about it through one of her students.

A close-knit family, Amelia once proudly praised the way Jeff helped raise their daughters. "He actually attended PTA meetings," she told Dora.

"Something went wrong," was all Dora would say. Today she asked, "And how are you, my dear?"

"I'm doing okay, Gran. Better than I expected."

"And the girls?"

"I think they've accepted what is. But it's July that surprised me the most. She's doing very well in school — thanks to you."

"I didn't do anything. She's always showed an interest in math…"

"Yes, but she was hiding it so boys would notice her. She told me straight out one night that boys don't like smart girls. Grandma, she was playing dumb!"

Pandora smiled, remembering how she had done the same thing in school when she discovered boys. "She'll be okay," she told her granddaughter. "Tell me how Marie is doing. I haven't seen or heard from her since she graduated."

"Sorry, Gran, but she's immersed in community college. She's taking a mechanical engineering course, of all things."

"How like her great-grandpa. You see, Amelia, things worked out for her, even without the grant program. But that may be the difference between the girls. You are so blessed. Have Marie drop me a note when she comes up for air. I still have some of Howard's books and tools; she may like to have them."

On Pandora's 95th birthday, the family gathered in San Jose — Bonnie and her new friend JoAnne; Hattie and Ford; Howard's daughter Holly; his granddaughter Amelia, and his great-granddaughters, Marie and July. While technically Howard's family, Dora liked to think of them as her own. Dora's sister, Iris Rosella now 84, came too, wheeled in by her 80-year-old brother Apollo, who never left her side.

Pandora's party was held at the Community Center where friends, teaching colleagues and miscellaneous well-wishers gathered to honor Pandora — professor, author, noted lecturer, (sometimes) sought-after TV personality, photographer, artist, mother, grandmother, and great-grandmother.

Dr. Pandora Whaley Chesterfield Cyzmanski looked about the room as the Happy Birthday chorus rang out. She smiled at the throng surrounding her, closed her eyes for a moment, and heard Mary Belle's voice singing "Good Morning to You." She breathed deeply, *Five more to go. Only five more.*

She looked about her, smiled, and responded, "I realize that you may be thinking this celebration may be my last… but, you'd be wrong. I've come this far; I'm determined to reach that hunnert year promise to myself. I'll see you here five years from now."

"I'm sticking with you, Sis," Iris offered.

"Me too," came from Apollo.

This was a time to think about her family and those who were no longer with her. Her youngest sister, Selene, the flower girl at Dora's wedding, had opened her own flower shop in Durand; she died of a heart attack in 1987. Their beloved older brother Jason died of a brain aneurism just after his fiftieth birthday. Apollo, her younger brother, joined the Merchant Marines at the start of WWII and returned to help with the family farm, where he was determined to outlive his older sisters.

Dora's siblings from Fayette's first marriage were all gone. Grace lived into her 80s. Lynna, who died at 71, had moved to California with her husband, where they raised three sons before her fatal car accident. Dear Andrew, confined to a wheelchair most of his life, lived to be 79. Adam finally gave up farming after WWII and retired to Florida, where he died a year later.

Billie? Ah, Billie. She wandered about the country, tasting life in many forms. She became a vaudeville actor in the '20s, tried the movies in the '30s, and then television in the '50s. She finally retired to do comedy routines at a Florida senior center, where she died in 1976.

"Perhaps we'll get a woman into the White House this time," Pandora commented as she watched the evening news in the spring of 1996. She sat in the chair in which she had held her daughters, rocking gently as she talked to Annette Gardner, her new assistant.

The writing student that Dora had encouraged back in the 1980s, returned to become Dora's listening apparatus, bouncing back her thoughts and helping her clarify the mysteries of daily life as the 21st century approached. The two reconnected after Dora emailed her student to congratulate her on a short story that had just appeared in an esteemed literature anthology.

"I'll be in San Jose next week. Can we talk?" Annette wrote back. And talk they did. Annette agreed to become Pandora's assistant, helping to keep her communications straight and her writing orderly.

"This fall will be the eighteenth — or is it nineteenth — Presidential election I've voted in. Makes me think. All these strange men, intent on becoming President, yet lacking… what… something," Dora commented. "What was it someone said the other day? 'When we were a nation of only a few million people, we came up with stately leaders like Washington, Jefferson, Lincoln, and the Roosevelts, two of them. Now we have nearly three hundred million people to choose from and we can't do better than this?'"

Annette laughed. "You're right. How bad will it have to get before this nation begins to tap its reservoir of competent women?"

Dora smiled and asked, "How are we doing on our Wish List, Nettie?" Pandora and Annette had accumulated a list of ways women's lives had changed over the twentieth century; now they were compiling a wish list for the next century.

"I've finished putting it into the computer. I'll get a printout in the morning. Oh, and I completed the mail. I believe it's up to date. If you'd just stay off television or out of lecture halls for a couple of weeks, I could catch up."

"Is it that bad?"

"Not bad, Ms. Dora, just heavy. Every time you do a TV show, the mail arrives in bags. I try to keep a log of what the responses say, but they're mostly the same. People support your views — women and men..."

"Well, that's progress!"

"... and they want to know what they can do."

"And you tell them... what?"

"Just like you said. I send them the letter you wrote and nearly always try to add a note to personalize it. By the way, you may want to re-write that letter to include a suggestion to come up with a woman candidate for President."

"Didn't I say that?"

"You suggested women run for public office. They're doing that, more every year with help from places like EMILY'S List, but mostly in local and state governments. It wouldn't hurt to suggest that someone come up with a Presidential candidate."

"Poor Ms. Ferraro. The first is always a scapegoat, it seems. Just like our first women governors and first women mayors. They are brave women, competent women, but they still run the men's gauntlet and are persecuted for their efforts. As was Gerry. I can only hope that these will be the heros that school children in the 21st century will idolize. The Firsts. Nettie, add that to my next lecture, a mention of "The Firsts" — and capitalize it."

"Will do. You might also point to some of the women who have served as governors — and senators."

"How many women do we have in the Senate?"

"Since the 1992 election, The Year of the Woman, we have six. I'm sure more fully qualified women are on the way and would fit the criteria set for Presidential hopefuls."

"Six out of a hundred. Isn't that just six percent representing fifty-one percent of the population? Progress moves about as fast as molasses!"

Dora let her mind roam for a moment. "You know, Nettie, it just occurred to me that many of the First Ladies of the past would have done as good a job as their husbands."

"Maybe better."

"Lou Hoover was the first I heard about. She was a friendly woman, I'm told. Very interested in people. But that old workaholic husband barely noticed."

"I read somewhere, maybe when I was a Girl Scout, that Mrs. Hoover wrote two school essays when she was a Girl Scout: 'Universal Suffrage' and 'The Independent Girl.' And how about Eleanor — the great Eleanor Roosevelt, who may have been able to bring The War to a close sooner than FDR?"

"Not sure about that, but she certainly was a strong woman. Look how she took off after her husband died." A moment later, "Bess? Bess Truman, maybe not so much. I don't think she ever left Kansas. But then, neither did Mamie Eisenhower. Ah, but Lady Bird, now there was a strong woman. Yes, Claudia Johnson, the woman who tried to dress up Texas."

"Wasn't Jackie next?"

"Oh, I can't believe I missed her. Back up. After Eisenhower came Kennedy — the Kennedys. Jackie did a lot to dress up the White House, but I'm not sure she was interested in politics very much."

"Then Johnson and oh-oh, Nixon."

"You know, I think Pat Nixon, without that husband of hers, might have done a grand job as President. I'll skip Betty Ford; she had her problems.

Rosalyn Carter? Yes. She would have made an excellent President, but her husband did rather well for himself."

"Is she still around?"

"My goodness, yes," Dora replied, smiling. "She is very much around. Now there's a couple living out their dream of growing old together. Then there's Nancy Reagan. She probably would have done about the same thing as Ronnie; in fact, I think that may be how it actually worked."

"Oh, Dora, you're joking now. Reagan was the first one I voted for; he didn't do so bad."

"No, but I'm not so sure all the decisions were his. That takes us up to Barbara Bush. I'll bet she'd do a good job, but would she want to? Now the Clintons…"

"I think Hillary would be a very good President; she seems determined to be fair, and she's well educated."

"Yes Hillary. I believe that young woman is going places. She seems to stand side-by-side with the folks in power and exude a bit of it herself. She has some very forward looking ideas."

The two sat back and mused over these ideas for a time. As Nettie noticed Dora's eyes fluttering, she softly added, "I wonder what the next century will bring."

"Yes, I wonder," Pandora sighed, and closed her eyes.

Dora's schedule slowed down considerably following her 97th birthday. She took her daily walk around the small lake near her home, tended to her herb garden, continued to cook her own meals — only two a day — and found plenty of time to read and have occasional lunches with friends. She watched the evening news on PBS, which seemed to be the only station offering news in a straightforward way without the need to entertain.

"The news is dramatic enough without those silly 'how-did-you-feel?' interviews," she had commented once during a television appearance. As soon as the cameras shut off, she was asked to amend her comment; she refused.

Hattie's husband Ford died during lung surgery that summer and Hattie flew to her mother. "I can't stand to be alone, Mother. Can I stay with you?"

"Hattie, dear Hattie. How I love you. And I know how alone you must feel right now. But no, you can't live with me. You can stay a couple of weeks, but that's all."

"But you have so much room, and you're alone too."

"And I like it that way, Precious."

"But Muh-ther!"

"Mother nothing. I know you think I need a keeper; I don't. I'm perfectly happy living alone with things the way I like them. More importantly, it's time you learned to live with yourself. You're 65 years old, for heaven's sake, old enough to take care of yourself. Darling, you need to let go of me. Go re-read my book!"

"I never lived alone before. Ford Junior's in Texas, and never visits. Now I wish we'd had more children."

"I know."

"Mom, I'm scared, really scared."

"I know."

"Are you psyching me?"

"No dear, I'm listening to you. And I hear you. You are faced with having to face yourself. That's too many faces, but you get the idea. I don't believe you have ever gotten to know the most important person in your life."

"Who?"

"You!"

Hattie sat back on her heels and looked to see if her mother was laughing at her. "You're serious, aren't you?"

"You bet. Honey, you lived with me until you found Ford. Then you lived with him. You've kept so busy with your activities, your clubs, your friends, and your travels that you have never stopped to face yourself."

Hattie couldn't answer. Something in her throat wouldn't release the words. Tears formed and she covered her eyes, moaning softly into her hands. "I'm sorry, Mother."

"Nothing to be sorry for, Hattie. You're human. You're wonderful. You have talent, personality, and great gobs of love to give."

Which sent Hattie into another round of heavy sobbing. "I let you down," she managed to blurt out. "I gave you only one grandchild. I am so sorry, I…"

"Oh Hattie, I don't need grandchildren. But you need someone to share your love with. And I'm suggesting it's you. Why not spread some of that love on yourself?"

"But that would be…"

"Generous. That would be very generous, very giving of you — a gift to yourself for a change. Lather yourself up in the love you have been giving away so generously all these years."

Again Hattie was silent, continuing to cry, her head resting in her mother's lap.

The next morning Hattie returned to her home and Dora began a new book. This one would record all her hopes for women in the twenty-first century — that Wish List she and Annette had compiled.

The proposal for *Out of the Bottle* was written and on her editor's desk in two weeks. The book followed in just a few months. After all, she had spent a lifetime in research; all Annette had to do was type it. Pandora dictated into a machine for Annette to type into the computer. Then she'd go over it the next day and have Annette print it out. She stopped once in the middle of a page, sitting back to remember how she wrote her first book. She had used a pencil on note pads before transferring the manuscript to a manual typewriter. *That was the one about marriages ending in "d". So long ago. Or was that yesterday?*

Each day Pandora rose early and dictated several pages before her breakfast of grapefruit and toast. She returned to the dictation before taking her walk. The single meal came after her mid-day nap. Then she enjoyed a session with her herb garden or a good book. Occasionally she went out for lunch and returned to dictate a few more pages. Those were high-energy days.

Her public appearances became rare, perhaps one or two a month. She loved to fly to New York or Chicago or just anyplace; she had loved airplanes ever since Dan took her up the first time. Still, she was just as happy to return home and celebrate by sleeping late the next morning.

Annette came in about ten each day and stayed until five or six, answering telephones, translating Dora's notes, answering mail, and listening to her ideas. Dora always introduced Annette as her invaluable assistant, and she treated her Nettie as a close friend.

"So much has changed over my lifetime," she repeated to Annette at least once a week. "The one element that doesn't change much is people. We still act like humans; we fight, we love, we make mistakes, we make up. Did I ever tell you about my first love? His name was Leo and he taught me about telephones and he taught me about automobiles — they were the new ways to connect back then. Now you're teaching me about the Internet. I can't help but wonder if another hundred years will find us talking to each other with just thoughts."

Dora sat back in her chair and rocked slowly. "Your thoughts…" her voice trailed off and she dozed. Annette gathered up her papers and quietly closed the door behind her.

Out of the Bottle became still another Pandora bestseller as the millennium approached, the turn of the century that raised fears alongside inevitable anticipation. The book brought a renewed surge of interest in Pandora's earlier books, especially *How To Hide a Woman*. For the new release, she used only her name, "Pandora", and included a sub-title: *How To Hide a Woman — Stuff Her Into a Bottle*.

"I've lived almost an entire century," Dora told interviewer Kelly Davidson on her late night television show in Chicago. "I've seen the fear that men have of strong, independent women. And I believe they have exhausted their ways to keep women in second place. At last. I believe men can no longer keep women hidden away at home and hobbled by men's rules."

Kelly leaned forward. "Do you honestly think of women as 'hobbled' by men?"

"Yes, some remain hobbled, maybe always will. Still, I have lived this century watching other women escape from their bottles, jars, and boxes. Now that they're free, they won't be put back."

"You may be right, Pandora," a male guest interjected, "but why do you believe that it's men's fear of women that keeps women 'in second place', as you put it?"

"Why else?" she countered. "Why else would men go to such lengths to keep women out of their way, out of their business?"

"You may be exaggerating," the host broke in. "Men don't keep women from doing anything. Women keep themselves from out front; it's risky there. Lots of women choose to stay home with their children, to provide the nurturing. They're content to let men protect them and take care of them. These are the choices of some... many women..."

Pandora could take no more. She interrupted. "Choice? Choice? Let me tell you something. My mother — like many women — had no choice. She was impregnated before she was sixteen, had four more children before she was thirty, and was mother to five older children who weren't even hers. She relied on my father to keep her and her children fed. She had neither time nor opportunity to complete her education, to find work that paid a salary, and she had no income of her own from family inheritance. She had no *choice*. When my father died, his property was handed to his oldest son — the boy from the first marriage, which left my mother and her brood penniless. If it hadn't been for my brother's generosity, we all would have been in the poorhouse. Not all women were so fortunate."

A speechless Kelly sat back, her mouth open, with nothing coming out.

Pandora grasped the moment. "My mother had no choice. And I determined early on that I would have choices, that I would be educated and not tied down with babies before I was ready, that I would earn my own money and spend it as I pleased. That was a big order in the early part of this century. Now, we don't even bat an eyelash at young women earning their keep, graduating from law school or medical college, discovering themselves before seeking a companion. We no longer penalize a woman for having a baby on her own, without a husband to take care of her. We no longer degrade a woman who chooses not to marry. We no longer regard a professional woman like you as an oddity. Can't you see how far we've progressed in just under a hundred years?" (She was tempted to pronounce the word "hunnert".)

"But *fear*, Pandora. That's a very strong word," the host persisted.

"And an accurate one. Why else would men fight so hard to keep women under their control? Give me one other reason." She paused, sat back, and waited.

"Well… er… uh…" Nothing came. Pandora waited longer.

A hand went up in the audience. The relieved host pointed at the same man who had spoken up earlier. A tall man with white hair rose slowly from his seat. "I have to agree with you, Pandora. I remember my mother and my sisters and the ways they were kept in line. The way you explain it… yes, I read your books… makes sense to an old duffer like me. I have to tell you that I stayed with my mother until I married. And I stayed with my wife until she died. Then suddenly, I was out on my own. My children grown and gone, not much family to return to…" his voice trailed off in an oddly familiar way.

Dora rolled her eyes at Kelly and shrugged her shoulders. Then she looked more closely at the monitor that was focused on the man's face. She thought she saw something familiar in his eyes. But then, a woman in her 90s has seen so many faces; they all look like someone she knows. This one seemed friendlier.

Her attention snapped back to his words as he continued. "When I last saw you, Pandora, I was one of those men who feared women. Now I can see…"

"Wendell? Is that you?" Pandora wiggled out of her chair and moved toward the audience. The cameraman spun his camera to follow her.

"Yes," the old man grinned and held out his arms. "Yes, it's me."

The two old friends clung together as the host broke for a commercial. When they pulled back and looked into each others tear-tired eyes, they both managed to sparkle with recognition. "You old goat," Dora said playfully as the audience chuckled behind them. She turned to the host,

"This is an old boyfriend from the... fifties? I mean — we were in our fifties back then. Wendell Westcott, this is Kelly..." she began the introduction.

"Yes, I know Mr. Westcott. He's been on my show. I'm well aware of who he is." Kelly pumped Wendell's hand. Dora looked on with surprise.

"I didn't know you knew... why... how do you know...?" she stammered.

"I still paint a bit, Dora. I've sold a few and I had a show in New York last spring, then one here in Chicago."

"And I'm always lucky to get him on my show."

Dora's mouth fell open. "I didn't know. I've been so busy with my own work I... I didn't know."

A nervous stage manager pulled the host and her guest back to the stage, and Dora promised to meet Wendell after the show.

Over a long dinner back at her hotel, the two old friends talked into the night. As dessert was served, Dora told him, "I lost track. But I often wondered what became of you, if you were even alive."

"Oh I had no difficulty keeping track of you. Your face stared back at me from every bookstore. And yes, I did buy them all, every book. When Joan died, I had to face myself for the first time in my life. There was much to get past, but I think I've done it pretty well."

"I'm impressed; I have to tell you that. I wouldn't have believed it was you admitting you admired the strengths of women. As I recall, you..."

"Oh, I don't agree with everything you write, but I have to take time to contemplate your views. Really, dear Pandora, you are one of a kind. And I still love you, old girl. Do you mind if I call you that?"

"No, not at all. I guess that's what I am." She suppressed a desire to giggle like a teenager.

The two sat quietly for a few moments, Dora reflecting on the *I still love you* part, as she pushed pieces of chocolate cake across her plate.

"Coffee?" a waiter interrupted.

"Not for me, thank you." Dora looked up.

"How about a nice Grand Marnier as a nightcap?" Wendell suggested.

Dora nodded. "I warn you, it might put me to sleep."

An hour later, Wendell dropped his napkin onto the table and said, "Dora, Pandora, I think they're ready to close the dining room. I can't tell you how much I've enjoyed this…"

"Me too, Wen," Dora returned. "I didn't know if you were even alive."

"Oh yes, very much so. Thank god I haven't had to wonder about you. You know, I don't think I could live in a world without you. I'm so glad we've had this chance to meet up again." He stopped then, thinking he had gone too far. Dora's eyes were filling with tears.

"Me too," was all she could squeak out. "Please keep in touch with me. I don't want to wonder again."

They stood together for several moments before he lightly kissed her forehead, then lowered his head to kiss her gently on her lips. "Goodnight, Pandora, my love," he murmured as he turned and walked away.

Pandora had to rush off to the airport the next morning to keep yet another scheduled interview in Houston, but she had promised Wendell to phone when she got home. On the plane she had a moment to recall her evening with her old college friend. *What was that he had said about me not liking men? What did he mean? Surely he could see I liked him, and that I had been married for years and had beaus that dated back to young what's-his-name and Leo. Of course I like men. I love my brothers, all of them, respect them, and… am I pretending? Are my books releases of anger against… who… what?*

She remembered the comments at some of her early lectures and the anonymous notes she received about being a "man-hater". All the while, what bothered her were the inequities, the lopsided balance of men's power and women's submissiveness.

"I know!" she blurted aloud to the surprise of her seatmate. "Sorry, just thinking out loud," she apologized, then continued with her bright idea — *I'll write an article titled "I Like Men!" That should settle the issue.*

Annette met Pandora at the airport. On the drive home she quietly asked, "Good trip? Good show?"

"Did you see it? Yes, it was good. I met an old friend…"

"Yes, I know. He called me."

"You? Why would he call you?"

"Didn't you know? Honestly?"

"Know what? Tell me, Nettie. What on earth are you talking about? And why would Wendell Westcott call you?"

"He's my grandfather. But I thought you knew." She waited for a response, sneaking a look out of the corner of her eye as she pulled up to a stoplight.

Pandora's mouth was open. "Nettie! No! You? Wen...? Why didn't you tell me?" Dora stammered and stuttered. "Yes, I remember now that you told me your grandfather was an artist, a painter, but I never thought for a moment... why didn't you tell me?"

"I did. I told you when we met that my grandfather had suggested I attend your lecture. I think he described you as a 'very moxie broad'... sorry." The light turned green and Annette pulled ahead, adding, "I may have mentioned that you were headed to Chicago when I last talked with him. Did I do wrong?"

"Of course not." They drove in silence until Annette turned the car into the driveway. Dora smiled broadly as she hugged her assistant and whispered, "Nettie, I couldn't be happier spending my days with Wendell's granddaughter."

The combination of celebrity, wisdom, and Dora's age — nearing one hundred — brought more requests for appearances than she could possibly fill, even if she were only thirty. She barely had time to put together the article about what she liked about men.

"There are enough requests here to keep you busy for another hundred years," Annette told her one morning as she riffled through the mail.

"Come on, Nettie, there aren't that many letters."

"No, but this doesn't include the emails and faxes. Haven't you noticed the fax machine buzzing long into the night?"

"Sorry, I'm a sound sleeper. I don't pay much attention to those gadgets anyway. But the email. Is that what you showed me on the computer?"

"That's right. You have a website that is filled with more comments than you ever received on any of your books. You have hit a nerve."

"Or perhaps the time is right."

"At least it's getting closer."

"Nettie, have you ever considered writing something longer than a short story — a book?"

"Um… well… yes." Annette blushed as her mentor gazed at her. "Yes, actually, I have begun a novel. I keep hearing you say there aren't enough good books written about strong women, so I'm writing one. I don't know if it's good or not, but I'm writing it anyway."

"Will you let me read what you've written?"

"Oh, I couldn't ask…"

"You didn't. *I'm* asking. Will you?"

The next day Annette shyly handed over the first pages of her novel to Dora and hid in the computer room while she read. When she returned home that night, she babbled excitedly to her boyfriend, "She likes it. She likes it. She wants me to finish it."

At the beginning of the 1998-1999 school year, the college opened a new course entitled, "The Wisdom of the Millennium". The cross-generational study was aimed at matching older students (those past fifty) with younger students (those under thirty) in discussing the importance of the changes during the closing century. The fall catalog read: *What can you offer from your own life as the 1900s disappear into the history books? Join a creative group and share your art, writing, poetry, music, ideas.*

Dr. Pandora Whaley was the first guest speaker to address the students before taking her lecture nationwide via the Internet.

"Could men be binding themselves together with their fears by becoming more aggressive?" she asked. She spoke vigorously before a crowded university audience at the taping in Boston. "Look at our prisons. They're full of angry men who rage against society and have to be locked up. I ask if you can't see an ironic parallel between the story of these locked-up men and the popular story of Pandora."

She paused a moment to let the idea sink in.

"I believe it's out of fear of that heady power — their own power.

"Consider for a moment. What would you do with uncontrolled power? The ability to order anything and anyone about, to make the rules and break them as you see fit, to have your way with whatever you fancy? That's probably the scariest notion that anyone, including Bram Stoker and Steven King, ever contrived.

"The answer? It's in the history books, if you look hard enough. There was a time, many many centuries ago, when women and men worked together to produce a society where pleasure was the norm and pain was the exception. Where humans — all of them — had equal chances to enjoy life, to work at whatever they chose and to excel according to their ability or desire.

"Sounds idyllic, doesn't it? Those are the ends I would seek if I had the power — the days when women again stand alongside men to determine their destinies and the destinies of their cultures. Powerful men working with powerful women to lead the 21st century.

"My message today is simple. The cap is off the bottle. The stopper is removed from the jar. The lid has been pried off the box. Women have been set free to discover their destiny. Men and women sharing their lives and responsibilities? Think about it. Wouldn't you have to call that paradise?

"This kind of society has become possible. Perhaps the twenty-first century will make it reality."

Silence filled the auditorium as Dora gathered her notes and bowed to her audience. Dead silence.

As she took a step away from the lectern, a thunderous applause broke out and the audience rose to its feet, smiles catching the tears that fell across their faces.

Dora stopped, turned to the audience, bowed slightly again with her hands together. She stood so for several minutes, feeling the possibilities she had just promised. For the first time, she wished she could live another hunnert years.

Pandora's Notes of the 19-nineties

The nation in the early 1990s was intrigued with the controversial response to the testimony of law professor **ANITA HILL** during the hearings to confirm Clarence Thomas to the Supreme Court. Her charges of sexual harassment by him when they both worked for the Equal Employment Opportunity Commission were discarded and the confirmation accepted by the all-male committee. Women across the nation reacted with a heightened awareness of workplace inequities and sexual harassment (1991).

MADELEINE ALBRIGHT was sworn in as U.S. Secretary of State, the first woman to hold this position, and the highest ranking woman in the U.S. government (1997).

SHARON PRATT KELLY was elected mayor of Washington DC, the first African American mayor of a major American city (1990).

DR. ROSELYN PAYNE EPPS was named as the first woman president of the American Medical Association (1990).

CAROL MOSELEY BRAUN became the first African American woman to be elected to the U.S. Senate (1992).

DR. ANTONIA C. NOVELLO was sworn in as U.S. Surgeon General, becoming the first woman and first Hispanic to hold that position (1990).

DR. M. JOYCELYN ELDERS became the first African American U.S. Surgeon General (1993).

JANET RENO was confirmed as the first woman U.S. Attorney General (1993).

RUTH BADER GINSBURG was sworn in as the second woman (after **SANDRA DAY O'CONNOR**) to serve on the U.S. Supreme Court (1993).

JUDITH RODIN became the first woman to head an Ivy League institution when she was named president of the University of Pennsylvania (1994).

RUTH J. SIMMONS was installed as president of Smith College, becoming the first African American president of one of the "Seven Sisters" colleges (1995).

ROBERTA COOPER RAMO took office as the first woman president of the American Bar Association (1995).

The MS. Foundation sponsored the first "**TAKE OUR DAUGHTERS TO WORK DAY**" (1993). Ten years later, the title would add "...and Sons..." to the occasion.

JULIA MONTGOMERY WALSH was the first woman inducted into the "Wall Street Week With Louis Rukeyser" Hall of Fame (1992).

DR. IRENE DUHART LONG was named to head the Biomedical Office of Florida's Kennedy Space Center, coordinating an array of medical and environmental programs (1994).

TONI MORRISON became the first African American woman to win the Nobel Prize for Literature for her body of work on behalf of black women (1993).

ANNIE PROULX received the Pulitzer Prize for Fiction with her novel, *The Shipping News* (1994).

CAROL SHIELDS received the Pulitzer Prize for Fiction for her novel, *The Stone Diaries* (1995).

RITA DOVE became the first African American poet laureate (1993).

MAYA ANGELOU, a black woman, was chosen to read a poem she wrote especially for the inauguration of President William Jefferson Clinton (1993).

ISABEL ALLENDE, an exiled Chilean author who wrote about family and politics, highlighted her work with her vision of what a woman's place in the world can be, *Aphrodite: A Memoir of the Senses* (1998).

ESMERALDA SANTIAGO, wrote *When I Was Puerto Rican,* about her young years in Puerto Rico and her move to New York (1993), and *Almost a Woman* (1998). She later became co-editor of two volumes of Latino literature.

MARTINA NAVRATILOVA, a native of Czechoslovakia, defected to the U.S. to play professional tennis. By 1990, she had surpassed a record number of Wimbledon wins to break the record set by **HELEN WILLS MOODY** in 1938.

JACKIE JOYNER-KERSEE became the first woman to win two Olympic heptathlons (1992).

CONNIE CHUNG became the second woman (after **BARBARA WALTERS**, 1976) to co-anchor the evening news — after a span of seventeen years (1993)!

Susan A. Maxman was elected as the first woman president of the American Institute of Architects in its 135-year history (1993).

Mary Schapiro became the first acting woman chair of the Securities Exchange Commission (1993).

Mae Jemison, astronaut, became the first African American woman in space (1992).

Lt. Col. Eileen Collins was the first woman astronaut to command a space shuttle mission (1999).

Ann Dunwoody, who would become the military's first 4-star general (2008), became the first woman to command a battalion, the Army's 82nd Division (1992).

Janet Wolfenbarger, who would become the first female 4-star general in Air Force history (2012), was promoted to colonel (1998).

Vice Admiral Michelle Howard took command of the USS Rushmore in San Diego harbor (1999). She was the first female graduate of the U.S. Naval Academy (1982) to be ranked admiral.

Lt. Kendra Williams, USN, became the first woman combat pilot to bomb an enemy target, during Operation Desert Fox in Iraq (1998).

Nancy Ruth Mace was the first female cadet to graduate from the Citadel, formerly an all-male military school in South Carolina (1999).

On Veterans Day, November 11, 1993, the **VIETNAM WOMEN'S MEMORIAL** was dedicated in Washington DC. The sculptor, **GLENNA GOODACRE**, created the memorial from an idea by army combat nurse **DIANE CARLSON EVANS** to honor the 265,000 women who served voluntarily during the Vietnam era.

With all the progress made by women during the 1990s, the world remained in masculine hands for the most part. In the U.S. the all-male world of baseball "suffered" a players' strike (September 1994), causing major consternation about the future of the World Series game, cancelled for the first time since 1904. You'd have thought the world was coming to an end without a baseball game!

Murder and mayhem flourished in the environment of masculinity. In 1994, O. J. Simpson, a football hero to fans, was accused and tried for the double murder of his wife and her boyfriend. After a 10-month trial, Simpson was acquitted. (One source wrote seven lines about his football career and only four lines about the murders.)

A bombing of the World Trade Center in New York City (1993) augured the rise of terrorism, raising suspicions over the bombing of the Murrah Federal Building in Oklahoma City that followed (1995).

Another war memorial — this time for the Korean War — was dedicated (July 27, 1995) on the 42nd anniversary of the armistice that ended the war. *How many memorials have been raised to honor the women who birthed and raised all those achieving men?* Zero!

In one Internet summary of the history of the 1990s, only two females are mentioned. One is **MONICA LEWINSKY**, involved in a White House scandal; the other is **DOLLY**, the sheep that was cloned in Scotland. Are these events indicative of a backlash against women?

WOMEN IN THE 106th **CONGRESS** at the close of the century numbered only 67, up from zero prior to 1917. The House of Representatives numbered 58, with only 9 women in the Senate (1999).

HILLARY RODHAM CLINTON was elected to the U.S. Senate, becoming the first First Lady ever to be elected to a national office (1999).

MICHELLE LAVAUGHN ROBINSON OBAMA earned a J.D. from Harvard Law School in 1988, where she took part in demonstrations demanding more minority students and professors. She married Barack Obama (1992) and became First Lady in 2009.

JILL TRACY JACOBS BIDEN, professor of English and holder of a Ph.D. from the University of Delaware, married Joe Biden in 1977. She founded the Biden Breast Health Initiative non-profit organization (1993) and became Second Lady in 2009.

Which direction are women headed? Will the new 21st century find women relinquishing their gains or standing firm and making more headway toward equal representation?

One thing you can be sure of — women will never be stuffed back into a box!

Pandora's Hundredth January

PANDORA at 100

Hello. My name is Pandora. Well, I made it — I have lived through a hunnert Januarys, just as I promised myself, lo those many years ago. While I haven't yet learned "everything", I have been fortunate to have lived a long — very long — and rather fruitful life, blessed with gifts that I pray I have put to good use. Along the way, I have witnessed a most spectacular phenomenon. My good wishes to all of you who have not yet burned up a birthday cake with 100 candles.

When the clock struck midnight in New York, changing the 1900s into the 2000s, Pandora sat before the television set, waiting to see what catastrophe would occur. For months, people around the world had prepared for the "Y2K Crisis" predicted to occur when computers would be confused by the date change and fall to pieces.

"Nothing happened so far, Nettie," Pandora whispered.

"Happy birthday, Ms. Dora," Nettie whispered back.

"They're cheering. Gee, it must be cold back there."

"Don't uncross your fingers just yet. It's only nine o'clock here. Anything can still happen."

"Don't be one of those hypo-scaredy-cats, Nettie." If it hasn't happened yet, it probably won't. I never thought a damn machine would foul up the world. I'm going to bed. Big day tomorrow."

"Yes, a big day, a very happy birthday day."

"Goodnight."

The family had gathered by mid-afternoon on New Years Day. Bonnie and JoAnne flew in (safely) from New York; Hattie, with Ford Jr. and Apollo, had arrived from Milwaukee in time to meet them. Apollo was Pandora's only surviving sibling; Iris Rosella had died the year before. Amelia and her daughters, Marie and July, drove down from San Francisco.

Annette bustled about the kitchen arranging food trays as Pandora caught up on family news.

"How does it feel to celebrate your hundredth year?" Marie asked.

"Let's see. I hadn't thought much about it. The years kind of go by and the numbers creep up, and finally you reach a hunnert."

"Hunnert?"

"That's the way I used to talk, when I was a mere toddler. I was, you know — a mere toddler."

Marie began, "That's hard to believe…" but caught her sister's look.

"Oh yes, when I was about four or five, I promised my pet kitten that I'd live 'for a hunnert years' and… here I am! The cat didn't make it."

The two laughed, and Pandora sat back, looking at her life spread about her: her daughters and grandson, her little brother, and Howard's family. *What a lovely birthd…*

Her thoughts were interrupted by the doorbell.

"That's probably someone from the college."

"I'll get it, Ms. Dora," Annette said, rushing past her.

In a moment, Pandora gasped to see Wendell Westcott enter the room on Annette's arm. "Granddad, these are my friends. I think you know the birthday girl."

Wendell shuffled over to Pandora and held out both hands. Pandora used them to stand up and wrap her arms around him. They simply held each other while the family attempted not to gape.

"Happy birthday, old girl."

Pandora hugged him closer, and they sat down on the sofa. "What a wonderful surprise. You have raised the best granddaughter ever."

The day couldn't get better. A few of Pandora's colleagues dropped by with birthday gifts and cheers, and the entire family took Wendell in as part of it. Pandora had stipulated that any gifts be of use to a woman over 65, and they were. Every gift was later re-wrapped and sent to a nursing home for retired college staff.

The birthday cake was another matter. It was rolled into the room, glowing with one over-sized candle that represented the century. Pandora's tears flowed silently as her family sang the happy birthday song. In her head, the words were Mary Belle's "Good morning to you..."

Afterwards, Wen returned home, and Dora's family settled in at a nearby hotel, planning to keep up the celebration as long as possible. While they spent a few days sightseeing, Pandora and Nettie were planning for the next "birthday" event.

In celebration, Pandora's beloved AAUW was throwing a party the following Saturday. "What will I talk about? They'll surely want a speech of some kind."

"Let's look at the computer and see what you have that would fit," Nettie suggested.

Pandora's whole life already was spread out in her own file inside her head. There was a film of childhood scenes, the primary colors intense — the Christmas holly with forest green leaves and red berries, and the cobalt blue, turquoise and copper of star-pointed jacks and shiny marbles, long lost under discarded leaves or buried in the garden.

Another file was filled with people she loved, every face as clear as when she last smiled at them.

Nettie provided the profession file: classes of admiring students and colleagues; patients who received honesty and hope from her; television stage managers, frowning at her; and readers, delighted to meet the woman who had shown them ways to independence.

She went over it again and again, each decade flashing by in a neat little package, covered and bound and placed on the shelves of her memory (not hanging on hooks in her head as Teacher once described them). Each decade contained a message; each decade offered a vision, combinations of truth and perception, memory and wishful thinking.

"Turn it into a new speech, Ms. Dora," Annette suggested. "You're being honored by the AAUW to celebrate your century. Why not take all these notes and photographs and turn them into a speech?"

"A kind of *Good-bye World* speech?" Dora joked.

"You know I didn't mean that! You have led… are leading… a gracious life, full of adventure and caring and good works. Perhaps this is the best opportunity to summarize it, a kind of birthday speech; they'll expect it." She paused just a moment before adding with a sly grin, "You're not getting any younger, you know."

"Hmmm. You're right. I've made it, Nettie! The world didn't end at midnight when I turned a *hunnert,* and I celebrated it the best way I know how." She closed her eyes and turned her head toward the ceiling. "Does it seem as if the world is speeding up at the same time I'm slowing down? Sometimes I feel as if the young folks who are keeping up with technology and progress are way ahead of me — you know, that feeling that 'nobody wants you when you're old and gray…', out of touch…"

"Oh, Ms. Dora, you are not slowing down. I don't know how you do it."

"I don't feel like a hundred. I don't believe it. I just…"

"C'mon, Ms. Dora. We have work to do!"

Annette sat down with the new voice recorder and Dora took a deep breath and put a smile on her face:

"Here's your history lesson for the day," Pandora began. "Straight from Pandora's eyes.

"Thousands of years passed since men grabbed power for themselves, claiming mastery over humans and animals and even the earth itself. Through the 2000 years of holy wars and feudal enslavement, men erased women's voices from history, claimed the arts for themselves, monopolized healing the ill, manipulated society's laws, and structured a male religion that kept women on their knees. To hold it all together, they developed languages that implied: *everything is male until proved otherwise.*

"Then came the experiment in democracy called the United States of America. Fore-*fathers* founded a new nation for themselves. Frontiers-*men* wandered west in search of adventure in the forests, following hazardous trails toward wealth in untamed land. The women who dared to follow were used as entertainment, accused of witchcraft, violated, raped, beaten, and shamed.

"Before the 20th century, men considered women evil, which explains why they kept women neatly stuffed into boxes or jars or bottles that restricted them to caring for the home and children. And men could do that; they made the rules!

"Men did not *allow* women to vote.

"Men did not *allow* women to own land.

"Men did not *let* women control their finances.

"Men *convinced* women to confine themselves tightly in corsets, long cumbersome hobbling skirts, and pointy high-heeled shoes.

"Men *denied* women an education.

"Men either *segregated* or *banned* women from participating in religious affairs.

"Men *squelched* women's desires to follow the arts.

"In short, men relegated women to the sidelines, where they were allowed to look, but not touch.

"The power of the patriarchy at the beginning of the 20th century was at its zenith. Men governed; men owned; men adventured; men wrote; men educated; men healed; men made the laws; and men took their armies off to war. In the parlor, men ruled their families with iron fists when they were present and the memory of that fist when they were absent. Very early in my life, I sensed *the way things were*, felt the uneasy restlessness, and was itching to raise the lid to get at the truth.

"In my first years, *the way it was* put my father in control of the house, the farm, and our lives. I saw my mother and sisters swooshing through the house in long skirts, disfigured by corsets and bustles, even afraid to cut their hair. I stood in the midst of the turmoil in a house full of children who kept Mother occupied and out of the way while Father and Sons did the *important* work that fed their self-esteem: providing for and protecting the 'helpless women'.

"Most women were content to be taken care of; I heard praise for the women who bore sons, and noticed the isolation of wives and daughters without husbands. I watched the ways men escaped to their fields (my father to his barn), their woods, their offices, their wars. I began to know these things, even before I learned to read.

"In the second decade, men once again tried to sell their idea that war was ennobling and courageous, even as men died of painful wounds and wandered aimlessly in a fog of poison gas, even as widows teetered on the edge of madness waiting to hear how their sons and husbands and brothers had died. Never mind how wives would continue without them, even as children grew up with fathers so badly maimed they could not be fathers anymore, or as children grew up with no fathers at all.

"I saw how men messed with women's minds, convinced them that men were the powers of everything from the household to the entire universe.

"Men became so sure of themselves that they agreed to toss women a crumb — the right to vote, believing that women would be content to stay home rather than use their vote, thus leaving the business of government to the men.

"By the 1920s, men proceeded to mess with women's bodies, to turn them into a confusion of madonnas and sex symbols — each fulfilling men's needs.

"You know how I learned about sex? I was a farm girl, and farm girls understand the way it works — except the emotional part. And my mother never discussed that with me. I had to learn it from Grace, my older half-sister. I blush when I admit that my own daughters learned about sex from… I don't know… it certainly wasn't from the Kotex booklet that I handed them when they were about *that* age.

"During those Roaring Twenties, feisty women entered the new world of politics to work their magic. When they brought about *The Prohibition Era*, men retaliated by proclaiming *The Flapper Era*. Single women were turned into molls — dressed up dollies with short hair, skimpy clothing, and no brains. 'If women want to be free, let them be f-r-e-e!' the men shouted as they gaped and gawked at their fancy women.

"The slowdown of the '30s decade was the result of the wild and roaring '20s. Men had been messing with women's money for years. When they lost their own, they contrived ways to get at their wives' inheritances, trust funds, and savings. When that money ran out, men ran out also. They took to the streets, wandered the nation looking for handouts, rode the rails away from responsibilities.

"At the top levels of government, a new generation of men was setting up new rules — rather like outlining a game. *Let women go to work; pay them a pittance, and treat them rough — like men. Give them the low-level, boring tasks. They won't last long in the marketplace, and men can resume their roles.* Results were slow in coming. No one was earning very much in those days.

"The answer to pushy women? Men's answer to most problems: war. Men beat their chests and took off to fight each other around the world. The 1940s became a decade for the glory of men, the glory that brings young men home in boxes and consoles the women with gold stars and black armbands. This was the decade that witnessed men try to wrest back control by losing their lives.

"Unexpectedly, with the men away, the women took charge of their lives and livelihoods by pitching in and filling men's abandoned jobs. Women built airplanes and tanks, flew those airplanes and drove taxis, operated companies and handled the finances, even served in public office. They flew out of their boxes!

"But not for long. As men returned from war, they tried to stuff women back in. It didn't work.

"During the decade of the '50s, men extended to women 'the respect and honor they deserved', cajoling them up onto pedestals to keep them out of the way, and ironically, expecting them to clean the toilets from up there. Women were brainwashed with June-Cleaver-like models, banished to lonely suburbs to think it over and feel useless by necessity. Quite a trick, eh? But it seemed to work — for a time. It did for me.

"As with bottles that are stopped up, devoid of air and isolated, something had to give. And it did.

"The bottles popped their corks in the '60s, and women came out fighting. I was only one of the many who insisted on claiming her space alongside men, working together, and playing house together. I did it by writing boldly about what I observed transpiring between men and women.

We women of the '60s battled for our 'rights' and for sexual freedom. Translate that to mean 'free love and free sex', which accounted for a phenomenal increase in flower children and single motherhood. Think 'baby boomers'!

"This was the decade when everybody went wacky; women bared their breasts and men beat theirs. Nobody and nothing worked. Turmoil — and terror — resulted.

"Once again, in an effort to regain control, men of the '70s resorted to intrigue and war. *Man*-ipulation was on a rampage as men reclaimed their animal dread of the Equal Rights Amendment, a bill that had lain dormant in Congress for fifty years. Women were defiled; women were degraded; *rape,* once unmentionable, became an everyday word in society's language, and great orations were made about *women's place* and where it was.

"Then, in my elder years…

[WINCE / WAIT FOR LAUGH]

…I could understand the angst of men and the frustration of women. Male power had been in effect for decades, centuries, millennia. And now it was crumbling as women poured out of their containers en masse.

"Echoing the '50s, the '80s dawned as a time for reflection, a drawing back from the edge to consider what was working and what wasn't. In the past, women had only talk to make their ways known. They cajoled, teased, manipulated, coaxed, pleaded, and begged. When their voices were raised together to demand, men looked for new weapons.

"Men changed the language. They doctored the language of the church; they obfuscated the language of law and finance, and they defiled the language of love.

"By using language, men placed women at the bottom of the economic ladder, their pay in the same pothole as their place in society. I watched women hesitatingly accept their new 'rights' as they walked into the trap of poverty. Women were working all right, but men were controlling their wages while laying on guilt trips about the disintegration of the home.

"*Children* were the next target that men attempted. *Children* were failing at school; *children* were going wrong; *children* were being abused. All because their mothers held jobs outside the home. *Mother* and *Motherhood* became dirty words.

"Now — here come the '90s. Men were still up to their old tricks, talking euphemistic gibberish that no one understands (not even themselves) and waging war whenever they talk themselves into a corner. You question *gibberish*? Consider the evolvement of communication: those marvelous inventions called *radio* and *television*, which promised education and enlightenment. Have you noticed how they have fallen into an abyss of posturing, lies, bad taste, and pure rubbish?

"News reporting — journalism — once an elevated profession, has become a cartoon show featuring pretty faces and words that belch… *gibberish*. Are you surprised that this happened after pressure was applied to include women in that esteemed lot of journalists? *Sure women can join us before the cameras, but they have to be young, very pretty and slim, with flowing hair, preferably blond.*

"A lone try at *allowing* a woman to run for President (at least Vice President) scared women away from politics when the candidate's personal life and family were violated. Not to be rebuffed, women grabbed at opportunities to try for lesser roles — Supreme Court, Senate, House, state, and local governments. They're gaining a foothold slowly, ever so slowly."

Dora rubbed her forehead and closed her eyes. "That's enough for today, Nettie. I'm quite worked up, and worn out. I think I'll take a little nap."

Annette turned off the recorder and headed for the computer to transcribe Pandora's words.

The following day, Dora continued:

"Increasingly during the twentieth century, the world became enchanted with the idea of driving about in a motor car, of people flying long distances in just a few hours, sending messages long distances in minutes by telegraph and telephone, lighting up the world with a newly discovered energy called electricity, fueling energy with atomic power, and finding ways to ease pain and suffering. The world woke up to new miracles each day.

"In the last decade before the 21st century, dreamers still managed to come up with new ideas to enchant: computers that allow instant communication with both sight and sound from any place in the world, utilizing new kinds of energy to operate magnificent new machines, extending life through new understanding of the human body, and making significant headway into knowing how we can know these things.

"We've come such a long way. When I look back to the years of growing up on that farm in Arkansaw, Wisconsin, I can't quite remember what the world was like without all these wonders. At ten, I wanted to know everything; now the limitless possibilities lie within the marvel of computers.

"I decided all those many decades ago to live to be a 'hunnert'. And here I am, across the threshold. All through my life I braved a male world to express my own femininity and to live my own life. Still this itch to widen the box opening carried me through.

"Just take a long look at the world today! I believe the time — and the new millennium — augurs change in the power that men have wielded over women.

"Do I want to destroy men? Of course not. I want women to pick up their ancient heritage and claim their place alongside men to keep this earth and all that's in it alive and well — as equals. Humans come in pairs, just like the other animals. Of course, men are different from women! Each of us has our own place, our special role, if you will, our strengths and our weaknesses. You see, that's the Great Truth of what lies inside Pandora's treasure box.

"You've been told that Pandora's box contained the *evils* of the world. This is all myth, you realize. However, you were told these stories by men, who regarded what was in the box — whatever it was — as *evil*.

"What actually was stuffed into Pandora's box? Could it have been Truth? And Imagination? And the Power of both women and men? All of these are grand forces. If sending Truth into the world doesn't convince men there's a better way, what else can a woman do?

"I'd like to ask a question — one simple question. Can you imagine a world where women and men — together — formulate the rules, lead negotiations and peacekeeping, supply physical protection, lead governments, manage business, nurture families, create art, play games, celebrate with music, write stories and plays — together? Can you imagine?

"Isn't that what one extraordinary young man of the '70s asked, 'Imagine!'?"

[LONG PAUSE]

"My friends. I won't be here to summarize the 21st century, but I *imagine* that some of you will. Science continues to offer fabulous solutions. My grand- and great-grandchildren will benefit. And yours. What kind of world will greet them in the year 2100? What kind of stories will be reviewed after the next *hunnert* Januarys?

"I've done all I could. I made it to a hundred, kicking and screaming at inequities as I saw them. Now it's up to you. Thank you for listening to me rant all these years."

Pandora handed the recorder to Annette. "I'm going to rest for a bit," she said. "We'll give them my big speech and see what happens."

"You'll wow 'em for sure," Annette said, taking Dora's arm and helping her to her room. "You're going to wow 'em!"

Pandora stopped at the door and turned toward her friend. "Nettie, you're darned tootin' I'm going to wow 'em. Isn't that what I came here to do?"

A week later, on Saturday afternoon, January 8, 2000, Pandora Whaley, with her family in tow, was greeted as the guest speaker at the birthday party arranged to honor her reaching the 100-year mark. She wore a new pantsuit of magenta satin, a light lavender blouse, and matching felt hat (which she immediately removed when she took her place at the podium. "Don't like hats," she muttered. She arranged her speech in front of her and began... "Here's your history lesson for the day..."

And yes, she wowed 'em!

Pandora's Notes prior to 1900

ANNE DUDLEY BRADSTREET, a native of Northamptonshire, England, emigrated to America with the Winthrop Puritan Group and became one of America's first poets. The mother of eight children wrote splendid verse, which allegedly was taken by her brother-in-law to England where it was published under the title *The Tenth Muse, Lately Sprung Up in America* (1650).

Did you know that 14-year-old SYBIL LUDINGTON rode 40 miles on horseback in the middle of the night to warn the American militia of the American Revolution that the British were invading (1777)?

Abolitionists and feminists have been quietly — and some not so quietly — on the move for decades.

ABIGAIL ADAMS may have started it, or at least moved it along in 1776, when she admonished her husband John, soon to be President, to "Remember the Ladies". More importantly, she purchased the first government bonds (1777).

MARY WOLLSTONECRAFT, a British feminist, published *A Vindication of the Rights of Women* in which she described marriage as "legal prostitution" (1792).

SACAGAWEA, a pregnant 16-year-old Native American woman, accompanied the Lewis and Clark Expedition as the interpreter — the only woman in the group (1804-1806). She gave birth along the way and didn't miss a day of work.

MARY PICKERSKILL designed and stitched (by hand) the flag that flew over Fort McHenry in 1812.

Oberlin College, a Presbyterian institution, coeducational from its founding (1833), admitted blacks in 1835, and opened its baccalaureate program to women in 1837. Admitted that year were **CAROLINE MARY RUDD, ELIZABETH PRALL, MARY HOSFORD,** and **MARY FLETCHER KELLOGG**.

MOTHER FRANCES XAVIER WARDE arrived in Pittsburgh with five nuns and established Irish foundations to care for the poor, uneducated, imprisoned, and abandoned in society (1843).

The first medical school for women — **NEW ENGLAND FEMALE MEDICAL SCHOOL** — opened in 1848.

The first women's rights convention was held in Seneca Falls NY in 1848. **VICTORIA WOODHULL** was nominated as the first woman candidate for U.S. president for the Equal Rights Party (1872).

ELIZABETH BLACKWELL became the first woman in America to graduate from medical school (New York's Geneva Medical College) and receive her medical degree (1849).

EMILY DICKINSON began publishing her poems in the 1850s.

SOJOURNER TRUTH, born into slavery, became a traveling preacher, speaking on the abolitionist movement and women's suffrage. She delivered her famous speech, "Ain't I a Woman?" at a women's rights convention in Ohio (1851).

HARRIET BEECHER STOWE'S novel *Uncle Tom's Cabin* became the best selling novel of the 19th century (1852).

HARRIET TUBMAN led hundreds of slaves to freedom through her Underground Railroad (1850s). During the Civil War, she was a nurse and cook for the Union Army and completed spy missions for the North (1860s).

JENNIE DOUGLAS was hired as the first woman employed by the U.S. Treasury (1862).

WYOMING became the first territory to give women voting rights (1869), followed closely by the **UTAH** Territory that same year and by **WASHINGTON** Territory in 1883.

ESTHER HOBART MORRIS became the first American woman Justice of the Peace (1870).

MARGARET KNIGHT invented the machine that makes paper bags while she worked at a Massachusetts factory (1871). She was taken to court by a challenger who argued that a woman could never design such an innovative machine. Her evidence won her the patent.

HELEN AUGUSTA BLANCHARD, an inventor, was often referred to as "Lady Edison"; she held 28 patents, 22 of which were related to sewing machines. Her first patent was for her most famous zigzag sewing machine (1873).

SUSAN B. ANTHONY was charged with illegally voting in a New York election (1873). Suffragists crashed the Centennial Celebration (1876) in Philadelphia to present Vice President William A. Wheeler of New York with the "Declaration of the Rights of Women", written by MATILDA JOSELYN GAGE.

When BELVA A. LOCKWOOD drafted a bill proposing Congress admit women to practice before the U.S. Supreme Court (1877), it was denied on the basis that no woman had ever been admitted to the Court. After a two-year lobbying effort, she was admitted to the Supreme Court bar (1879). This extraordinary woman drafted an equal pay bill in 1870, which wasn't passed until 1963. She was nominated by the Equal Rights Party as the second woman candidate for President (after VICTORIA WOODHULL, 1884).

CLARA BARTON risked her life to bring supplies and support to soldiers in the field during the Civil War. At age 60, she founded the American Red Cross (1881) and led it for the next 23 years.

LOUISA STEPHENS became president of the First National Bank of Marion IA, predecessor of Wells Fargo (1883).

LUCRETIA MOTT took up the cause for women's rights in the mid-1880s.

AMELIA BLOOMER, women's rights activist, created *The Lily*, a temperance newspaper (1849). The publication tackled pressing women's issues, especially advocating women's dress reform. After writing about looser tops and knee-length skirts with a pair of pants underneath, she was deluged with requests for patterns for the "bloomers".

THE NATIONAL COUNCIL OF WOMEN of the United States was organized in 1888 by SUSAN B. ANTHONY, CLARA BARTON, JULIA WARD HOWE, and SOJOURNER TRUTH, among others, becoming the oldest non-sectarian women's organization in the country.

ELIZABETH COCHRANE, a New York journalist known as NELLIE BLY, sailed around the world in 72 days to beat the fictional record set by a male hero in Jules Verne's *Around the World in Eighty Days* (1889).

JANE ADDAMS founded Hull House in Chicago (1889).

Suffragists formed the NATIONAL AMERICAN WOMAN SUFFRAGE ASSOCIATION (1890) and rallied in New York City in March 1908, the same year that garment workers held a massive demonstration in New York for fair treatment at work and a demand to end child labor.

Have you heard about FAY FULLER, a journalist not quite 21, who was the first woman to climb Mt. Rainier to its summit, over 14,000 feet? She wore skirts, a costume she devised especially for the climb (1890).

QUEEN ISABELLA of Spain was the first woman to appear on a U.S. commemorative postage stamp (1893). The first postage stamp was issued in 1847. The first woman to be specifically honored was MARTHA WASHINGTON, her face on the 8-cent stamp (1902). The second woman so honored was POCOHONTAS (1907).

PATTY SMITH HILL and her sister MILDRED J. HILL, of Louisville KY are credited with writing a classroom greeting song, "Good Morning to All", which would become "Happy Birthday To You". Patty, a faculty member at Columbia University Teachers

College, wrote the lyrics and Mildred, an educator who later became a composer, pianist, and organist, wrote the melody. It was published in a book of songs for kindergarteners (1893).

MARY FIELDS was the first African American woman employed to carry mail (1895). She traveled the mail route in central Montana for more than ten years.

FANNY FARMER'S first cookbook was published in 1896.

Then came women of the 1900s. Standing on the shoulders of 1800s women, they could feel their own powers of possibilities and they itched to release them from the containers that had held them for so long. Women in America became restless at home, longing to know what their men were doing "out in the world" and eager to join them.

Sometime, early in 1900, the lid popped ajar, and women started to explore, tentatively at first. In mid-century, they exploded. The lid was lost in the explosion of World War II and cannot ever be replaced!

What had Pandora released into the world? Men considered it *evil*. Women considered it *truth — freedom, opportunity, good fortune — their rights*.

Pandora's Vessels

A woman has often been described as a "vessel". She carries within her the pieces of life, mysteries unsolved by men. Goddesses are like that, full of mystery and the pieces that make up life.

Pandora was such a goddess. Mythology sketches her vaguely as the woman entrusted with a container of all ills that could ever befall humans and told never to open it. Unable to fight the temptation to learn what was inside the vessel, this curious goddess opened it and released… what?… into the world. Some versions call it *Evils*; other versions refer to *Problems* or *Troubles* or *Ills*.

One version of the myth, often repeated, claims that Pandora was created as punishment for an errant god, Prometheus, who stole from Mount Olympus. As punishment to the thief, Zeus, head god, created "a woman".

Another version credits Hephaestus, god of fire, with the creation of Pandora. Directed by Zeus to create a "new kind of human" (because mortals at the time consisted of only one gender — male), Hephaestus was told to form the first woman from clay. He named her *Pandora*.

The bountiful earth goddess then opened that supernatural vessel believed to contain the ills of humankind. Horrified at what she had done, even though it was what she was designed to do, Pandora could not slam the lid back quickly enough. The only thing left in the jar was *Hope*.

One has to wonder about Pandora's name. The Greek derivative means "having all gifts" (pan = *all*; doron = *gift*), or "one who gives all gifts".

The Bible version (and many other religious writings) blames Eve for stealing an apple and punishes the newly created woman by tossing all humans out of The Garden. *What does that tell you about gods' opinions of women?*

Oh so many questions are raised with this little story (remember it's a myth). No answers have surfaced through the ages. None that anyone in the 21st century would believe.

Look at *vessels* for a moment. Such a variety to choose from. Some versions of the Pandora myth refer to a *box*; some call it a *jar* or *earthenware vessel* (probably the most likely, given the early Greek era); or it could be a *bottle*, even a *pot*. The only requirement was that the container have a cover, lid, stopper — something to hold in the contents, but one that could be removed to allow escape. The ultimate requirement was that the curious would find difficulty in returning the escaped contents to the vessel.

Who placed those *Things* in the vessel? Well, who do you think? One must conclude that the great god of the world — Zeus — might have had something to do with it. Certainly it wouldn't have been a woman; he hadn't created her yet!

What was the purpose behind tucking away these ills/evils? If the gods cared at all for humanity, those nasty Evils would never have been created. Okay, theories of anti-matter, opposites, *what goes in must come out,* are possible. But, c'mon, a god creating a universe of humans would certainly possess some degree of compassion for what "he" created — i.e., life. Wouldn't you think?

And now, the big question: where did the Evils come from? Were there none before Pandora came along? This is the question that philosophers and other great minds have debated for centuries — nay, millennia. Ironically, this is an excellent question for the 21st century: how did the world manage before women came out of the box?

Pandora has become a conundrum, a mystery, a woman, a goddess (if indeed she were created by Zeus). All her female descendents — women — must therefore be conundrums, mysteries, and goddesses.

Which is what Pandora Whaley is trying to tell you. Humanity hasn't changed much since the days of Zeus, her namesake Pandora, Hephaestus, and Prometheus. We still harbor gods and idols, that profess to be-know-do everything, alongside thieves and evil-doers. Women, who are aware of what is going on, understand their men and aren't afraid to deal with the bad stuff. (Have you ever watched a pair of first-time parents about to change their baby's diaper?)

The 20th century Pandora Whaley knew what she was doing. She was a curious child who wanted to know everything, an ambitious young woman who wanted to explore the world, and a wise old woman who knew how much she didn't know — all wrapped up in a modern goddess — a 20th century woman who was curious, who knew what she wanted and how to get it.

Arkansaw

Pandora Nelle Whaley wrote this at age 70 after visiting her hometown to bury her mother in the Arkansaw Cemetery.

This is Arkansaw. The town everyone thinks is misspelled. It's been around for a long time, a northern Wisconsin village inhabited mostly by French Canadians and a few Irish. Ironically, the only church in town is the quaint white Methodist church that looks like every other Methodist church built in the late 1800s — square with corner steps leading to large wooden double doors, always unlocked and always open all day Sundays. Can't you just imagine a bride and groom coming down those steps after posing at the top for photographs?

Surrounding the church are small warm homes full of growing families. They love kids here. The school across the street now goes all the way through high school. There were only eight grades when I went there.

Walk down the dirt streets — muddy slogs after rain and rutted horrors when they dry — and you'll see lots of space around the houses. Some lots used to be bigger — farm-sized, with horses, cows, and chickens (oh yes, you'll still hear roosters at sunrise). See fields of hay and corn and oats and… over there is a wild strawberry field. Yup, just like the Beatles' song, but this one had real strawberries in it. I used to sit in that field and stuff my mouth with berries until the juice spilled down my chin.

Arkansaw is a two-layered town. Half of it sits high above the rushing Arkansaw River amid grassy farmland, with homes safe from occasional floods, and half sits about a hundred feet lower, cut in two by the creek and, now, Arkansaw Creek Park, added after World War II to honor fallen soldiers.

Follow me and you'll find the hill road down to the shopping area, though it won't be what you expect. I always loved skipping down the steep tree-lined hill, kicking up sand and singing silly songs. Half-way down you can hear the creek bubbling its way over rocks, a tributary of the Eau Galle River. Upstream, if you stretch your neck, you can see the flour mill, maybe even hear the wheel churning the creek water. It was a sawmill when the community was getting started, just before the Civil War, but it's been gone since the big flood of 1907.

At the bottom of the hill sits an old rusty bridge, with room to walk on both sides; only one car can cross at a time. Horses used to wheeze crossing that bridge, out of breath from the swift ride down the hill. My cousins and I used to throw our string fishing lines over the railing, but they never were long enough to touch the water. Still, it was fun to watch the fish in the clear water, knowing we could join them on hot summer days. Which we did.

My cousins lived downstream where the river narrowed and turned into a bed of mud in the summer. Alongside the roots of a great fir tree at the creek's edge sat a hole deep enough to cool off four of us as we took turns jumping from the grassy shore into the waiting muddy water.

The river in Spring wasn't as friendly; swollen waters rushed, tore, and pushed their way through town, threatening the bridge. Once, when I was seven, the flooding waters were so strong they wiped out three dams across Arkansaw Creek, sending water adult-knee deep into the lower streets. Our farm got soggy, but was on ground too high for the flood waters to reach.

Here's the *town*, where most folks come on Saturdays — "go-to-town day" — when farmers come in for weekly supplies at the grain and feed store over there and Hartung's General Store next to the bridge, where you can buy everything from groceries to wheelbarrows and dress fabric. The smell of new cloth and new shoes, mixed with the aroma of fresh vegetables, is worth the trip inside. Garden gloves still hold that scent for me. (The candy that Mr. Hartung gave us kids added sweet reason to behave while our parents shopped.)

Across the street is the Rialto Theater, which some say was the first theater for miles around. It opened in the early 1920s, and many a Saturday afternoon I sat in the magnificent dark, holding hands with my latest beau while we watched Theda Bara or Clara Bow or the wonderful Barrymores do their stuff on the silver screen.

Main Street in Arkansaw now sports a barber shop, a tack shop (once a blacksmith shop), and a gas station — that showed up in the early 1920s. Arkansaw farmers were well ahead of the national trend towards motorized equipment — trucks and tractors and plows — dutifully stocked and promoted at the Grain and Feed Store.

Arkansaw was put together by farmers, who needed the mill for their grain, and the traders for supplies, back in the 1800s. It never was a big place; right now it harbors only a couple hundred people. When I was born, twice as many people lived here, including my parents, grandparents, three older half-brothers and two half-sisters from Dad's first family, my own two brothers and two sisters, and cousins galore.

Arkansaw became my hometown early one morning in January at the start of the 20th century. It will remain my home for a hunnert Januarys.

About the Author

Val Dumond is not 100 years old, but she is closing in on it. Her mother was the one actually born on the cusp of the 20th century, living into the 1970s. Val lived the last 70 years of the century. A writer and historian during the explosive years that found women discovering their strengths, she recognized the strides made by women in her lifetime. She combined her findings with her mother's stories to cover the progress of women throughout the 1900s. Events of that entire century affect not only the lives of women who lived it, but those who are their descendents.

Continuing to write in her 80s, Val stays young and healthy and very much aware of the distance still ahead for women. [Just before this book went to press, a woman in the United States was denied credit to buy a car without the co-signature of her father or husband (January 2014).]

Val's greatest wish is for final ratification of the Equal Rights Amendment to the U.S. Constitution — while she is still alive to celebrate it.

Other Books by Val Dumond

The Anarchist's Guide to Grammar
Grammar For Grownups
Just Words — The US and THEM Thing
Elements of Nonsexist Usage
Grammar In Your Pocket Series
Imagine! Breathe!
Are You Singing Your Song?
When Roosters Fly
Cloudbursts
A Little Rebellion…
Sugar, Spice, and Stone
Mush On and Smile
Ahlam's Stories
How We Fought WWII at
Wm T Sherman Elementary School
The Sun Never Rises
Dream Makers

(All available at Amazon.com and Kindle.com)

Follow Val at www.valdumond.com
Facebook, LinkedIn, Twitter
Blogs: grammaranarchist.blogspot.com
pandoras100januarys.com

Index

www.ingramcontent.com/pod-product-compliance
Lightning Source LLC
Chambersburg PA
CBHW060255100426
42742CB00011B/1757